YEADON'S REGISTER

of

L N E R

LOCOMOTIVES

Volume Twenty-One

Class A5 to A8, H1, H2, L1(L3), L2, M1 & M2 Tank Engines

YEADON'S REGISTER OF L.N.E.R. LOCOMOTIVES - VOLUME 21

EDITOR'S NOTE & ACKNOWLEDGEMENTS

This the twenty-first volume of *Yeadon's Register of LNER Locomotives* is the most ambitious so far published. Within the 128 printed pages no less than ten classes are featured all of which are tank engines - most are of the larger variety and although many were pre-Grouping designs, the majority saw service on British Railways.

Within the ten classes there are three which were inherited in 1937 from the London Passenger Transport Board which constituted the engines of the former Metropolitan Railway. These engines, though none-standard to any LNER designs, enjoyed virtually a decade of further work on the LNER - one class actually left their 'home counties' patch and went north to Nottinghamshire to find further work during wartime. Three of the ten classes were of Great Central origin although one of these, the M1's, started life on the former Lancashire, Derbyshire & East Coast Railway before that small company was absorbed by the GCR. One of the GC classes, the A5's, was further expanded by the LNER shortly after Grouping in a bid for further reliable motive power in the interim period before LNER designs bagan to appear. The other four classes were all of North Eastern design and one of these, the H1's, was subject to rebuilding from 4-4-4T to the more successful 4-6-2T Class A8.

Photographically this volume far exceeds any that have gone before it and nearly 400 photographs have been used to illustrate the various major and detail changes carried out on the engines during their lifetime - space was something of a premium even though the volume has been enlarged by more than thirty percent over previous volumes.

However, in producing this volume we have finished off a number of the LNER class letter designations - the A, H, L and M's are now completed - not to mention those which have already been completed by earlier volumes in the series. Volume One started with the A1/A3's and now twenty volumes later we have completed the A's; not bad going! There are lots more to come.

Eric Fry not only checks the endless amount of paperwork generated during the production of each volume, he also guides the editor safely through the minefield of LNER locomotive history whilst his experience and maturity lends an authority enabling a thorough job to be carried out. Brian Dyson and his staff at the University of Hull Archive Department have once again been patient and professional in answering our requirements - thanks.

Thanks to Mike and Mick; was it grand or premier cru? The lads at Amadeus who do a superb job with the printing never get a mention but this time they have - thanks.

The people who probably know more about the Registers than most but have little to do with the production - Annie, Jean and Simon - are thanked for their tolerance; we will get there yet. And not forgetting you the reader; hopefully this volume will get your blessing.

The next Register, Volume 22, will feature the balance of the Q classes - those 0-8-0's of the former North Eastern, and Hull & Barnsley railways - Q5 to Q7 and Q10.

The Yeadon Collection is available for inspection and anyone who wishes to inspect it should contact:-
The Archivist
Brynmor Jones Library
University of Hull
Hull
HU6 7RX
Tel: 01482-465265
A catalogue of the Yeadon collection is available.

First published in the United Kingdom by
BOOKLAW/RAILBUS 2001 in association with CHALLENGER
382 Carlton Hill, Nottingham, NG4 1JA.
Printed and bound by The Amadeus Press, Cleckheaton, West Yorkshire.

INTRODUCTION

A5

The Robinson 4-6-2 tank engine was introduced in 1911 primarily to work the suburban services from Marylebone. By Grouping twenty-one engines (GCR Class 9N) were in service with another ten being built at Gorton. The LNER ordered a further thirteen for work in the former North Eastern Railway area and these were delivered from the maker, Hawthorn, Leslie & Co. during 1925 and 1926. So as to bring them within the LNER Loading Gauge, the last thirteen engines varied considerably from the Gorton built engines though it was not too apparent in appearance. They were in fact some two inches narrower across the engine at the side tanks, cab and bunker which brought a decrease in fuel and water capacity by three hundredweight and 180 gallons respectively. Also they had lower chimney, dome and cab roof whilst the wheelbase was lengthened by four inches between the rear wheels of the bogie and the leading coupled wheels. This made the engines 3¾ inches longer than the GC engines.

Those engines built by Hawthorns for the N.E.Area had left-hand drive whereas the Gorton built engines were right-hand. Eventually, but not until the first year of the BR period, the differences were recognised by classifying the GC engines A5/1 and the LNER engines A5/2. Another difference between the two batches was that the Hawthorn engines were fitted with Westinghouse brake but this was removed during the early 1930's.

The 9N class were the first class of GC engines built with superheaters. The first eight had Schmidt type whilst the remainder were fitted with Robinson's own design of superheater and by 1917 the eight with Schmidt superheaters had been changed to Robinson type. The boiler used on the 9N was later used on the rebuilt D9 class 4-4-0's. Though Ramsbottom safety valves were fitted at first to the GC engines, they were all changed to Ross 'pop' valves by Grouping; the later built engines including the ten built at Gorton in 1923 all came new with Ross 'pops'.

In September 1921 No.450 was fitted with side windows to its cab and consequently all the new engines from 1923 onwards were fitted with cab side windows at building; the earlier members of the class were altered to cab side windows as they went to works between 1924 and 1926.

During the 1921 coal strike ten of the class were fitted for oil burning using the 'Unolco' system and again, during the 1926 strike, six of that same batch were altered to oil burning using the same apparatus.

'Reliostop' ATC apparatus was used on a number of the Neasden based engines from 1919 until that type of ATC was discarded. Later ATC equipment was tried out in the London area using the Hudd and Great Western systems during the period between 1947 and 1949.

Intended for suburban and local passenger workings, the A5's carried out such duties throughout their lives; those of GC origin being employed exclusively by Neasden shed up to Grouping. From 1923 the Gorton built engines started to stray to other districts first to Woodford and Annesley then in 1924 six went to the West Riding where they settled at Ardsley shed for a couple of years. There were other instances of A5's working from Bradford and Copley Hill sheds during the summer periods of the late 1930's and in 1941 five of the class were sent there

again. King's Cross shed got four in 1928 and used them for outer suburban work but by 1935 only two remained and these then went to Hitchin. King's Cross got a couple more in the late 1930's but they went to Colwick in 1940. Neasden continued to have the largest allocation of these capable engines and when the LNER took over the London Passenger Transport Board working northwards from Rickmansworth in 1937, the Neasden A5's were soon taking over from the ex-LPTB engines.

All the GC built engines (except for No.5447 withdrawn in 1942) were allocated to Neasden at the beginning of 1948 and they were even joined by two of the NE Area engines from 1943 to 1945; the first instance of these Hawthorn built engines leaving the NE Area. However, the A5's began to depart Neasden as the new Thompson L1's gradually took over the Marylebone services and by June 1954 they had all left. During the intervening period the A5/1's had gone to Boston, Grantham and Lincoln sheds. Langwith Junction got a couple as did Colwick once again. A couple went even further north up to the NE Region at Saltburn shed eventually ending their days working from Botanic Gardens shed in Hull. The Manchester area had use for some of them from 1954 and they could be seen working the Liverpool to Hull and the daily Liverpool to Harwich passenger trains from Central station round the Fallowfield loop to Guide Bridge where electric traction took over as far as Sheffield. The A5's also worked the suburban services from London Road over the former LNER lines to the south and east of the city in this period.

The Hawthorn built engines were employed specifically in the North Eastern Area when introduced in 1925. Blaydon, Gateshead and Heaton sheds sharing the thirteen engines between them. In the first instance some were tried out at Darlington, Starbeck, York and Leeds before settling down on Tyneside. Saltburn shed had seven of them from mid-1928 to replace H1's on the Darlington and later, the Scarborough services. In 1930 Middlesbrough got two of the class from Heaton and in 1938 got three more from that shed. In 1939 the eight at Saltburn and the five at Middlesbrough all moved to Darlington where they remained concentrated until 1949 with the exception of the two which went to Neasden for two years during the war. In 1949 four of the A5/2's moved back from Darlington to Saltburn and in February 1951 five of the class went to Norwich; a month later four of those were sent to Stratford along with six of the Teeside based engines to work the Liverpool Street - Southend Victoria service whilst the turntable at Livrpool Street was out of use being modified to take the new 'Britannia' class Pacifics. By August all ten had returned north and resumed passenger workings from Saltburn, Middlesbrough, Stockton and Darlington sheds. Hull Botanic Gardens shed gained three of the North East engines in July 1952 when Nos.69835, 69836 and 69837 arrived to work alongside the two former GC A5's drafted away from Neasden.

Maintenance was split between Darlington and Gorton works; the former having charge of the NE Area engines and the latter the Gorton built engines, however, during BR days this changed and Darlington took over maintenance of the whole class although occasional forays to Gorton by some engines saw them receiving anything from light to general repairs.

The first withdrawal took place in 1942 when No.5447 was discovered to have had badly cracked frames. In September 1944 No.5165 was also found to have the same condition but a

(left) Sixteen engines were built by the Great Central Railway at their Gorton workshops in 1911/12. Designated GCR Class 9N, they were fitted with four-column Ramsbottom safety valves which were still in place at Grouping. The GC introduced this class to cope with the heavy and increasing residential traffic in and out of Marylebone on both the High Wycombe and Rickmansworth routes.

(below) Ten engines, Nos.686 to 695 entered Grouping as seen here, rebuilt from original 4-6-0T between September 1914 (No.688) and January 1917 (No.687). At rebuilding they kept the original boiler with Ramsbottom safety valves and no superheater.

At Grouping thirteen of the twenty engines in the A7 class still had the original boiler which supplied saturated steam. The last of these Gateshead built boilers was cut up in June 1932. Some retained Ramsbottom safety valves (*see* page 55 top, left) and even when superheater was put in (*see* page 52, top).

new set of frames were constructed and the engine was returned to traffic. The cracked frames problem continued from there on and subsequently nine more engines had to be dealt with. The next withdrawals did not take place until 1957 when two engines went for scrap. 1958 saw the largest inroads into the class and all the remaining North Eastern Region engines succumbed in that year. The last A5's were withdrawn in November 1960 when 69808, 69814 and 69820 went for scrap making Class A5 extinct.

A6

The North Eastern railway Class W 4-6-0T comprised ten engines built at Gateshead between December 1907 and April 1908. Primarily intended for work on the hilly coastal route in Yorkshire between Teeside, Whitby and Scarborough, they were found to be lacking in both coal and water capacities. In 1914 a start was made to give them larger tanks and bunkers and the rebuilding necessitated an extended frame and a pair of trailing wheels. Their overall weight rose by nearly ten tons but coal capacity increased from 2½ to 4 tons whilst water capacity went from 1500 to nearly 1900 gallons. The rebuilding did not require a different boiler and was completed by 1917.

Three types of boiler were used on this class, all of the same basic size (4ft 9in. diameter). The boiler types were: (1) *Diagram 61* - the type first fitted and also interchangeable with Class T1 4-8-0T engines. None of these boilers were superheated but spares and replacements were built up to 1930. (2) *Diagram 63C* - this was the redesigned Diagram 63 boiler carried by Class A8 engines. In 1936 it was made such that it was interchangeable between classes A6, A7, A8, H1 and T1. Five of these superheated boilers were built and three fitted to A6 Nos.689, 693 and 695 in 1937. No.687 received a second hand Diagram 63C boiler in 1943, and 9796 (692) was so treated in 1946. (3) *Diagram 63B* - this superheated and final version of Diagram 63, appeared in 1939 and was characterised by having the dome set 1ft 9in. further back, and with a squarer cover. Seven of the class carried this type of boiler. Within the tables the 63B and 63C boilers are indicated where relevant. The final position within the A6 class was that three remained saturated, carrying Diagram 61 boilers to the end. Four received Diagram 63C superheated boilers before eventually getting the 63B type, whilst three engines went direct from Diagram 61 to Diagram 63B superheated boilers. One of these temporarily carried a 63C boiler before reverting to 63B.

Westinghouse brakes were fitted when new and steam brakes replaced these on all but No.687 (9791) between 1944 and 1948. The bogies were equipped with brakes at rebuilding but these had been removed by 1938.

Up to 1934, Saltburn, Scarborough and Whitby sheds used these engines during the summer months over the heavily graded route along the Yorkshire coast. In the winter period some would move to Leeds primarily due to lack of work on the coast. With the arrival of the A8's in the mid 1930's some of the A6's were ousted from the most strenuous jobs and sent to Heaton or Hull as a temporary measure but at the outbreak of war they scattered to all parts of the NE Area with just a few remaining by the seaside. Besides Neville Hill, the sheds at Darlington, Northallerton, Stockton and West Auckland made use of these large engines during the war years. During the closing months of the conflict, all the class except No.694 were sent to Starbeck to help move the heavy goods trains around the hilly districts of Harrogate, albeit late in the day for this awkward section of railway which during wartime saw a large

amount of traffic 'bottlenecked' on many occasions. In 1947 three went to Hull Botanic Gardens for further passenger work on the branches to Hornsea and Withernsea, besides pilot work at Paragon station. Whitby got one back in October of the same year in the shape of No.9792 which stayed until May 1948.

Only one withdrawal took place during the LNER period when No.9790 was condemned in June 1947. Of the remainder all but two got 60,000 added to their numbers. The last to go was No.69796 in March 1953, ending its days as Hull (Paragon) pilot. All were cut up at Darlington.

A7

Another large North Eastern Railway tank design having its origins during the Wordsell period but this class (NER Class Y) was built during Raven's tenure as C.M.E.. Designed primarily for mineral traffic, these hefty engines with three cylinders were intended to release tender engines from the short haul coal working from the collieries to the staithes.

Twenty were turned out from Darlington between October 1910 and June 1911 and put to work as intended. However, by the beginning of the LNER period they were used mainly on hump shunting duties, throughout the NE Area, where their immense power was extremely useful.

As with Class A6, three types of boiler were used on Class A7. The original type was Diagram 55 and was 5ft 6in. in diameter. At first all twenty engines were without superheater, but this was introduced in 1917. Although some new superheated boilers were made, seven of the original boilers were altered to superheater type. From 1943 the Diagram 63B boiler (and one 63C) began to be fitted to Class A7 - a most unusual case of rebuilding to smaller boiler. However, in their later days, the A7's were undertaking rather different duties to those that they were originally designed to do. The rebuilding merited reclassification and Part 1 was given to them. To summarise the final position: *(1)* Seventeen received superheated Diagram 55 boilers of which four were not further changed. *(2)* One engine (No.1176) never received a superheater and carried a Diagram 55 saturated boiler to withdrawal. *(3)* Fifteen became Class A7/1. Fourteen of these carried Diagram 63B superheated boilers, and one of them (No.1191/69786) ran for a time, in the early 1950's, with one of the earlier Diagram 63C boilers: whilst another (No.1182/69782) had its superheater removed in 1954. *(4)* The remaining A7/1 (No.1192/69787) was given a Diagram 63B saturated boiler when rebuilt (thus never carrying a superheater). This pattern was introduced specially for Class T1.

Ross 'pop' safety valves replaced the original Ramsbottom type when engines received the later built boilers, the shaped casing being removed usually at the same time.

None were fitted with Westinghouse brakes and steam brakes, along with three-link couplings, sufficed the whole class for their intended work. However, in 1934 one engine, No.1179, was equipped with vacuum ejector, screw coupling, heating gear and brake pipe connections at both ends; this in connection with passenger train trials on the Newcastle to Blackhill line which came to nothing and the superfluous equipment was removed in 1943.

At Grouping the class was distributed the length and breadth of the former NER system a trend which continued for most of the LNER period except for two engines, Nos.1129 and 1190, which went to the Southern Area in 1926, staying there until 1943 when they returned to Starbeck. During those years the engines had stints at Doncaster, Frodingham,

Immingham and Northwich, the latter shed using them banking the ICI trains from Hartford to Winnington Park. During WWII many of the class worked in the Hull area with a pair allocated to Cudworth. Starbeck, Stockton and York also had some in this period. Once hostilities were ended and with the onset of Nationalisation, the class gathered at Hull with Dairycoates having the lion's share and Springhead shed having a number for trip work over the former Hull & Barnsley line.

Withdrawals started with No.9789 in May 1951, this engine never receiving a BR number. From there on condemnations became steady each year, except 1953, and in December 1957 the last three were retired making Class A7 extinct.

A8

Rebuilt by Gresley from the forty-five Class H1 locomotives of NER origin, these engines remained engaged on the work for which they had been originally intended to perform putting in better performances than ever before and no doubt repaying the cost of rebuilding.

The boiler carried at first by the A8's was either the original Diagram 63 or its modification, the 63A, which had been designed in 1929 with a one piece barrel as opposed to the three sections of the Dia.63 boiler. It was also fitted with a Robinson superheater in preference to the Schmidt type used in the Dia. 63. Nineteen of the 63A boilers were built between 1930 and 1935 purely for the A8 and their predecessor the H1. However, one 63A was put on a T1 class engine, minus superheater and later, in 1935, the 63A was redesigned to make it interchangeable between classes A6, A7, A8, T1 and the remaining H1 engines. This became known as the 63C and was sans superheater when installed on the T1 class engines. The final boiler type appeared in 1937, the Diagram 63B, which was again interchangeable between the A6, A7, A8 and T1 classes. Some seventy of these boilers were made, ten of them saturated for the T1 class, the others all fitted with Robinson superheaters. The dome on the 63B boiler was positioned further back towards the cab and was no longer in line with the front end of the side tanks.

Group Standard buffers were fitted to the whole class at rebuilding. Some of the class had a coal hopper built onto the cages situated over the bunkers, thus enabling them to be coaled at the overhead mechanical coaling plants whilst others were not so fitted and tended to be sent to sheds where the old coaling stages still existed.

The Tyneside sheds lost most of their allocation when the A8's went to work on the coastal line in North Yorkshire, their adhesion and power being ideal for the arduous grades over this route. Though weighing half a ton less than the H1 type, they now had thirteen tons more adhesion weight to their advantage. By the time rebuilding was completed the distribution was still 'Area wide' but there were only three on Tyneside at Gateshead, Sunderland had a couple whilst in the area between Darlington and Middlesbrough, including Stockton, there were twenty-six at the three sheds. Whitby and Scarborough had three each as did Neville Hill, and Dairycoates had four. A solitary engine was stationed at Middleton-in-Teesdale.

Short distance express passenger work still kept the class busy up to the outbreak of war. Thereafter Scarborough and Whitby lost their A8's and redistribution saw them at places where they had never before worked albeit still in the NE Area. West Auckland, West Hartlepool and Selby were recipients

during the conflict and Starbeck too had a number for piloting the heavy goods trains in the Harrogate district. During the BR period a few went back to the coastal towns but many found work on the stiff grades in County Durham either banking or still hauling passenger trains. In the late 1950's, like many other steam locomotives, they were put into store as dieselisation swept through the North Eastern Region. Sunderland shed had eighteen examples at one point though little passenger work could be found for them except lightweight through services. Some ended their working days as bankers at Durham shed where they pushed southbound expresses - an inglorious end for a capable class overtaken by modernisation.

No.69876 was the first to be withdrawn in October 1957 followed a few weeks later by No.69868. From thereon the steady condemnations continued until June 1960 when the last eleven were withdrawn en masse and Class A8 became extinct.

H1

This class of three-cylinder 4-4-4 tank engines was built by the North Eastern Railway at Darlington in various batches and classified D. The first twenty came out between October 1913 and April 1914 and had consecutive numbers from 2143 to 2162. Another ten engines should have been constructed but the order was cancelled by the intervention of WWI. Twenty-five more Class D were authorised in 1919 but shortage of materials ensured that the last one did not enter traffic until May 1922. The numbering of these engines was more haphazard than the previous batch and took the numbers of withdrawn older engines.

Intended purely for passenger work, they had a full weight in excess of 87 tons but less than a half of that was available for adhesion. But, they were useful machines though not wholly popular with enginemen.

The original superheated Diagram 63 boiler was updated to 63A in 1931 and this latter type only saw service on classes H1 and the A8 derivative. Fourteen H1's received the 63A type, which had the Robinson pattern of superheater in place of the Schmidt type on Diagram 63.

Westinghouse brakes were standard throughout the class but in the first year of the LNER No.1500 was given a vacuum ejector also. One more was so treated in 1924 and between 1928 and 1930 the rest of the class were equipped similarly. The Westinghouse equipment was removed in most cases during rebuilding but some engines had it removed before being changed to 4-6-2T.

The majority of the class were to be found working in the area north and east of Darlington with most at Tyneside sheds. Neville Hill and Starbeck had ten between them for working the fast and semi-fast trains between Leeds and Harrogate and surrounding districts. Saltburn had nine for working to Darlington and along the coastal route to Whitby and Scarborough. Things stayed pretty much that way until 1934 when No.2160 went to Duns for a couple of years working over former North British territory.

In July 1931 No.2162 emerged from Darlington rebuilt to a 4-6-2T type and was evaluated over the following year. The engine was found to be superior to its earlier 4-4-4 form and the go-ahead was given for further rebuilding. Thereafter from January 1933 to August 1936 the whole class of H1's were dealt with and reclassified A8, all now with left-hand drive.

In June 1931 No.2162 was rebuilt to 4-6-2T from Class H1 4-4-4T, and ultimately the other forty-four were dealt with in the same way. Changes which applied to them all were fitting of screw in place of steam reverse, left hand instead of right hand drive, Group Standard instead of NER design buffers, and the addition of a drain pipe from the vacuum ejector exhaust. No.2162 was the only A8 until January 1933. Rebuilding was completed when No.1517 was ex works on 12th August 1936 and all first carried a Diagram 63 or 63A boiler.

Class H1 comprised forty-five engines built at Darlington in various batches: Nos.2143 to 2162 from October 1913 to April 1914, and Nos.1326 to 1330, 1499 to 1503 and 1517 to 1531 between May 1920 and May 1922.

H2

Along with Metropolitan Class K (LNER L2) and Class G (LNER M2), these eight Class H 4-4-4 tank engines became LNER property on 1st November 1937 when they were purchased from the London Passenger Transport Board as part of the arrangements whereby the LNER took over operation of the line northwards from Rickmansworth where the LPTB electrification ended.

The Class H became LNER Class H2 and their LPTB running numbers 103 to 110 were changed in 1938 to 6415-6422. Originally supplied to the Metropolitan during 1920 and 1921, these large 4-4-4T engines carried Kerr, Stuart & Co., Stoke-on-Trent works numbers 4088 to 4095. The boiler was similar to that used on the Class M2 0-6-4T engines and was interchangeable.

From new all were superheated with the Robinson type and were fitted with piston valves. Before the LNER take-over the original Ramsbottom safety valves were replaced by Ross 'pops'. The LNER reduced the height of the boiler fittings in 1941 to bring them into line with the composite gauge.

Throughout their lives in the Metropolitan area they were used primarily on passenger work and were based at Neasden LT shed before moving across the main line to Neasden LNER shed in 1937. In December 1941 the whole class moved away from London and were reallocated to Colwick and Langwith Junction sheds for further passenger work on the Nottingham suburban lines and the Lincoln-Chesterfield route. Whilst at Langwith one of the three working from that shed, No.6421, was withdrawn and the other two ended up at Colwick with the rest of the class.

Stratford works was entrusted with their upkeep during LNER days and even after their move to the East Midlands they continued to be 'shopped' at Stratford. Colwick shed looked upon the H2's in a bad light but they continued in use throughout the wartime period with only one other engine, No.6419, being condemned before the cessation of hostilities. The last to go was No.7511 (6416) in November 1947; along with 7512 (6417), these were the only two to be renumbered in 1946.

L1 (L3)

The Great Central Railway Class 1B consisted of twenty engines, built at Gorton in various batches during the years between 1914 and 1917. Like most of the GC locomotive fleet, these engines were not built with consecutive numbers although numerically they did conform to some sort of date order. Nos.272 and 273 came out in 1914 whilst the next batch 274 to 276 and 336 to 340 came out in 1915. Nos.341 to 344 followed in 1916, and 345 with 366 to 370 appeared in 1917.

The inside cylinder 2-6-4T's were large by any standard and weighted just under 97½ tons with a maximum axle load of 20 tons. The 1B class was also the first 2-6-4T type to run in this country being employed by the GCR on heavy goods and mineral traffic, however, their braking power could not match their haulage capacity.

Superheated from the outset, the boilers were similar to those fitted on the 'Director' class 4-4-0's though the top feed on the 2-6-4T was fitted in front of the dome. During the early LNER period the top feed apparatus was removed. Those engine built between 1914 and 1916 had Wakefield mechanical lubricators whilst later engines had the Robinson 'Intensifore'

type; in the period from 1939 to 1944 the 'Intensifore' lubricators were changed in favour of the Wakefield type.

Beside the normal steam brakes for the coupled wheels the bogies had steam actuated brakes also but these eventually became redundant and were removed during WWII.

It was intended that these engines should work the export coal traffic from the Nottinghamshire and Derbyshire mining districts to the GC port at Immingham but the First World War practically wiped out that export so other work was found for them. As mentioned earlier, braking became something of a problem for these engines when working heavy goods trains and when used on the Woodhead route before Grouping they caused many a hair to turn grey. By the time the class was complete the allocations saw fourteen at Gorton and six at Sheffield but in 1919 most of them were sent away to Annesley and Woodford. At the former shed they were employed on pick-up goods and colliery trips whilst Woodford used them on goods trains down to London. Neasden shed eventually got a handful for working similar traffic to Woodford besides employing them on passenger work.

Staveley acquired two of the Annesley engines which they employed as assisting engines on heavy coal trains to Dunford Bridge. Langwith Junction got the Staveley pair and used them on the same work assisting coal trains to Dunford Bridge. The same shed also used M1 0-6-4T's on this very same job. In 1923 Immingham gained six of the class for working the local yards and various members of the class settled down on these duties for the next twenty years. Mexborough got the Annesley engines in 1929 and used them for banking coal trains to Dunford Bridge but this time from Wath. Eventually seven L1's were allocated to Mexborough for this work which they performed on and off until 1948. 1929 saw four of the class sent to March shed where until 1931, when they returned to the GC Section, they worked coal trains from Peterborough to Whitemoor yard. Two of the Immingham engines went to Keady shed for further banking duties and when that shed closed they went to the replacement depot at Frodingham. Gorton shed lost its sole example in 1940 when No.5275 went to Mexborough. Its twenty-five year spell at Gorton had hardly taxed its power as it was virtually continuously employed as Guide Bridge No.10 Pilot working to Ashton Moss sidings and back, trips to Hyde Road goods yard, down to Park Bridge and back to Dewsnap.

Between 1942 and 1944 three of the Mexborough engines were sent to Sheffield to bank coal trains up to Dunford Bridge just as they had done when at Annesley and Langwith Junction sheds before Grouping. Further banking duties between Hartford and Winnington Park in Cheshire brought two of the class to Northwich shed in 1943; they stayed there until withdrawn in the 1950's. Towards the end of the LNER period Neasden had fourteen L1's allocated, the rest were at Sheffield (Darnall) shed.

In 1945 the class was reclassified L3, Thompson's new 2-6-4 tank engines taking over the L1 title.

Withdrawals started in July 1947 when 9063 went for scrap but it was another eight years before the last examples were withdrawn. But, the class lived on for a couple of years; No.69060 went to Stratford Carriage works in June 1954 performing stationary boiler duties until September 1957 whilst No.69052 did a similar job at Gorton from 1954 to 1956.

Eight 4-4-4T engines, Nos.103 to 110, were built for the Metropolitan Railway during the period between October 1920 and June 1921. All were allocated to that company's Neasden shed and worked the outer suburban services north of Harrow. On 1st November 1937 they were taken over by the LNER and classified H2. Shortly after the take-over all the class moved across to the LNER's Neasden shed on the west side of the mainline. Note the large maker's plate on the smokebox saddle.

(above) Twenty engines numbered 272 to 276, 336 to 345 and 366 to 370, were built at Gorton between December 1914 and May 1917. They were fitted with combined blower and circulating valve, also top feed. The first fourteen had Wakefield mechanical lubricator but before Grouping they had been changed to Robinson 'Intensifore' lubricator which Nos.345 and 366 to 370 had from new.

(right) Six engines, Nos.111 to 116, were built in March 1925 by Armstrong Whitworth & Co. from parts made at Woolwich Arsenal and boilers made by Robert Stephenson & Co. These engines were owned by the Metropolitan Railway until 1933 when it was absorbed by London Passenger Transport Board.

L2

The Class K were the last locomotives built for the Metropolitan Railway and all six were delivered in March 1925 from Armstrong Whitworth & Co. put together with parts supplied by Woolwich Arsenal. Designed by G.Hally, the Met's C.M.E., they had a look of the Maunsell N class 2-6-0 tender engines which wasn't surprising as R.E.L.Maunsell had designed the Woolwich engines in the first instance. Weighing some 87 tons, they were substantial machines and easily handled the goods work for which they were purchased.

Like the other former LPTB under review here, the K's were superheated from the outset and had piston valves with Walschaerts valve gear.

Numbered 111 to 116 on the Met, they became Nos.6158 to 6163 on the LNER. Stratford was again chosen as the main works for this further class of ex LT engines and renumbering took place as they went for general repairs in 1938 and 1939.

They spent all their lives on the former Metropolitan lines and could be seen hauling goods trains or shunting the yards between Finchley Road and out as far as Aylesbury. Although their height above rail level was within the LNER Composite Load Gauge, some aspects of their width caused them to be banned from the tunnels south of Finchley Road.

Black livery became the norm during LNER days and withdrawals started in 1943 as the wartime NE came into general usage. Two of the class were renumbered under the 1943 scheme whilst two others were allocated numbers but failed to get them before withdrawal. 9070 (6158) and 9071 (6160) lasted until October 1948 before they were condemned. No doubt their lives were prolonged by the shortages of motive power during wartime and the period immediately afterwards.

M1

The nine engines of LNER Class M1 were the only 0-6-4 tank engines employed by the company until 1937 when another four ex-London Transport engines of the same wheel arrangement (LNER Class M2) were added to stock.

The nine M1's had been part of the Great Central locomotive fleet inherited by the LNER at Grouping but the GCR itself had inherited the nine when it absorbed the Lancashire Derbyshire & East Coast Railway in 1907.

The 0-6-4T's were essentially goods engines purchased by the LD&ECR in two batches from Kitson & Co. of Leeds in 1904 and 1906. The 1904 batch consisted six engines (Works Nos.4246 to 4251) and were numbered 29 to 34 in the LD&ECR roster of Class D. The three engines of the 1906 batch (Works Nos.4435 to 4437) were given the numbers 1 to 3 but with an A prefix. When taken over by the GCR these engines took up the number block 1145 to 1153 starting with A1 to A3 and then 29 to 34.

As already mentioned these engines were purchased to haul goods trains, mainly coal, from the East Midlands area coal mines served by the LD&EC to Grimsby, via the GCR from Lincoln, but once the GCR took over they were relegated to trip working and shunting from either Langwith Junction or Tuxford sheds where the class were allocated. Their work on the long coal hauls now being entrusted to 0-6-0 and 0-8-0 tender engines probably more suited to job. However, one of the Langwith Junction duties saw them on a lodging turn working a goods to Woodford and empties back. Another of that sheds duties had them assisting coal trains as far as Dunford Bridge, and on the last section from Sheffield (Victoria) they were used to bank the coal trains; the return to Langwith was light engine.

None of the engines were ever superheated but the boilers of the two batches differed slightly in that the later batch had fewer tubes installed and therefore less heating surface. This was changed over the years as Gorton built new boilers which were standardised and eventually all had Diagram 19A boilers as per the former GCR series, working at 160 pound pressure.

Besides the steam brake on the engine and vacuum ejector for train working, Nos.29, 30, A1, A2 and A3 had steam actuated brakes on their bogies but these were taken off before Grouping.

All received their LNER numbering during 1924 and 1925 when 5000 was added to their former GC numbers.

Tuxford works carried out the maintenance on the M1's until that works closed in 1927, Doncaster then took over for a few years until Gorton became responsible for them and all the other former LD&ECR engines, in 1931.

When the LNER came into being it was usual for certain types of engines to be tested out at other sheds far from the engines usual haunts and one Class M1 engine followed this trend. No.6149 went first to Ardsley in August 1927 where it found work for a month on the Wakefield to Bradford portion of the morning express from London to Leeds. It was apparently quite successful on this turn but it was returned to Tuxford after touching the platform at Batley Carr. Its next move was to Lincoln in November 1934 where it spent just two weeks before moving back to Tuxford.

Tuxford shed became the home for the entire class in 1928 and other than No.6149's short stay at Lincoln and No.6147's move to Langwith in 1930, things remained that way. The first withdrawal was No.6152 which went for scrap in February 1939 but the intervention of war stopped the wholesale withdrawal of the class and though a few succumbed during WWII, four managed to survive to the end of hostilities. No.6145 which was withdrawn in September 1941, was partly dismantled by Gorton then after the boiler, cab and side tanks were removed the remaining portion of the locomotive, including the bunker, was left intact and used to carry and transport a large air cylinder around the works. This 'portion' of 6145 survived until 1958 when, after outliving all the other M1's by more than ten years, it was eventually cut up for scrap. Five engines were allocated new numbers in the 1943 scheme but only one No.6151 carried its new number 9082 which was applied in May 1946. That same engine was also the last to be withdrawn when in July 1947 LNER Class M1 became extinct.

M2

These four 0-6-4 tank engines became LNER property in 1937 under the same circumstances as the H2 and L2 classes described earlier. All four were built by the Yorkshire Engine Co. and supplied to the Metropolitan Railway during the winter months of 1915-16 being designated Class G.

Robinson superheaters and mechanical lubricators were installed from new and these were the first Met locomotives to receive them. Piston valves were also fitted from new. Maintenance was carried out at the Neasden works of the Metropolitan Railway until the LNER period when they then visited Stratford for major repairs. It was during their tenure on the LNER when the engines had their Ramsbottom safety valves replaced by Ross 'pop' valves.

Though classified as mixed traffic, these engines spent most of their lives working goods trains on the Metropolitan line, their use on passenger trains being somewhat rare after the 4-4-4T's of Class H (LNER H2) arrived in 1920. The LNER altered the heights of the chimney, dome and cab to conform to the LNER gauge but the engines never strayed away from their usual radius of operation.

Numbered 94 to 97 on the Met, they also carried names on curved brass plates fixed to the front driving wheel splashers. Other than the North Eastern Railway 2-2-4T AEROLITE, these were the only LNER owned tank engines to carry names. On becoming London Passenger Transport Board property in 1933 they retained their names and numbers but the LNER renumbered them 6154 to 6157 during 1938/9. In January 1943 Stratford works withdrew No.6157 but the next withdrawal was not until May 1946 when 6154 was scrapped. Miraculously, the other two engines 6155 (9076) and 6156 (9077) survived until October 1948 and were even allocated BR numbers. Being such non standard engines they were hardly likely to last much longer and Stratford condemned them making Class M2 extinct.

(below) **Six tank engines for the Lancashire, Derbyshire & East Coast Railway were built during the May and June of 1904 by Kitson & Co., Leeds. Numbered 29 to 34, they had an 0-6-4 wheel arrangement and were intended for coal train haulage. When the L.D & E.C.R. was taken over by the Great Central from 1st January 1907 they became Nos.1148 to 1153. At Grouping they were in black, with red and double white lining. No.1153, to October 1924, was the last with the original two-column Ramsbottom safety valves.**

(above) **Between 29th November 1915 and 14th March 1916, the Metropolitan Railway took delivery of four engines from Yorkshire Engine Co. Ltd., Sheffield to which they gave Nos.94 to 97. Note the brackets at each side of the apron plate to carry destination boards.**

(above) **A further five engines of the same design were built at Gorton in 1917 but had two Ross 'pop' safety valves on shallow mountings and were also fitted with ATC on the 'Reliostop' system.**

(left) **Ten more engines to the same design as the 1917 batch, except that these had double side windows on the cab, were built by Gorton in 1923 to fulfil an order issued by the GCR before Grouping.**

By Grouping and in early LNER years, the whole class, including the ten 1923-built engines, were fitted with Robinson's combined blower and steam circulating valve on the left hand side of the smokebox.

CLASS A 5

5165

Gorton.

To traffic 18/3/1911.

REPAIRS:
Gor. 2/6—15/9/17.**G.**
Gor. 27/5—5/8/22.**G.**
Gor. 21/6—18/10/24.**G.**
Cab side windows fitted.
Gor. 17/4—24/7/26.**G.**
Gor. 31/7/26.**L.**
Converted to fuel oil.
Nea. 2/3/27.**N/C.**
Fuel oil app. removed.
Gor. 8/12/28—9/2/29.**G.**
Gor. 28/2—4/4/31.**G.**
Gor. 20/8—24/9/32.**G.**
Gor. 3/2—17/3/34.**G.**
Intensifore removed.
Eureka fitted.
Gor. 7—28/3/36.**G.**
Fountain lubrication to
axleboxes.
Gor. 30/10—20/11/37.**G.**
Gor. 27/1—2/3/40.**G.**
Gor. 14/11—6/12/41.**H.**
Special examination.
Gor. 15/4—29/5/43.**H.**
Gor. 24/6—30/9/44.**G.**
New frames & cylinders.
Gor. 22/6—3/8/46.**G.**
Gor. 29/3—5/4/47.**L.**
Gor. 27/9—18/10/47.**G.**
Gor. 29/1—5/3/49.**G.**
W.P.U. gear removed.
Dar. 1/5—8/6/51.**G.**
Gor. 24/4—12/6/54.**G.**
Gor. 10—16/6/54.**N/C.**
Dar. 13/9—16/10/56.**G.**
Dar. 20/3—29/4/57.**C/H.**
Dar. 22/8/59. *Not repaired.*

BOILERS:
  1419.
  1420 *(ex5166)* 15/9/17.
  1421 *(ex5168)* 18/10/24.
   343 *(ex5371)* 24/9/32.
   390 *(ex5088)* 28/3/36.
   444 *(ex5169)* 20/11/37.
   718 *(ex5452)* 2/3/40.
   964 *(ex5030)* 29/5/43.
   845 *(ex9803)* 3/8/46.
   672 *(ex9807)* 18/10/47.
  3848 *(ex9824)* 5/3/49.
 22377 *(ex69825)* 8/6/51.
 22039 *(ex spare)* 12/6/54.
 22397 *(ex69818)* 16/10/56.

SHEDS:
Annesley.
Ardsley 5/1/24.
Neasden 21/4/24.
Woodford 4/10/38.
Colwick 17/8/39.
Neasden 8/11/40.
Ardsley 27/10/41.
Neasden 30/5/43.
Immingham 26/3/50.
Colwick 23/10/55.
Leicester 15/6/57.
Staveley 26/1/58.
Annesley 8/6/58 *o/l.*
Leicester 15/6/58.
Colwick 11/1/59.

RENUMBERED:
5165 18/10/24.
9800 24/3/46.
69800 5/3/49.

CONDEMNED: 24/8/59.
Cut up at Darlington.

5166

Gorton.

To traffic 15/4/1911.

REPAIRS:
Gor. 6/1—24/3/17.**G.**
Gor. 22/4—17/6/22.**G.**
Gor. 10/11/23—9/2/24.**G.**
Cab side windows fitted.
Gor. 24/10—31/12/25.**G.**
Nea. 23—30/7/26.**L.**
Converted to fuel oil.
Nea. 9/3/27.**N/C.**
Fuel oil app. removed.
Gor. 22/10—31/12/27.**G.**
Gor. 15/6—3/8/29.**G.**
Gor. 25/4—30/5/31.**G.**
Gor. 10/2—10/3/34.**G.**
Gor. 4/4—9/5/36.**G.**
Gor. 27/11—31/12/37.**G.**
Gor. 14/1—4/2/39.**G.**
Gor. 25/1—15/2/41.**G.**
Gor. 8/5—10/7/43.**G.**
Gor. 3—31/3/45.**G.**
Gor. 12/4—24/5/47.**G.**
Gor. 23/10—27/11/48.**G.**
W.P.U. gear removed.
Dar. 10/1—10/2/51.**G.**
Dar. 3—27/10/51.**C/L.**
Dar. 20/5—17/6/52.**C/L.**
Dar. 8/1—2/7/53.**C/H.**
Dar. 15/3—28/5/55.**G.**
Dar. 16—21/6/55.**N/C.**

Dar. 12/3—25/4/58.**G.**
Dar. 1/3/60. *Not repaired.*

BOILERS:
  1420.
  1665 *(new)* 24/3/17.
  1597 *(exD9 6037)* 9/2/24.
   557 *(exD9 5107)* 30/5/31.
   714 *(ex5006)* 10/3/34.
   844 *(ex5170)* 9/5/36.
   390 *(ex5165)* 31/12/37.
   276 *(exD9 6036)* 4/2/39.
   384 *(ex5450)* 15/2/41.
   719 *(exD9 6029)* 31/3/45.
   800 *(ex9829)* 24/5/47.
   968 *(exD9 2332)* 27/11/48.
 22365 *(ex9817)* 10/2/51.
 22398 *(ex spare)* 2/7/53.
 22380 *(ex spare)* 25/4/58.

SHEDS:
Neasden.
Colwick 30/12/49.
Darlington 18/2/51.
Colwick 1/7/51.
Gorton 7/10/56.

RENUMBERED:
5166 9/2/24.
9801 24/3/46.
69801 27/11/48.

CONDEMNED: 1/3/60.
Cut up at Darlington.

5167

Gorton.

To traffic 6/5/1911.

REPAIRS:
Gor. 3/6—19/8/16.**G.**
Robinson superheater boiler.
Gor. 26/11/21—4/2/22.**G.**
Gor. 12/8—2/9/22.**L.**
New cylinders.
Gor. 18/6—11/10/24.**G.**
Cab side windows fitted.
Gor. 5/6—28/8/26.**G.**
Gor. 19/7/27—21/1/28.**G.**
Gor. 23/6—18/8/28.**G.**
Gor. 18/10—29/11/30.**G.**
Gor. 4/6—9/7/32.**G.**
Gor. 17/6—15/7/33.**G.**
Gor. 16/2—16/3/35.**G.**
Gor. 27/6—25/7/36.**G.**
Gor. 4/9—9/10/37.**G.**
Gor. 25/3—22/4/39.**G.**
Gor. 9/7—16/8/41.**G.**

Gor. 22/9/42—2/1/43.**G.**
Gor. 30/8—14/10/44.**G.**
Gor. 11/5—14/9/46.**G.**
New frames & cylinders.
Gor. 8/5—5/6/48.**G.**
Dar. 2/11—10/12/49.**C/H.**
Dar. 3/1—9/2/52.**G.**
Gor. 22/5—3/7/54.**G.**
Dar. 14/6—15/9/55.**C/L.**
Dar. 30/1—1/3/58.**G.**
Dar. 3—5/3/58.**N/C.**
Dar. 24/12/58. *Not repaired.*

BOILERS:
  1421.
  1624 *(new)* 19/8/16.
   138 *(exD9 6041)* 4/2/22.
   983 *(new)* 29/11/30.
   719 *(ex5128)* 15/7/33.
   796 *(exD9 6030)* 16/3/35.
   799 *(ex5372)* 25/7/36.
   941 *(ex5373)* 9/10/37.
   392 *(exD9 5108)* 22/4/39.
  3853 *(new)* 16/8/41.
   984 *(ex5128)* 14/10/44.
  3866 *(new)* 14/9/46.
  3861 *(ex9811)* 5/6/48.
   984 *(exD9 62332)* 10/12/49.
 22382 *(ex spare)* 9/2/52.
 22370 *(ex69826)* 3/7/54.
 22381 *(ex69819)* 1/3/58.

SHEDS:
Neasden.
Ardsley 20/11/24.
King's Cross 15/2/28.
Neasden 12/9/28.
Saltburn 4/6/50.
Hull Botanic Gardens 19/8/51.
Bridlington 9/1/55.
Hull Botanic Gardens 29/5/55.

RENUMBERED:
5167 11/10/24.
9802 24/3/46.
69802 5/6/48.

CONDEMNED: 24/12/58.
Cut up at Darlington.

5168

Gorton.

To traffic 20/5/1911.

REPAIRS:
Gor. 28/10—23/12/16.**G.**
Gor. 1/4—1/7/22.**G.**
Ross Pops fitted.

For superheater protection, the circulating valves were replaced in the mid-1920's by the simpler Gresley anti-vacuum valve. On some this was connected to the front of the header and mounted on the side of the smokebox. Note the pillar bases for control rod to the circulating valve have not been taken off but the boiler top feed has gone and its opening plated over.

During the 1939-45 war, Gorton made dome covers with a flatter profile, and some were put on the A5/1 class.

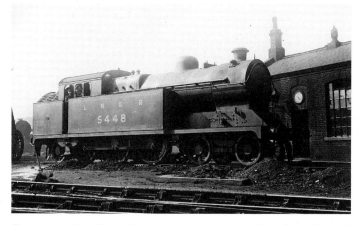

On some engines the anti-vacuum valve was located on the right hand side of the smokebox.

On some replacement boilers with low dome, the original high cover remained in use, although it gave a height of 13ft 5in.

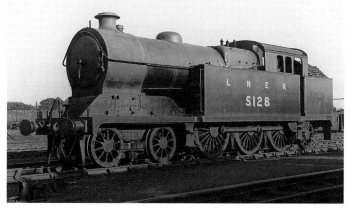

In due course the whole class had the Gresley anti-vacuum valve in the normal position behind the chimney and mounted on top of the header. No attempt was made in LNER days to bring A5/1 class within the 13ft 0in. load gauge, but when replacement boilers were built, they had to be suitable for use also on Class D9 engines where 13ft 0in. maximum height was required. Therefore, these replacement boilers had low dome, and the whistle was placed in front of the cab instead of above it.

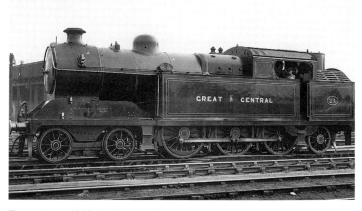

From about 1920 the Ramsbottom safety valves, fitted originally, were replaced by Ross 'pop' type which then became standard. At first short 'pops' were used, on the original mounting.

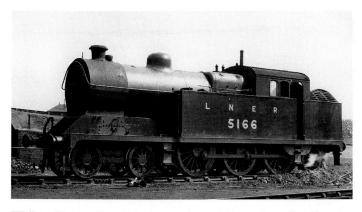

Whilst still using the original mounting, a taller and smaller diameter valve became standard. On replacement boilers, no mounting pad was provided (*see* page 12 right, centre).

The 'Intensifore' type suffered from air locks and between 4th January 1930 (5448) and 22nd February 1936 (5411), all A5 class had them removed and replaced by the Detroit or Eureka hydrostatic lubricator. Feed pipes from the cab to the front end were then clearly to be seen.

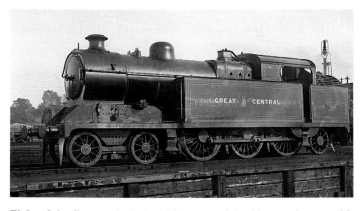

Eight of the first ten built had 18-element Schmidt superheater with element protection by flue dampers operated by the small steam cylinder on the smokebox side. Wakefield mechanical lubricators served the cylinders and valves.

In the original batch, one at least had steam operated bogie wheel flange lubrication fitted. Note the vacuum ejector exhaust pipe is through the boiler, only possible with the original 18-element superheater. Note also that no top feed is fitted.

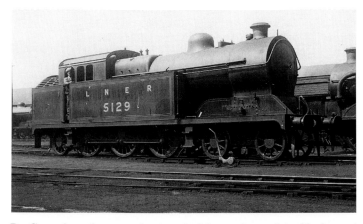

By Grouping, the superheaters had been changed to 22-element Robinson type and lubrication changed to Robinson's 'Intensifore' pattern. This was sight feed but pressure fed and all the class got it.

Both above features had been removed from No.170 by Grouping, probably at its November 1918 shopping.

5168 cont./

Gor. 15/3—28/6/24.**G.**
Gor. 4/9—25/12/26.**G.**
Cab side windows fitted.
Gor. 16—30/4/27.**L.**
Gor. 31/8—19/10/29.**G.**
Gor. 9/9—24/10/31.**G.**
Gor. 17/3—19/5/34.**G.**
Intensifore removed.
Eureka fitted.
Gor. 9—30/5/36.**G.**
Fountain lubrication to
axleboxes.
Gor. 24/7—21/8/37.**G.**
Gor. 28/5—2/7/38.**G.**
Gor. 9/3—27/4/40.**G.**
Gor. 20/7—5/9/42.**G.**
Gor. 30/11/43—1/1/44.**G.**
Gor. 6/1—10/2/45.**L.**
Gor. 13/4—25/5/46.**G.**
Gor. 21—28/9/46.**L.**
Gor. 30/11—7/12/46.**L.**
Gor. 7/2—6/3/48.**G.**
Ghd. 24/3—29/4/49.**C/L.**
Dar. 22/5—14/7/51.**G.**
Dar. 16/7—4/9/53.**G.**
Dar. 12/5—8/7/55.**G.**
Dar. 18—20/7/55.**N/C.**
Dar. 3—4/10/55.**N/C.**
Dar. 23/6/59. *Not repaired.*

BOILERS:
1422.
1421 *(ex5167)* 23/12/16.
1624 *(exD9 6038)* 28/6/24.
392 *(exD9 6037)* 24/10/31.
557 *(ex5003)* 30/5/36.
168 *(ex5088)* 21/8/37.
719 *(exD9 6013)* 2/7/38.
984 *(ex5158)* 27/4/40.
396 *(ex5373)* 5/9/42.
845 *(ex5024)* 1/1/44.
843 *(ex5003)* 25/5/46.
91 *(ex9820)* 6/3/48.
22375 *(ex69805)* 14/7/51.
22368 *(ex69809)* 4/9/53.
22351 *(ex69814)* 8/7/55.

SHEDS:
Neasden.
Ardsley 20/11/24.
Neasden 28/7/27.
Lincoln 11/7/48.
Grantham 10/7/49.
Boston 29/10/50.
Immingham 28/8/55.
Langwith Jct. 24/6/56.
Staveley 28/10/56.
Sheffield Darnall 13/4/58.
Lincoln 8/6/58.

RENUMBERED:
5168 28/6/24.
9803 24/3/46.
E **9803** 6/3/48.
69803 29/4/49.

CONDEMNED: 23/6/59.
Cut up at Darlington.

5169

Gorton.

To traffic 27/5/1911.

REPAIRS:
Gor. 17/4—12/6/20.**G.**
Gor. 7/1—4/3/22.**G.**
Ross Pops fitted.
Gor. 28/7—13/10/23.**G.**
Gor. 10—17/11/23.**L.**
After collision.
Gor. 23/1—3/4/26.**G.**
Cab side windows fitted.
Gor. 22/10—24/12/27.**G.**
Gor. 21/12/29—8/2/30.**G.**
Gor. 16/4—14/5/32.**G.**
Gor. 5/8—16/9/33.**G.**
Gor. 24/8—28/9/35.**G.**
Fountain lubrication to
axleboxes.
Gor. 10/7—14/8/37.**G.**
Gor. 21/1—25/2/39.**G.**
Gor. 8/2—1/3/41.**G.**
Gor. 10/11/42—13/2/43.**G.**
Gor. 25/11/44—6/1/45.**G.**
Gor. 21/9—26/10/46.**G.**
Gor. 28/2—3/4/48.**G.**
Dar. 11/12/48—8/1/49.**C/H.**
Dar. 5/11/49—5/1/50.**G.**
Dar. 10/12/51—22/1/52.**G.**
Gor. 11/12/54—5/2/55.**G.**
Dar. 3/1—2/2/56.**C/L.**
Dar. 27/8—11/10/57.**C/L.**
Dar. 31/3/58. *Not repaired.*

BOILERS:
1423.
1530 *(ex5450)* 12/6/20.
1532 *(ex5128)* 24/12/27.
1843 *(ex5006)* 14/5/32.
1597 *(ex5045)* 16/9/33.
444 *(exD9 6023)* 28/9/35.
410 *(exD9 6040)* 14/8/37.
168 *(ex5024)* 1/3/41.
3853 *(ex5167)* 6/1/45.
964 *(ex9800)* 26/10/46.
3869 *(new)* 3/4/48.
806 *(ex9821)* 5/1/50.
22387 *(ex69812)* 22/1/52.
22391 *(ex69827)* 5/2/55.

SHEDS:
Neasden.
Woodford 6/12/39.
Neasden 30/12/39.
Lincoln 23/4/50.
Immingham 20/2/55.
Boston 24/4/55.
Langwith Jct. 15/5/55.
Colwick 23/10/55.

RENUMBERED:
169c 3/10/23.
5169 3/4/26.
9804 31/3/46.
69804 3/4/48.

CONDEMNED: 7/4/58.
Cut up at Darlington.

5170

Gorton.

To traffic 10/6/1911.

REPAIRS:
Gor. 31/8—9/11/18.**G.**
Gor. 16/9—4/11/22.**G.**
Gor. 29/3—7/6/24.**G.**
Cab side windows fitted.
Gor. 29/5—21/8/26.**G.**
Gor. 21/7—22/9/28.**G.**
Gor. 1/11—6/12/30.**G.**
Gor. 29/10—3/12/32.**G.**
Gor. 25/8—29/9/34.**G.**
Gor. 21/3—11/4/36.**G.**
Fountain lubrication to
axleboxes.
Gor. 26/6—24/7/37.**G.**
Gor. 29/4—20/5/39.**G.**
Gor. 24/5—12/7/41.**G.**
Gor. 26/5—25/9/43.**G.**
Gor. 7/7—25/8/45.**G.**
Gor. 26/4—31/5/47.**G.**
Gor. 31/12/48—5/2/49.**G.**
W.P.U. gear removed.
Gor. 3—27/8/49.**C/H.**
Dar. 26/4—1/6/51.**G.**
Dar. 5/12/52—21/3/53.**G.**
Dar. 23—24/3/53.**N/C.**
Dar. 30/3—17/4/53.**N/C.**
Dar. 29/6—30/7/55.**G.**
Dar. 23/4—30/5/58.**G.**

BOILERS:
1424.
1533 *(ex5128)* 9/11/18.
253 *(exD9 6028)* 21/8/26.
984 *(new)* 6/12/30.
844 *(ex5451)* 29/9/34.
816 *(exD9 5110)* 11/4/36.

366 *(exD9 6028)* 24/7/37.
941 *(ex5167)* 20/5/39.
3852 *(new)* 12/7/41.
3858 *(ex5006)* 25/8/45.
171 *(ex9824)* 31/5/47.
708 *(exD9 2312)* 5/2/49.
22369 *(ex69806)* 1/6/51.
22046 *(new)* 30/7/55.
22041 *(ex69819)* 30/5/58.

SHEDS:
Annesley.
Ardsley 5/1/24.
Gorton 25/3/24.
Neasden 7/7/24.
Colwick 29/1/50.
Neasden 30/7/50.
Gorton 13/6/54.
Colwick 19/5/57.

RENUMBERED:
5170 7/6/24.
9805 31/3/46.
69805 5/2/49.

CONDEMNED: 23/9/59.
Into Dar. for cut up 10/10/59.

5023

Gorton.

To traffic 24/6/1911.

REPAIRS:
Gor. 21/4—23/6/17.**G.**
Gor. 18/10—21/11/19.**G.**
Gor. 16/4—14/5/21.**G.**
Gor. 21/10—9/12/22.**G.**
Gor. 12/7—4/10/24.**G.**
Cab side windows fitted.
Nea. 5—11/8/26.**L.**
Converted to fuel oil.
Gor. 11/12/26—26/2/27.**G.**
Fuel oil app. removed.
Gor. 11/8—6/10/28.**G.**
Gor. 28/6—2/8/30.**G.**
Gor. 14/5—11/6/32.**G.**
Gor. 13/5—17/6/33.**G.**
Gor. 13/10—3/11/34.**G.**
Gor. 25/7—15/8/36.**G.**
Fountain lubrication to
axleboxes.
Gor. 19/2—19/3/38.**G.**
Gor. 9/12/39—6/1/40.**G.**
Gor. 26/3—18/4/42.**G.**
Gor. 1/10—6/11/43.**G.**
Gor. 5/5—23/6/45.**G.**
Gor. 29/6—27/7/46.**L.**
Gor. 17/5—21/6/47.**G.**
Gor. 5/2—5/3/49.**G.**

WORKS CODES:- Cw - Cowlairs. Dar- Darlington. Don - Doncaster. Ghd - Gateshead. Gor - Gorton. Inv - Inverurie. Str - Stratford. Tux - Tuxford.
REPAIR CODES:- **C/H** - Casual Heavy. **C/L** - Casual Light. **G** - General. **H**- Heavy. **H/I** - Heavy Intermediate. **L** - Light. **L/I** - Light Intermediate. **N/C** - Non-Classified.

14

For a short time in the middle 1920's, some of the 1923 batch were fitted with ash ejector. These smokebox ash ejectors were soon taken off in cases where they had been fitted.

Until after the LNER took over, the first twenty-one engines had their cab front windows in two portions, the larger around the top corner of the firebox with a smaller square portion below.

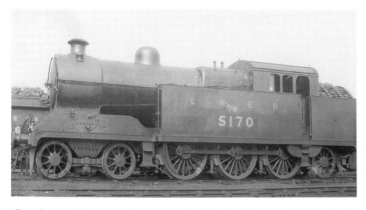

Gravity sanding was fitted ahead of the leading, and behind, the trailing coupled wheels, and all were so fitted.

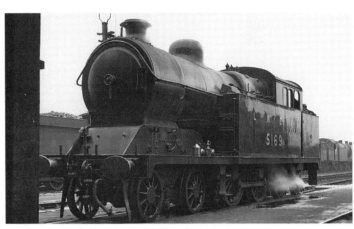

Most, but not all of these twenty-one subsequently acquired single piece front windows. The ten 1923 engines had the single window from building.

Until September 1948 all A5/1 had water pick-up gear for both directions of running. Note the plate to protect it from being damaged by a swinging coupling. Removal then began and by March 1949 Gorton had taken it off thirteen of the thirty-one. Later maintenance was done by Darlington, and on their repair sheets they did not record removal of the WPU gear.

At least four are known to have kept the original style front windows through to withdrawal.

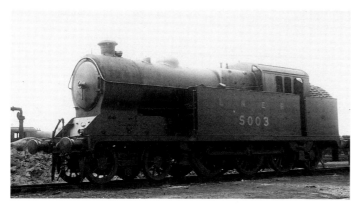

One boiler was fitted in June 1914 with top feed between the dome and chimney. The rest of the class had been so fitted by Grouping. The ten boilers for the 1923 engines were built with top feed, and eight of them later served on D9 class engines from 1929 but no D9's carried a boiler with top feed.

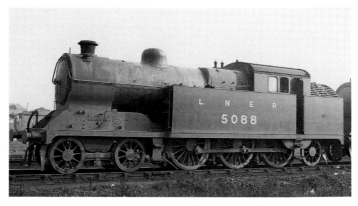

These Robinson chimneys proved prone to cracking and where this occurred from 1925, the replacement chimney was the straighter sided 'flowerpot' type, which was fitted to most of the class. The 'flowerpot' was 1ft 9in. high, the same as the original.

Breakage of feed pipes and sticking clack valves caused top feed to be discarded so by 1929 it had virtually disappeared.

In the early 1930's the 'flowerpot' type was superseded by a design much more akin to the original but 1ft 5½in. tall against the 1ft 9in. Robinson design. When a low dome boiler was used, this brought the engine below 13ft 0in.

The twenty-one pre-Grouping engines all carried the Robinson design of chimney, over which the height from rail level was 13ft 3in. The ten engines built in 1923 had the same design of chimney.

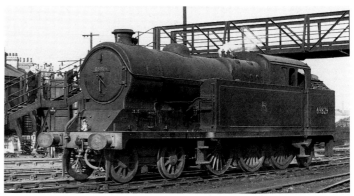

To release three V1's from Norwich for transfer to Scotland, three A5's got low dome boilers and were fitted with a built-up chimney to bring them to the G.E. gauge. Nos.69824, 69826 and 69829 were all altered in May, 1952.

5023 cont./
W.P.U. gear removed.
Dar. 25/1—3/3/51.**G.**
Dar. 4—6/4/51.**N/C.**
Ghd. 5/11—6/12/52.**C/H.**
Dar. 4/9—3/10/53.**G.**
Dar. 14—17/10/53.**N/C.**
Dar. 10/12/53—21/1/54.**C/H.**
Dar. 16/10—29/11/56.**G.**

BOILERS:
1425.
1426 *(ex5024)* 23/6/17.
1424 *(ex5170)* 21/11/19.
1423 *(ex5169)* 14/5/21.
1530 *(ex5169)* 6/10/28.
1532 *(ex5169)* 11/6/32.
410 *(exD9 6034)* 17/6/33.
696 *(exD9 6036)* 3/11/34.
964 *(new)* 15/8/36.
278 *(ex5046)* 19/3/38.
986 *(ex5448)* 6/1/40.
210 *(ex5449)* 18/4/42.
1825 *(ex spare)* 6/11/43.
983 *(exD9 6032)* 23/6/45.
718 *(ex9809)* 21/6/47.
3852 *(ex9825)* 5/3/49.
22364 *(ex69818)* 3/3/51.
22374 *(ex69830)* 3/10/53.
22388 *(ex69808)* 29/11/56.

SHEDS:
Neasden.
Colwick 12/2/50.
Gorton 13/6/54.

RENUMBERED:
5023 4/10/24.
9806 27/7/46.
69806 5/3/49.

CONDEMNED: 3/3/60.
Into Dar. for cut up 3/3/60.

5024

Gorton.

To traffic 1/7/1911.

REPAIRS:
Gor. 17/3—19/5/17.**G.**
Gor. 26/3—7/5/21.**G.**
Ross Pops fitted.
Gor. 17/2—19/5/23.**G.**
Gor. 4/4—27/6/25.**G.**
Cab side windows fitted.
Nea. 28/7—6/8/26.**L.**
Converted to fuel oil.
Gor. 22/1—2/4/27.**G.**
Fuel oil app. removed.
Gor. 6/8—24/9/27.**G.**
Gor. 9/2—20/4/29.**G.**
Gor. 31/12/30—31/1/31.**G.**
Gor. 1/7—5/8/33.**G.**

Gor. 16/9/33.**L.**
Gor. 20/7—31/8/35.**G.**
Fountain lubrication to
axleboxes.
Gor. 27/3—17/4/37.**G.**
Gor. 24/9—22/10/38.**G.**
Gor. 19/10—16/11/40.**G.**
Gor. 26/9—31/10/42.**G.**
Gor. 13/11—11/12/43.**G.**
Gor. 14--28/10/44.**L.**
Gor. 17/11—21/12/45.**G.**
Gor. 9/8—13/9/47.**G.**
Fitted with GWR A.T.C.
Dar. 18/3—6/5/49.**G.**
GWR A.T.C. removed.
Dar. 19/2—7/4/51.**G.**
Ghd. 3—22/11/52.**C/L.**
Gor. 2/10—4/12/54.**G.**
Ghd. 9—23/11/56.**C/L.**
After collision.
Dar. 24/1—26/2/57.**G.**
Dar. 3/7/58. *Not repaired.*

BOILERS:
1426.
1699 *(new)* 19/5/17.
444 *(new)* 19/5/23.
383 *(ex5411)* 20/4/29.
983 *(ex5167)* 5/8/33.
321 *(ex5447)* 17/4/37.
168 *(ex5168)* 22/10/38.
1825 *(ex5374)* 16/11/40.
845 *(exD9 6039)* 31/10/42.
846 *(ex5452)* 11/12/43.
672 *(ex5156)* 21/12/45.
983 *(ex9806)* 13/9/47.
3845 *(ex9810)* 6/5/49.
22372 *(ex spare)* 7/4/51.
22041 *(new)* 4/12/54.
22357 *(ex69810)* 26/2/57.

SHEDS:
Neasden.
Colwick 29/1/50.

RENUMBERED:
5024 27/6/25.
9807 11/8/46.
69807 6/5/49.

CONDEMNED: 14/7/58.
Cut up at Darlington.

5447

Gorton.

To traffic 15/7/1911.

REPAIRS:
Gor. 23/6—13/10/17.**G.**
Gor. ?/?—10/10/19.**L.**
Reliostop fitted.
Gor. 13/1—10/3/23.**G.**
Gor. 17/1—28/3/25.**G.**

Cab side windows fitted.
Gor. 21/5—16/7/27.**G.**
Gor. 19/10—7/12/29.**G.**
Gor. 28/11/31—9/1/32.**G.**
Gor. 11/11—16/12/33.**G.**
Gor. 3/8—21/9/35.**G.**
Fountain lubrication to
axleboxes.
Gor. 13/3—10/4/37.**G.**
Gor. 17/12/38—14/1/39.**G.**
Gor. 5—26/10/40.**G.**
Gor. 21/12/42. *Not repaired.*

BOILERS:
1427.
1425 *(ex5023)* 13/10/17.
1685 *(ex5373)* 28/3/25.
384 *(exD9 6024)* 9/1/32.
321 *(exD9 6018)* 16/12/33.
985 *(ex5450)* 10/4/37.
800 *(exD9 5105)* 14/1/39.
3842 *(ex5156)* 26/10/40.

SHED:
Neasden.

RENUMBERED:
5447 28/3/25.

CONDEMNED: 21/12/42.
Cut up at Gorton.

5448

Gorton.

To traffic 12/8/1911.

REPAIRS:
Gor. 17/11/17—2/2/18.**G.**
Gor. 3/9—29/10/21.**G.**
Gor. 5/1/22.**L.**
Ross Pops fitted.
Gor. 3/3—9/6/23.**G.**
Gor. 28/11/25—13/2/26.**G.**
Cab side windows fitted.
Gor. 26/11/27—11/2/28.**G.**
Gor. 16/11/29—4/1/30.**G.**
Gor. 7/11—12/12/31.**G.**
Gor. 2/12/33—13/1/34.**G.**
Gor. 6/7—3/8/35.**G.**
Fountain lubrication to
axleboxes.
Gor. 26/12/36—23/1/37.**G.**
Gor. 5/2—12/3/38.**G.**
Trip cock gear fitted.
Gor. 28/10—2/12/39.**G.**
Gor. 16/10—6/12/41.**G.**
Gor. 12/3—11/4/42.**L.**
Collision damage.
Gor. 28/1—4/3/44.**G.**
Gor. 3—21/10/44.**L.**
Gor. 13/4—1/6/46.**G.**
Gor. 13/12/47—17/1/48.**G.**
Dar. 22/6—6/12/49.**G.**

Dar. 3—22/3/52.**G.**
Dar. 24—26/3/52.**N/C.**
Gor. 15/5—26/6/54.**H/I.**
Gor. 27/6—5/7/54.**N/C.**
Dar. 24/8—2/10/56.**G.**
Dar. 17/11/60. *Not repaired.*

BOILERS:
1428.
1427 *(ex5447)* 2/2/18.
1683 *(ex5371)* 9/6/23.
1784 *(exD9 6037)* 4/1/30.
1624 *(ex5168)* 12/12/31.
416 *(exD9 6027)* 13/1/34.
383 *(ex5158)* 3/8/35.
986 *(ex5128)* 23/1/37.
843 *(exD9 6015)* 2/12/39.
3849 *(ex5451)* 6/12/41.
696 *(exD9 6019)* 4/3/44.
658 *(exD9 6039)* 1/6/46.
3841 *(ex9822)* 17/1/48.
22388 *(ex69828)* 22/3/52.
22362 *(ex69822)* 2/10/56.

SHEDS:
Annesley.
Ardsley 5/1/24.
Neasden 21/4/24.
King's Cross 22/2/28.
Neasden 8/1/30.
Ardsley 16/10/41.
Neasden 15/2/43.
Immingham 26/3/50.
Boston 6/8/50.
Immingham 19/2/56.
Boston 26/2/56.
Lincoln 1/3/59.

RENUMBERED:
5448 13/2/26.
9808 1/6/46.
ᴇ 9808 17/1/48.
69808 6/12/49.

CONDEMNED: 17/11/60.
Into Dar. for cut up 17/11/60.

5449

Gorton.

To traffic 19/10/1912.

REPAIRS:
Gor. 7/2—8/5/20.**G.**
Gor. 12/3/22.**L.**
Ross Pops fitted.
Gor. 18/11—16/12/22.**G.**
Gor. 27/10/23—26/1/24.**G.**
Gor. 6/3—12/6/26.**G.**
Cab side windows fitted.
Gor. 10/12/27—4/2/28.**G.**
Gor. 31/5—26/7/30.**G.**
Gor. 4/6—2/7/32.**G.**
Gor. 30/6—21/7/34.**G.**

5449 cont./
Gor. 13/6—25/7/36.**G.**
Fountain lubrication to
axleboxes.
Gor. 20/11—11/12/37.**G.**
Gor. 2/3—6/4/40.**G.**
Gor. 7—31/1/42.**G.**
Gor. 16/10—20/11/43.**G.**
Gor. 19/8—2/9/44.**L.**
Gor. 29/12/45—26/1/46.**G.**
New frames & cylinders.
Gor. 8/3—5/4/47.**G.**
Gor. 28/8—25/9/48.**G.**
W.P.U. gear removed.
Dar. 5/6—10/8/50.**C/L.**
Dar. 10/2—10/3/51.**G.**
Dar. 2—14/4/51.**N/C.**
Dar. 11/5—6/6/53.**G.**
Dar. 8—9/6/53.**N/C.**
Dar. 18—19/6/53.**N/C.**
Gor. 6—27/11/54.**C/L.**
Gor. 30/11—3/12/54.**N/C.**
Dar. 20/2—20/3/56.**G.**
Dar. 1/5/59. *Not repaired.*

BOILERS:
  1529.
  1534 *(ex5129)* 8/5/20.
  1825 *(ex5450)* 4/2/28.
  1530 *(ex5023)* 2/7/32.
   278 *(exD9 6017)* 21/7/34.
   325 *(exD9 5106)* 25/7/36.
   947 *(exD9 5107)* 11/12/37.
   210 *(exD9 5112)* 6/4/40.
   843 *(ex5448)* 31/1/42.
    91 *(exD9 5105)* 20/11/43.
   718 *(ex5374)* 26/1/46.
   936 *(exD9 2313)* 5/4/47.
  3856 *(ex9815)* 25/9/48.
  22368 *(ex spare)* 10/3/51.
  22399 *(ex spare)* 6/6/53.
  22047 *(new)* 20/3/56.

SHEDS:
Annesley.
Neasden 22/4/24.
Woodford 3/10/38.
Neasden 3/12/38.
Woodford 25/6/39.
Colwick 31/7/39.
Neasden 9/9/41.
Boston 30/1/49.
Colwick 11/12/49.
Annesley 7/10/56.
Colwick 14/12/58.

RENUMBERED:
  5449 26/1/24.
  9809 18/8/46.
  69809 25/9/48.

CONDEMNED: 4/5/59.
Cut up at Darlington.

5450

Gorton.

To traffic 2/11/1912.

REPAIRS:
Gor. 15/11—27/12/19.**G.**
Gor. 25/6—3/9/21.**G.**
Cab side windows fitted.
Gor. 20/10/21.**L.**
Ross Pops fitted.
Gor. 24/3—2/6/23.**G.**
Gor. 24/10—31/12/25.**G.**
Don. 24—29/1/27.**L.**
Gor. 14/5—9/7/27.**G.**
Gor. 11/5—6/7/29.**G.**
Gor. 29/8—10/10/31.**G.**
Gor. 13/5—17/6/33.**G.**
Gor. 4—25/5/35.**G.**
Intensifore removed.
Fountain lubrication to
axleboxes.
Gor. 30/1—27/2/37.**G.**
Gor. 27/8—8/10/38.**G.**
Gor. 3—17/12/38.**L.**
Gor. 30/11—21/12/40.**G.**
Gor. 15/4—5/6/43.**G.**
Gor. 10/3—14/4/45.**G.**
New frames & cylinders.
Gor. 15/3—19/4/47.**G.**
Gor. 6/11—11/12/48.**G.**
W.P.U. gear removed.
Dar. 14/3/51. *Weigh.*
Dar. 22/8—21/9/51.**G.**
Dar. 27/5—14/6/52.**C/L.**
After collision.
Dar. 30/3—19/5/53.**C/H.**
Gor. 4—.26/9/53**C/L.**
Gor. 29/9—3/10/53.**N/C.**
Gor. 13—27/3/54.**C/H.**
Gor. 30/3—8/4/54.**N/C.**
Gor. 27/11/54—5/3/55.**H/I.**
Gor. 8—15/3/55.**N/C.**
Dar. 31/10—5/12/56.**G.**

BOILERS:
  1530.
  1825 *(new)* 27/12/19.
  1420 *(ex5165)* 9/7/27.
  1826 *(ex5030)* 10/10/31.
   672 *(ex5046)* 17/6/33.
   985 *(exD9 6015)* 25/5/35.
   653 *(exD9 6027)* 27/2/37.
   384 *(exD9 6025)* 8/10/38.
   800 *(ex5447)* 21/12/40.
   210 *(ex5371)* 14/4/45.
  3845 *(exD9 2319)* 19/4/47.
   783 *(ex9818)* 11/12/48.
  22379 *(ex69820)* 21/9/51.
  22357 *(ex69821)* 27/3/54.
  22039 *(ex69800)* 5/12/56.

SHEDS:
Annesley.

Ardsley 5/1/24.
Neasden 21/4/24.
Ardsley 5/2/26.
Neasden 18/7/27.
Woodford 6/12/39.
Neasden 30/12/39.
Boston 30/1/49.
Colwick 11/12/49.
Darlington 4/2/51.
Colwick 8/7/51.

RENUMBERED:
  5450 31/12/25.
  9810 18/8/46.
  69810 11/12/48.

CONDEMNED: 23/10/58.
Into Dar. for cut up 23/10/58.

5451

Gorton.

To traffic 16/11/1912.

REPAIRS:
Gor. 22/11—27/12/19.**G.**
Gor. 23/9—18/11/22.**G.**
Gor. 13/9—13/12/24.**G.**
Gor. 18/8—27/11/26.**G.**
Cab side windows fitted.
Gor. 15/9—10/11/28.**G.**
Gor. 3/1—21/2/31.**G.**
Gor. 15/10—19/11/32.**G.**
Gor. 2—23/6/34.**G.**
Gor. 28/3—25/4/36.**G.**
Gor. 18/12/37—8/1/38.**G.**
Gor. 29/7—26/8/39.**G.**
Gor. 27/10—29/11/41.**G.**
Gor. 23/3—29/5/43.**G.**
Gor. 6—27/1/45.**G.**
New frames & cylinders.
Gor. 26/10—16/11/46.**G.**
Gor. 13/3—24/4/48.**G.**
Dar. 9/1—17/2/50.**G.**
Dar. 27/2—8/3/50.**N/C.**
Dar. 16/6—12/7/52.**G.**
Gor. 13/11/54—15/1/55.**G.**
Dar. 22/10—22/11/56.**H/I.**

BOILERS:
  1531.
  1826 *(new)* 27/12/19.
   720 *(new)* 27/11/26.
   149 *(new)* 21/2/31.
   844 *(exD9 6025)* 19/11/32.
  1683 *(ex5373)* 23/6/34.
   343 *(ex5165)* 25/4/36.
   325 *(ex5449)* 8/1/38.
  3849 *(new)* 26/8/39.
   392 *(ex5167)* 29/11/41.
   708 *(exD9 6030)* 27/1/45.
  3861 *(exD9 2332)* 16/11/46.
   658 *(ex9808)* 24/4/48.
  3858 *(ex69820)* 17/2/50.

22393 *(ex69829)* 12/7/52.
22044 *(new)* 15/1/55.

SHEDS:
Neasden.
Ardsley 11/2/26.
Neasden 13/1/27.
Saltburn 4/6/50.
Hull Botanic Gardens 19/8/51.

RENUMBERED:
  5451 13/12/24.
  9811 18/8/46.
  69811 24/4/48.

CONDEMNED: 6/10/58.
Into Dar. for cut up 6/10/58.

5452

Gorton.

To traffic 30/11/1912.

REPAIRS:
Gor. 20/10—1/12/17.**G.**
Gor. 29/10/21—4/2/22.**G.**
Gor. 9/4/22.**L.**
Ross Pops fitted.
Gor. 31/3—25/8/23.**G.**
Gor. 21/11/25—30/1/26.**G.**
Cab side windows fitted.
Gor. 21/4—16/6/28.**G.**
Gor. 11/10—15/11/30.**G.**
Gor. 14/7—11/8/34.**G.**
Intensifore removed.
Gor. 4/9—16/10/37.**G.**
Fountain lubrication to
axleboxes.
Gor. 30/10/37.**L.**
Trip cock gear fitted.
Gor. 18/11—9/12/39.**G.**
Gor. 16/12/41—24/1/42.**G.**
Gor. 18/10—11/12/43.**G.**
Gor. 27/9—7/10/44.**L.**
Gor. 10/2—3/3/45.**L.**
Gor. 23/2—30/3/46.**G.**
Gor. 27/9—25/10/47.**G.**
Dar. 30/11/49—11/1/50.**G.**
Dar. 7/6—8/7/50.**C/H.**
Dar. 23/11—29/12/51.**G.**
Dar. 1—4/1/52.**N/C.**
Dar. 4—25/10/52.**C/L.**
Gor. 10/7—18/9/54.**G.**
Dar. 4/9—12/10/57.**G.**
Dar. 19—20/10/57.**N/C.**

BOILERS:
  1532.
  1419 *(ex5165)* 1/12/17.
   414 *(exD9 6025)* 25/8/23.
   558 *(exD9 6029)* 15/11/30.
  1825 *(exD9 6039)* 11/8/34.
   718 *(exD9 6015)* 16/10/37.
   846 *(exD9 6041)* 9/12/39.

No.5156 is believed to be one which never had a 'flowerpot' chimney as this 1932 photograph shows it still with the original 1ft 9in. type, and by 1936 it had a similar style but in the later 1ft 5½in. variety. Note hose connection at front end for carriage heating, also the angle iron strengthening stay fixed to the end of the side tank and curving under the boiler.

All thirty-one engines had, and retained, GC design buffers which had parallel shanks with a pronounced collar at the outer end. There was some appreciable variation in the shape of buffer head which could be circular, as in this photo, elliptical (*see* page 15 top, left), or a wide oval (*see* page 15 centre, right).

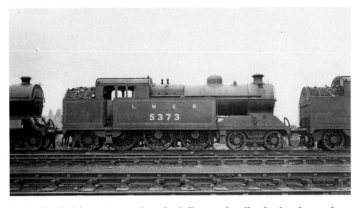

As built all thirty-one engines had five coal rails sloping inward on the top of the bunker, and an opening which was adequate for hand controlled filling.

In April 1921 Nos.167 and 372 were fitted to burn oil fuel on the 'Unolco' system. Note it is fitted with the 'Reliostop' train control system beneath the cab.

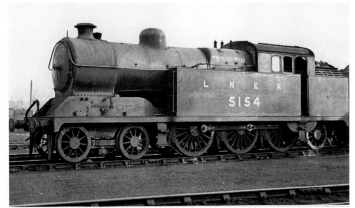

The large scale introduction of mechanical coaling plants in 1932 needed a bigger opening and the rails were reduced to three, the top one being a substantial angle iron. All were so altered.

Due to the coal strike of 1921 at least nine more A5 class, Nos.23, 24, 128, 165, 166, 168, 371, 373, and 374 were similarly fitted to burn oil but had larger capacity cylindrical containers.

5452 cont./

720 (ex5128) 11/12/43.
149 (exD9 6036) 30/3/46.
796 (ex9823) 25/10/47.
3849 (ex spare) 11/1/50.
22383 (ex spare) 29/12/51.
22382 (ex69802) 18/9/54.
22043 (ex69815) 12/10/57.

SHEDS:
Neasden.
Woodford 20/9/24.
Neasden 23/9/24.
Gorton 21/12/27.
King's Cross 30/6/28.
Hitchin 29/11/35.
Bradford 6/5/37.
Neasden 16/10/37.
London Passenger Transport
Board 1/11/37.
Neasden 2/10/38.
Grantham 14/5/48.
Langwith Jct. 23/1/49.
Lincoln 24/10/54.
Immingham 13/2/55.
Boston 11/3/56.
Colwick 29/7/56.

RENUMBERED:
452c 29/9/23.
5452 30/1/26.
9812 18/8/46.
69812 11/1/50.

CONDEMNED: 7/7/59.
Into Dar. for cut up 7/7/59.

5128

Gorton.

To traffic 21/12/1912.

REPAIRS:
Gor. 11/5—6/7/18.**G.**
Gor. 21/1—11/3/22.**G.**
Gor. 9/5/22.**L.**
Ross Pops fitted.
Gor. 29/3—28/6/24.**G.**
Cab side windows fitted.
Gor. 13/3—17/7/26.**G.**
Gor. 4/8—29/9/28.**G.**
Gor. 13/12/30—24/1/31.**G.**
Gor. 8/4—6/5/33.**G.**
Gor. 17/11—8/12/34.**G.**
Intensifore removed.
Gor. 26/9—17/10/36.**G.**
Fountain lubrication to
axleboxes.
Gor. 12/3—2/4/38.**G.**
Gor. 13/4—11/5/40.**G.**

Gor. 1/9—24/10/42.**G.**
Gor. 1/7—15/8/44.**G.**
Gor. 18/5—22/6/46.**G.**
Gor. 17—24/8/46.**L.**
After collision.
Gor. 17/1—28/2/48.**G.**
Gor. 31/7—14/8/48.**C/H.**
Dar. 8/12/49—26/1/50.**G.**
Dar. 5/9—11/10/52.**G.**
Dar. 23/6—5/8/55.**G.**

BOILERS:
1533.
1532 (ex5452) 6/7/18.
719 (new) 17/7/26.
800 (new) 6/5/33.
986 (ex5372) 8/12/34.
984 (ex5374) 17/10/36.
964 (ex5023) 2/4/38.
720 (ex5045) 11/5/40.
984 (ex5168) 24/10/42.
3849 (ex5448) 15/8/44.
3851 (exD9 5108) 22/6/46.
844 (ex9817) 28/2/48.
171 (ex9805) 26/1/50.
22361 (ex69838) 11/10/52.
22393 (ex69811) 5/8/55.

SHEDS:
Annesley.
Neasden 7/7/24.
Ardsley 20/11/24.
Neasden 1/10/28.
Lincoln 23/4/50.
Immingham 26/9/54.
Lincoln 2/1/55.
Retford 19/2/56.
Immingham 26/2/56.
Lincoln 2/12/56.
Gorton 16/12/56.

RENUMBERED:
5128 28/6/24.
9813 22/6/46.
E **9813** 28/2/48.
69813 14/8/48.

CONDEMNED: 1/3/60.
Into Dar. for cut up 1/3/60.

5129

Gorton.

To traffic 28/12/1912.

REPAIRS:
Gor. 7—28/2/20.**G.**
Gor. 5/11/21—28/1/22.**G.**
Ross Pops fitted.
Gor. 3/11/23—16/2/24.**G.**

Cab side windows fitted.
Gor. 28/11/25—13/2/26.**G.**
Gor. 11/2—28/4/28.**G.**
Gor. 28/9—9/11/29.**G.**
Gor. 3/10—14/11/31.**G.**
Gor. 3/2—24/3/34.**G.**
Intensifore removed.
Eureka fitted.
Gor. 16/11—7/12/35.**G.**
Fountain lubrication to
axleboxes.
Gor. 13/6—4/7/36.**H.**
Gor. 28/8—2/10/37.**G.**
Gor. 4/3—1/4/39.**G.**
Gor. 19/4—24/5/41.**G.**
Gor. 21/7—11/9/43.**G.**
Gor. 28/4—9/6/45.**G.**
Gor. 14/12/46—18/1/47.**G.**
Gor. 12/6—24/7/48.**G.**
Gor. 8—18/9/48.**C/H.**
Dar. 1/8—6/9/50.**G.**
Dar. 12—14/9/50.**N/C.**
Dar. 8/8—5/9/51.**C/H.**
Dar. 20/8—26/9/52.**G.**
Dar. 1—7/10/52.**N/C.**
Dar. 9/2—11/3/55.**G.**
Dar. 13—17/9/55.**N/C.**
Dar. 18/2—21/3/58.**G.**

BOILERS:
1534.
1843 (new) 28/2/20.
1533 (ex5170) 28/4/28.
395 (ex5156) 14/11/31.
939 (new) 7/12/35.
816 (ex5170) 2/10/37.
1597 (exD9 6032) 1/4/39.
772 (ex5371) 24/5/41.
156 (ex5158) 9/6/45.
3859 (exD9 2329) 18/1/47.
3854 (ex9827) 24/7/48.
22350 (ex69811) 6/9/50.
22351 (ex69815) 26/9/52.
22360 (ex69835) 11/3/55.
22383 (ex69837) 21/3/58.

SHEDS:
Annesley.
Bradford 25/3/24.
Neasden 21/4/24.
Ardsley 20/11/24.
King's Cross 7/5/28.
Neasden 18/11/29.
Colwick 30/12/49.
Neasden 29/4/51.
Grantham 16/5/54.
King's Cross 27/12/59.
Lincoln 12/6/60.
Colwick 19/6/60.

RENUMBERED:
5129 16/2/24.
9814 11/8/46.
69814 24/7/48.

CONDEMNED: 14/11/60.
Into Dar. for cut up 14/11/60.

5371

Gorton.

To traffic 30/6/1917.

REPAIRS:
Gor. 8/7—23/9/22.**G.**
Gor. 1/11—27/12/24.**G.**
Cab side windows fitted.
Gor. 27/11/26—19/2/27.**G.**
Gor. 28/9—23/11/29.**G.**
Gor. 26/7—6/9/30.**G.**
Gor. 21/5—11/6/32.**G.**
Gor. 28/7—25/8/34.**G.**
Gor. 2—23/5/36.**G.**
Fountain lubrication to
axleboxes.
Gor. 21/8—2/10/37.**G.**
Gor. 25/2—18/3/39.**G.**
Gor. 20—27/5/39.**L.**
Gor. 8/3—12/4/41.**G.**
Gor. 7/10/43—22/1/44.**G.**
Gor. 27/1—10/3/45.**G.**
Gor. 17/8—21/9/46.**G.**
Gor. 5/6—31/7/48.**G.**
Dar. 8/8—9/9/50.**G.**
Dar. 22/4—24/5/52.**G.**
Dar. 1—23/9/53.**C/L.**
Dar. 21/12/54—28/1/55.**G.**
Dar. 25/6/57. Not repaired.

BOILERS:
1683.
343 (new) 23/9/22.
1638 (exD9 6017) 11/6/32.
558 (ex5452) 25/8/34.
957 (new) 23/5/36.
557 (ex5168) 2/10/37.
772 (exD9 6031) 18/3/39.
118 (exD9 6039) 12/4/41.
210 (ex5023) 22/1/44.
968 (ex5030) 10/3/45.
3856 (ex9826) 21/9/46.
3850 (ex9828) 31/7/48.
22351 (ex69827) 9/9/50.
22392 (ex69824) 24/5/52.
22043 (new) 28/1/55.

SHEDS:
Neasden.
Ardsley 5/1/25.
Neasden 20/9/27.

WORKS CODES:- Cw - Cowlairs. Dar- Darlington. Don - Doncaster. Ghd - Gateshead. Gor - Gorton, Inv - Inverurie. Str - Stratford. Tux - Tuxford.
REPAIR CODES:- C/H - Casual Heavy. C/L - Casual Light. G - General. H - Heavy. H/I - Heavy Intermediate. L - Light. L/I - Light Intermediate. N/C - Non-Classified.

20

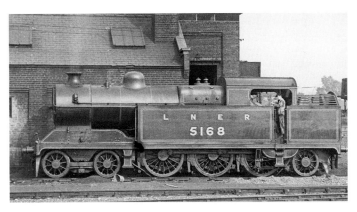

The oil burning apparatus taken off in October and November 1921 was stored and during the 1926 coal strike, six sets were used again on the following engines: 5023 (August 1926 to February 1927), 5024 (August 1926 to April 1927), 5165, 5166 (both July 1926 to March 1927), 5372 (August 1926 to April 1927), and 5373 (August 1926 to March 1927) - all having been so equipped in 1921. The 'Reliostop' equipment was then still fitted for train control.

Some of the class got their 1924 LNER number and livery before any change was made to the cab. No.5168 was ex works unaltered on 28th June 1924 although the change had begun in February, and No.5451 was not altered when out on 13th December 1924.

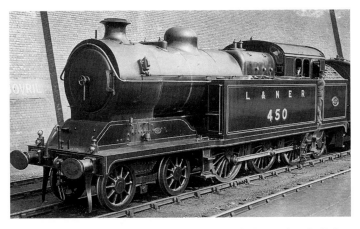

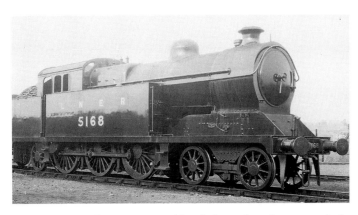

No.5168 was the last one to get side window cab - when ex works in December 1926.

The first twenty-one engines had no cab side windows when built but in September 1921 No.450 got a new cab with two side windows although no more were done before Grouping.

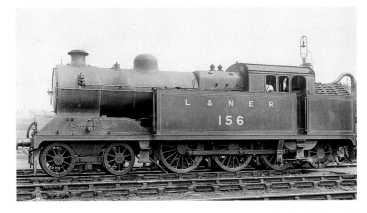

The ten engines built in 1923 all had the double side window cab when new. They also had 'Reliostop' train control as original equipment.

During 1937 seven of the class: Nos.5003, 5046, 5372, 5374, 5411, 5448 and 5452, were fitted with trip cock apparatus as required for working over London Passenger Transport Board lines north of Rickmansworth.

5371 cont./
Boston 6/1/49.
Langwith Jct. 16/1/49.
Immingham 7/11/54.
Gorton 11/9/55.

RENUMBERED:
5371 27/12/24.
9815 21/9/46.
69815 31/7/48.

CONDEMNED: 15/7/57.
Cut up at Darlington.

5372

Gorton.

To traffic 28/7/1917.

REPAIRS:
Gor. 25/11/22—3/2/23.**G**.
Gor. 21/2—2/5/25.**G**.
Cab side windows fitted.
Nea. 14—23/8/26.**L**.
Converted to fuel oil.
Gor. 5/2—16/4/27.**G**.
Fuel oil app. removed.
Gor. 1/12/28—2/2/29.**G**.
Gor. 31/12/30—7/2/31.**G**.
Gor. 26/11/32—14/1/33.**G**.
Gor. 4—11/3/33.**L**.
After collision.
Gor. 13/10—10/11/34.**G**.
Gor. 13/6—11/7/36.**G**.
Fountain lubrication to axleboxes.
Gor. 29/1—26/2/38.**G**.
Trip cock gear fitted.
Gor. 18/3—15/4/39.**G**.
Gor. 9—26/7/41.**G**.
Gor. 13/10—25/12/43.**G**.
Gor. 2—23/12/44.**L**.
Gor. 12/1—9/2/46.**G**.
Gor. 7/2—6/3/48.**G**.
Dar. 14/9—2/11/51.**G**.
Dar. 28/10—4/12/53.**G**.
Dar. 28/12/55—27/1/56.**G**.
Dar. 2—6/2/56.**N/C**.
Dar. 16/1/59. *Not repaired.*

BOILERS:
1684.
1341 *(exD9 6020)* 3/2/23.
986 *(new)* 7/2/31.
799 *(ex5374)* 10/11/34.
558 *(ex5371)* 11/7/36.
1825 *(ex5452)* 26/2/38.
557 *(ex5371)* 15/4/39.
713 *(ex5046)* 26/7/41.
985 *(exD9 6017)* 9/2/46.
720 *(exD9 2324)* 6/3/48.
22381 *(ex spare)* 2/11/51.
22380 *(ex69833)* 4/12/53.
22369 *(ex69805)* 27/1/56.

SHEDS:
Neasden.
Lincoln 11/7/48.
Grantham 29/5/49.
Lincoln 15/10/50.
Boston 29/10/50.
Immingham 11/3/56.
Lincoln 9/12/56.

RENUMBERED:
5372 2/5/25.
9816 11/8/46.
E9816 6/3/48.
69816 2/11/51.

CONDEMNED: 19/1/59.
Cut up at Darlington.

5373

Gorton.

To traffic 25/8/1917.

REPAIRS:
Gor. 22/1—1/4/22.**G**.
Gor. 15/3—31/5/24.**G**.
Gor. 9/1—27/3/26.**G**.
Cab side windows fitted.
Nea. 9—18/8/26.**L**.
Converted to fuel oil.
Nea. 22/3/27.**L**.
Fuel oil app. removed.
Gor. 21/4—16/6/28.**G**.
Gor. 26/7—30/8/30.**G**.
Gor. 2/4—7/5/32.**G**.
Gor. 28/4—9/6/34.**G**.
Gor. 16/11—14/12/35.**G**.
Fountain lubrication to axleboxes.
Gor. 12/6—10/7/37.**G**.
Gor. 5/8—2/9/39.**G**.
Don. 12/8—5/9/41.**L**.
Gor. 29/4—30/5/42.**G**.
Gor. 8/4—20/5/44.**G**.
Gor. 6/4—4/5/46.**G**.
Gor. 29/11/47—10/1/48.**G**.
Dar. 25/9—4/11/50.**G**.
Ghd. 26/8—26/9/52.**C/H**.
Dar. 21/11/52—10/1/53.**G**.
Dar. 29/3—6/5/55.**G**.
Dar. 11/1—13/2/58.**G**.

BOILERS:
1685.
185 *(exD9 5106)* 31/5/24.
1683 *(ex5448)* 30/8/30.
843 *(ex5003)* 9/6/34.
941 *(new)* 14/12/35.
713 *(ex5156)* 10/7/37.
396 *(ex5411)* 2/9/39.
3850 *(exD9 6018)* 30/5/42.
558 *(ex5411)* 20/5/44.
844 *(exD9 5105)* 4/5/46.
149 *(ex9812)* 10/1/48.

22356 *(ex69823)* 4/11/50.
22395 *(ex69813)* 10/1/53.
22387 *(ex69804)* 6/5/55.
22390 *(ex69824)* 13/2/58.

SHEDS:
Neasden.
Gorton 20/12/27.
Neasden 30/6/28.
Bradford 10/7/37.
Neasden 28/10/37.
Bradford 19/5/38.
Copley Hill 29/7/38.
Neasden 24/11/38.
King's Cross 20/9/39.
Colwick 25/5/40.
Neasden 7/11/40.
Ardsley 5/9/41.
Neasden 15/2/43.
Grantham 9/5/48.
Boston 23/1/49.
Colwick 11/12/49.
Gorton 13/6/54.

RENUMBERED:
5373 31/5/24.
9817 4/5/46.
69817 4/11/50.

CONDEMNED: 4/4/60.
Into Dar. for cut up 4/4/60.

5374

Gorton.

To traffic 29/9/1917.

REPAIRS:
Gor. 8/7—14/10/22.**G**.
Gor. 1/11—27/12/24.**G**.
Cab side windows fitted.
Gor. 26/3—28/5/27.**G**.
Gor. 1/6—6/7/29.**G**.
Gor. 24/1—28/2/31.**G**.
Gor. 8/4—6/5/33.**G**.
Gor. 29/9—20/10/34.**G**.
Intensifore removed.
Gor. 22/8—26/9/36.**G**.
Fountain lubrication to axleboxes.
Gor. 18/9—23/10/37.**H**.
Gor. 30/10/37.**L**.
Trip cock gear fitted.
Gor. 10/6—8/7/39.**G**.
Gor. 14/9—5/10/40.**G**.
Gor. 15/6—24/7/43.**G**.
New frames & cylinders.
Gor. 4/8—22/9/45.**G**.
Gor. 28/9/46.**L**.
Gor. 1—29/3/47.**G**.
Gor. 11/9—16/10/48.**G**.
WPU gear removed.
Dar. 19/12/50—27/1/51.**G**.
Dar. 6—7/2/51.**N/C**.

Gor. 30/7—2/8/52.**C/L**.
Dar. 18/5—19/6/53.**G**.
Dar. 16/3—25/4/56.**G**.

BOILERS:
1686.
366 *(new)* 14/10/22.
156 *(new)* 28/2/31.
799 *(new)* 6/5/33.
984 *(ex5170)* 20/10/34.
696 *(ex5023)* 26/9/36.
1825 *(ex5372)* 8/7/39.
291 *(ex5154)* 5/10/40.
718 *(ex5165)* 24/7/43.
3852 *(ex5170)* 22/9/45.
783 *(ex9821)* 29/3/47.
936 *(ex9809)* 16/10/48.
22362 *(ex69815)* 27/1/51.
22397 *(ex69823)* 19/6/53.
22045 *(new)* 25/4/56.

SHEDS:
Neasden.
Ardsley 8/1/25.
Neasden 15/9/27.
London Passenger Transport
Board 1/11/37.
Neasden 17/4/38.
Boston 7/1/49.
Langwith Jct. 16/1/49.
Darlington 28/1/51.
Colwick 1/7/51.
Annesley 21/10/56.

RENUMBERED:
5374 27/12/24.
9818 11/8/46.
69818 16/10/48.

CONDEMNED: 16/12/58.
Into Dar. for cut up 16/12/58.

5411

Gorton.

To traffic 27/10/1917.

REPAIRS:
Gor. 21/10/22—3/2/23.**G**.
Gor. 22/11/24—21/2/25.**G**.
Cab side windows fitted.
Gor. 16/10/26—15/1/27.**G**.
Gor. 15/9—27/10/28.**G**.
Gor. 31/12/30—14/2/31.**G**.
Gor. 16/9—14/10/33.**G**.
Gor. 25/1—22/2/36.**G**.
Intensifore removed.
Fountain lubrication to axleboxes.
Gor. 17/4—22/5/37.**G**.
Don. 22—25/11/37.**L**.
Trip cock gear fitted.
Gor. 24/6—22/7/39.**G**.
Gor. 1/11—13/12/41.**G**.

5411 cont./
Gor. 3/3—22/4/44.**G.**
Gor. 30/3—4/5/46.**G.**
Gor. 29/11—20/12/47.**G.**
New frames & cylinders.
Dar. 3/8—2/9/49.**G.**
Dar. 12/11—8/12/51.**G.**
Gor. 20/3—1/5/54.**G.**
Dar. 4/6—6/7/57.**G.**
Dar. 14—19/7/57.**N/C.**
Dar. 24—28/7/57.**N/C.**
Dar. 5/2/58. *Not repaired.*

BOILERS:
1694.
  383 *(new)* 25/11/22.
 1534 *(ex5449)* 27/10/28.
 1843 *(ex5169)* 14/10/33.
  395 *(ex5129)* 22/2/36.
  396 *(ex5030)* 22/5/37.
  808 *(exD9 6029)* 22/7/39.
  558 *(ex5006)* 13/12/41.
 3854 *(ex5007)* 22/4/44.
  720 *(ex5452)* 4/5/46.
 3868 *(new)* 20/12/47.
  672 *(ex9800)* 2/9/49.
22384 *(ex spare)* 8/12/51.
22381 *(ex69816)* 1/5/54.
22041 *(ex69807)* 6/7/57.

SHEDS:
Neasden.
Bradford 20/5/37.
Neasden 12/11/37.
London Passenger Transport
Board 14/11/37.
Neasden 17/4/38.
Ardsley 27/10/41.
Neasden 15/2/43.
Immingham 26/3/50.
Boston 6/8/50.
Lincoln 16/12/56.

RENUMBERED:
5411 21/2/25.
9819 4/5/46.
69819 2/9/49.

CONDEMNED: 3/3/58.
Cut up at Darlington.

5003

Gorton.

To traffic 27/1/1923.

REPAIRS:
Gor. 31/3—14/4/23.**L.**
After collision.
Gor. 26/7—18/10/24.**G.**

Gor. 30/6—2/10/26.**G.**
Gor. 17/3—19/5/28.**G.**
Gor. 16/11/29—4/1/30.**G.**
Gor. 31/12/31—6/2/32.**G.**
Gor. 17/3—14/4/34.**G.**
Gor. 7—28/3/36.**G.**
Fountain lubrication to
axleboxes.
Gor. 6—27/11/37.**G.**
Trip cock gear fitted.
Gor. 23/9—21/10/39.**G.**
Gor. 23/1—21/2/42.**G.**
Gor. 15/12/43—15/1/44.**G.**
Gor. 25/11—16/12/44.**L.**
Gor. 2/2—2/3/46.**G.**
Gor. 27/9—25/10/47.**G.**
Gor. 18/9—9/10/48.**L.**
WPU gear removed.
Dar. 26/5—11/7/49.**G.**
Dar. 28/5—6/7/51.**G.**
Gor. 27/2—10/4/54.**G.**
Gor. 11—16/4/54.**N/C.**
Gor. 31/7—28/8/54.**C/L.**
Gor. 31/8—3/9/54.**N/C.**
Dar. 4/3—17/4/58.**H/I.**

BOILERS:
384.
 843 *(new)* 19/5/28.
 557 *(ex5166)* 14/4/34.
 808 *(exD9 5107)* 28/3/36.
 386 *(exD9 6038)* 27/11/37.
 325 *(ex5451)* 21/10/39.
 808 *(ex5411)* 21/2/42.
 843 *(ex5449)* 15/1/44.
  91 *(ex5449)* 2/3/46.
3858 *(ex9805)* 25/10/47.
 799 *(exD9 2305)* 11/7/49.
22376 *(ex69800)* 6/7/51.
22364 *(ex69806)* 10/4/54.

SHEDS:
Neasden.
London Passenger Transport
Board 16/1/38.
Neasden 2/10/38.
Lincoln 23/4/50.
Immingham 10/2/52.
Lincoln 2/12/56.
Immingham 10/7/60.

RENUMBERED:
5003 18/10/24.
9820 21/7/46.
69820 9/10/48.

CONDEMNED: 14/11/60.
Into Dar. for cut up 14/11/60.

5006

Gorton.

To traffic 10/2/1923.

REPAIRS:
Gor. 21/3—30/5/25.**G.**
Gor. 2/4—28/5/27.**G.**
Gor. 27/10—8/12/28.**G.**
Gor. 31/5—5/7/30.**G.**
Gor. 26/3—23/4/32.**G.**
Gor. 20/1—24/2/34.**G.**
Intensifore removed.
Eureka fitted.
Gor. 8—29/8/36.**G.**
Fountain lubrication to
axleboxes.
Gor. 26/3—16/4/38.**G.**
Gor. 10/2—16/3/40.**G.**
Gor. 7/10—22/11/41.**G.**
Gor. 18/10—20/11/43.**G.**
Gor. 22/7—5/8/44.**L.**
Gor. 9/6—28/7/45.**G.**
Gor. 18/1—1/3/47.**G.**
Gor. 4—18/10/47.**L.**
After collision.
Gor. 18/12/48—5/2/49.**G.**
WPU gear removed.
Fitted with GWR ATC.
Dar. 16/11—30/12/50.**G.**
Dar. 2—20/1/51.**N/C.**
Gor. 22/12/52—14/2/53.**C/L.**
Gor. 17/2—8/3/53.**N/C.**
Dar. 24/8—3/10/53.**G.**
Dar. 6—26/10/53.**N/C.**
Dar. 10/7—30/8/56.**G.**

BOILERS:
386.
 1843 *(ex5129)* 8/12/28.
  714 *(new)* 24/3/32.
 1644 *(exD9 5110)* 24/2/34.
  796 *(ex5167)* 29/8/36.
  558 *(ex5372)* 16/4/38.
  557 *(ex5372)* 22/11/41.
 3858 *(new)* 20/11/43.
  783 *(exD9 6018)* 28/7/45.
  806 *(ex9828)* 1/3/47.
  800 *(ex9801)* 5/2/49.
22357 *(ex69814)* 30/12/50.
22375 *(ex69803)* 3/10/53.
22049 *(new)* 30/8/56.

SHEDS:
Neasden.
Ardsley 16/10/41.
Bradford 13/12/41.
Ardsley 15/3/42.
Neasden 15/2/43.
Colwick 26/3/50.

Langwith Jct. 4/2/51.
Boston 10/2/52.
Langwith Jct. 20/4/52.
Lincoln 24/10/54.
Immingham 13/2/55.
Langwith Jct. 10/7/55.
Colwick 23/10/55.
Immingham 17/2/57.
Lincoln 16/6/57.

RENUMBERED:
5006 30/5/25.
9821 21/7/46.
69821 5/2/49.

CONDEMNED: 19/5/60.
Cut up at Stratford.

5007

Gorton.

To traffic 24/2/1923.

REPAIRS:
Gor. 17/1—28/3/25.**G.**
Gor. 5/3—16/4/27.**G.**
Gor. 21/7—25/8/28.**G.**
Gor. 19/10—7/12/29.**G.**
Gor. 24/10—28/11/31.**G.**
Gor. 2—23/7/32.**L.**
Gor. 24/8—21/9/35.**G.**
Fountain lubrication to
axleboxes.
Gor. 30/1—20/2/37.**G.**
Gor. 14/10—4/11/39.**G.**
Gor. 18/5—20/6/42.**G.**
Gor. 24/1—25/3/44.**G.**
Gor. 9—23/12/44.**L.**
Gor. 16/2—16/3/46.**G.**
Gor. 12—26/10/46.**L.**
Gor. 25/10—29/11/47.**G.**
Dar. 9/5—14/7/49.**G.**
Dar. 23/12/49—4/2/50.**C/L.**
Dar. 13/4—18/5/51.**G.**
Dar. 24/5—7/6/51.**N/C.**
Dar. 8/10—7/11/53.**G.**
Dar. 17/11—1/12/53.**N/C.**
Dar. 21/12/53—8/1/54.**C/L.**
Dar. 25/10—30/11/55.**G.**
Gor. 20/6—6/7/57.**C/L.**
Dar. 28/10/58. *Not repaired.*

BOILERS:
390.
 391 *(ex5030)* 25/8/28.
 411 *(ex5156)* 7/12/29.
1533 *(ex5129)* 28/11/31.
 416 *(ex5448)* 21/9/35.
1826 *(ex5158)* 20/2/37.
 386 *(ex5003)* 4/11/39.

WORKS CODES:- Cw - Cowlairs. Dar- Darlington. Don - Doncaster. Ghd - Gateshead. Gor - Gorton. Inv - Inverurie. Str - Stratford. Tux - Tuxford.
REPAIR CODES:- **C/H** - Casual Heavy. **C/L** - Casual Light. **G** - General. **H** - Heavy. **H/I** - Heavy Intermediate. **L** - Light. **L/I** - Light Intermediate. **N/C** - Non-Classified.

23

5007 cont./
3854 *(new)* 20/6/42.
3860 *(new)* 25/3/44.
3841 *(exD9 6031)* 16/3/46.
810 *(exD9 2333)* 29/11/47.
22373 *(ex69807)* 18/5/51.
22362 *(ex69818)* 7/11/53.
22368 *(ex69803)* 30/11/55.

SHEDS:
Neasden.
King's Cross 5/12/29.
Hitchin 29/11/35.
Bradford 7/5/37.
Neasden 27/11/37.
Bradford 19/5/38.
Copley Hill 29/7/38.
King's Cross 26/2/39.
Colwick 25/5/40.
Neasden 27/6/40.
Colwick 5/3/50.
Neasden 30/7/50.
Colwick 7/12/52.
Gorton 17/2/57.

RENUMBERED:
5007 28/3/25.
9822 21/7/46.
69822 14/7/49.

CONDEMNED: 3/11/58.
Cut up at Darlington.

5030

Gorton.

To traffic 17/3/1923.

REPAIRS:
Gor. 18/4—11/7/25.**G.**
Gor. 16/7—3/9/27.**G.**
Gor. 17/8—5/10/29.**G.**
Gor. 25/7—29/8/31.**G.**
Gor. 14/10—11/11/33.**G.**
Gor. 30/3—20/4/35.**G.**
Fountain lubrication to
axleboxes.
Gor. 30/1—20/2/37.**G.**
Gor. 28/5—2/7/38.**G.**
Gor. 1—29/6/40.**G.**
Gor. 15/1—20/2/43.**G.**
Gor. 6—23/10/43.**L.**
Gor. 16/12/44—20/1/45.**G.**
Gor. 3—31/8/46.**G.**
Gor. 14/6—5/7/47.**G.**
A.C. Eureka fitted.
Gor. 25/9—23/10/48.**G.**
WPU gear removed.
Ghd. 22/9—1/11/49.**C/L.**
Ghd. 20—23/11/49.**N/C.**
Dar. 24/6—12/8/50.**G.**
Dar. 20/6—15/8/51.**C/H.**
Dar. 9/3—11/4/53.**G.**
Dar. 13—16/4/53.**N/C.**

Dar. 27/2—3/4/56.**G.**
Dar. 22/8—19/9/57.**C/L.**
Frames straightened after
collision.

BOILERS:
391.
1826 *(ex spare)* 3/9/27.
1905 *(exD9 6032)* 29/8/31.
704 *(exD9 6029)* 11/11/33.
396 *(exD9 6042)* 20/4/35.
3841 *(new)* 20/2/37.
796 *(ex5006)* 2/7/38.
964 *(ex5128)* 29/6/40.
968 *(exD9 6020)* 20/2/42.
168 *(ex5169)* 20/1/45.
796 *(exD9 6013)* 31/8/46.
210 *(ex9810)* 5/7/47.
3844 *(exD9 2313)* 23/10/48.
3847 *(ex69828)* 12/8/50.
22356 *(ex69817)* 11/4/53.
22361 *(ex69813)* 3/4/56.

SHEDS:
Neasden.
Colwick 13/1/50.
Gorton 13/6/54.

RENUMBERED:
5030 11/7/25.
9823 31/8/46.
69823 23/10/48.

CONDEMNED: 5/4/60.
Into Dar. for cut up 5/4/60.

5045

Gorton.

To traffic 7/4/1923.

REPAIRS:
Gor. 21/3—30/5/25.**G.**
Gor. 25/6—27/8/27.**G.**
Gor. 6/4—15/6/29.**G.**
Gor. 13/6—25/7/31.**G.**
Gor. 8/7—5/8/33.**G.**
Gor. 6/4—4/5/35.**G.**
Fountain lubrication to
axleboxes.
Gor. 11/7—8/8/36.**G.**
Gor. 12/2—12/3/38.**G.**
Gor. 2/3—6/4/40.**G.**
Gor. 20/7—15/8/42.**G.**
Gor. 18/10—13/11/43.**G.**
Gor. 4—26/2/44.**L.**
After collision.
Gor. 30/6—11/8/45.**G.**
New frames & cylinders.
Gor. 29/3—10/5/47.**G.**
Gor. 23/10—13/11/48.**G.**
WPU gear removed.
Dar. 9/5—16/7/49.**C/L.**
Gor. 16—26/8/50.**C/H.**

Dar. 29/3—2/5/52.**G.**
Part 2 built-up chimney fitted.
Gor. 25/9—13/11/54.**H/I.**
Dar. 20/8—21/9/57.**G.**

BOILERS:
392.
86 *(exD9 6024)* 15/6/29.
1597 *(ex5166)* 25/7/31.
1826 *(ex5450)* 5/8/33.
704 *(ex5030)* 4/5/35.
720 *(exD9 6024)* 12/3/38.
278 *(ex5023)* 6/4/40.
947 *(ex5158)* 15/8/42.
3859 *(new)* 13/11/43.
171 *(exD9 6034)* 11/8/45.
3848 *(exD9 2311)* 10/5/47.
210 *(ex9823)* 13/11/48.
3861 *(ex69802)* 26/8/50.
22390 *(ex spare)* 2/5/52.
22399 *(ex spare)* 21/9/57.

SHEDS:
Neasden.
Ardsley 29/4/27.
Neasden 16/6/27.
Boston 30/1/49.
Lincoln 13/2/49.
Grantham 11/9/49.
Boston 15/10/50.
Lincoln 27/5/51.
Norwich 11/5/52.
Lowestoft 30/10/55.
Immingham 17/2/57.
Grantham 13/4/58.
Lincoln 8/6/58.

RENUMBERED:
5045 30/5/25.
9824 21/7/46.
69824 13/11/48.

CONDEMNED: 16/12/58.
Into Dar. for cut up 16/12/58.

5046

Gorton.

To traffic 28/4/1923.

REPAIRS:
Gor. 11/4—20/6/25.**G.**
Gor. 30/7—1/10/27.**G.**
Gor. 21/1—11/2/28.**L.**
After collision.
Gor. 23/3—8/6/29.**G.**
Gor. 23/5—27/6/31.**G.**
Gor. 29/4—27/5/33.**G.**
Gor. 16/3—6/4/35.**G.**
Fountain lubrication to
axleboxes.
Gor. 5/9—3/10/36.**G.**
Gor. 12/2—5/3/38.**G.**
Trip cock gear fitted.

Gor. 28/10—18/11/39.**G.**
Gor. 28/6—26/7/41.**G.**
Gor. 26/6—9/10/43.**G.**
Gor. 4/8—8/9/45.**G.**
Gor. 28/6—16/8/47.**G.**
Hudd ATC fitted.
Gor. 25/12/48—29/1/49.**G.**
WPU gear removed.
Gor. 21/11—3/12/49.**C/L.**
Dar. 12/4—26/5/51.**G.**
Dar. 4—7/6/51.**N/C.**
Dar. 11/9—4/10/52.**C/H.**
Dar. 21/11—22/12/53.**G.**
Dar. 29/11—2/12/55.**N/C.**
Dar. 31/5—9/7/56.**G.**
Dar. 26/11/59. *Not repaired.*

BOILERS:
395.
386 *(ex5006)* 8/6/29.
672 *(new)* 27/6/31.
156 *(ex5374)* 27/5/33.
845 *(exD9 6031)* 6/4/35.
278 *(ex5449)* 3/10/36.
1795 *(exD9 5106)* 5/3/38.
713 *(ex5373)* 18/11/39.
714 *(exD9 6023)* 26/7/41.
174 *(ex5156)* 9/10/43.
772 *(ex5129)* 8/9/45.
3852 *(ex9818)* 16/8/47.
3853 *(ex9829)* 29/1/49.
22367 *(exD9 62332)* 26/5/51.
22373 *(ex69822)* 22/12/53.
22048 *(new)* 9/7/56.

SHEDS:
Neasden.
Ardsley 29/4/27.
Neasden 19/7/27.
Colwick 5/1/50.
Annesley 14/10/56.
Colwick 14/12/58.

RENUMBERED:
5046 20/6/25.
9825 21/7/46.
69825 29/1/49.

CONDEMNED: 30/11/59.
Cut up at Darlington.

5088

Gorton.

To traffic 12/5/1923.

REPAIRS:
Gor. 4/4—13/6/25.**G.**
Gor. 25/6—13/8/27.**G.**
Gor. 13/4—20/7/29.**G.**
Gor. 9/5—6/6/31.**G.**
Gor. 7—28/10/33.**G.**
Gor. 21/12/35—18/1/36.**G.**
Intensifore removed.

In August 1947, No.9825 was fitted with Hudd type Automatic Train Control for trials on the line from Marylebone to Neasden.

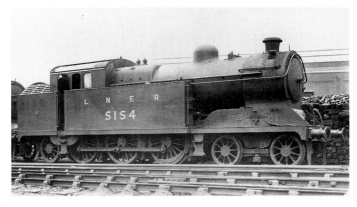

The original fastening for the smokebox door was by a wheel and handle. The top lamp iron was mounted above the smokebox. These features were not disturbed before 1945.

No.9807 was fitted in September 1947, and No.69821 in February 1949, with Great Western Railway type of train control, for trials of the established system. The apparatus was removed from 9807 in May 1949 at Darlington.

From 1946 a second handle began to supersede the wheel, all being so changed. A lamp iron was also fitted on the door for easier access, but the first few retained the iron on top of the smokebox (*see* page 15 bottom, right).

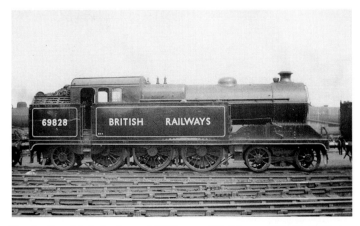

For further trials, in August 1948 a modified type of Hudd ATC was fitted to No.69828.

By 1947 the redundant top iron was being removed and this was then normal practice.

In 1925 thirteen more A5's were built by an outside contractor for service in the North Eastern Area. They were all under 13ft 0in. in height where such restriction was un-necessary. They were also 2in. narrower and 3¾in. longer than the earlier engines and, they were fitted for left hand drive. These A5's became Part 2 of the class whilst the Gorton built engines became Part 1.

At least the first four had frames similar in profile to the Part 1 engines but N.E.Area enginemen complained that this made oiling difficult and an alteration was requested.

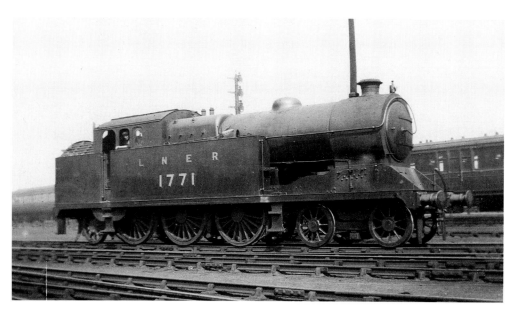

Later engines had the top edge of the frame cut away behind the smokebox when they were delivered by the makers, Hawthorn Leslie & Co.

5088 cont./
Fountain lubrication to
axleboxes.
Gor. 10/7—7/8/37.**G.**
Gor. 21/1—18/2/39.**G.**
Gor. 15/3—12/4/41.**G.**
Gor. 22/4—20/6/42.**G.**
Gor. 17/6—29/7/44.**G.**
Gor. 29/6—10/8/46.**G.**
Gor. 19/4—17/5/47.**G.**
Gor. 13/3—15/5/48.**G.**
Gor. 12—28/8/48.**C/L.**
Dar. 27/6—12/8/49.**G.**
Dar. 12/3—19/4/51.**G.**
Dar. 30/4—1/5/51.**N/C.**
Dar. 2/4—7/5/52.**C/L.**
Part 2 built up chimney fitted.
Gor. 3/4—15/5/54.**G.**
Gor. 18—27/5/54.**N/C.**
Gor. 3—19/6/54.**N/C.**
Dar. 24/2—18/3/55.**N/C.**
Dar. 21/5/58. *Not repaired.*

BOILERS:
　396.
　1694 *(exD9 6018)* 20/7/29.
　390 *(ex5158)* 28/10/33.
　168 *(exD9 6039)* 18/1/36.
　1905 *(exD9 6032)* 7/8/37.
　390 *(ex5166)* 18/2/39.
　410 *(ex5169)* 12/4/41.
　3856 *(ex5154)* 29/7/44.
　984 *(ex5167)* 10/8/46.
　3846 *(exD9 6031)* 15/5/48.
　714 *(exD9 2329)* 12/8/49.
22370 *(ex spare)* 19/4/51.
22376 *(ex69820)* 15/5/54.

SHEDS:
Neasden.
Colwick 19/3/50.
Darlington 4/2/51.
Colwick 26/8/51.
Norwich 25/5/52.
Lowestoft 29/1/56.
Immingham 17/2/57.

RENUMBERED:
5088 13/6/25.
9826 24/3/46.
69826 15/5/48.

CONDEMNED: 2/6/58.
Cut up at Darlington.

5154

Gorton.

To traffic 26/5/1923.

REPAIRS:
Gor. 22/8—14/11/25.**G.**
Gor. 24/9—19/11/27.**G.**
Gor. 15/6—10/8/29.**G.**
Gor. 9/5—20/6/31.**G.**
Gor. 25/2—25/3/33.**G.**
Gor. 19/1—9/2/35.**G.**
Intensifore removed.
Fountain lubrication to
axleboxes.
Gor. 7—21/11/36.**G.**
Gor. 25/6—16/7/38.**G.**
Gor. 6—27/7/40.**G.**
Gor. 30/9—7/11/42.**G.**
Gor. 29/4—24/6/44.**G.**
Gor. 21—28/4/45.**L.**
Gor. 8/6—10/8/46.**G.**
Gor. 13/9—4/10/47.**L.**
Gor. 13/3—10/4/48.**G.**
Dar. 7/2—4/3/49.**C/L.**
Dar. 25/11/49—11/4/50.**G.**
Dar. 10/7—16/9/50.**H.**
Dar. 8/4—15/5/52.**G.**
Gor. 23/1—20/2/54.**C/H.**
Gor. 23—26/2/54.**N/C.**
Gor. 16/10—27/11/54.**G.**
Gor. 1—6/12/54.**N/C.**
Dar. 14/11—14/12/56.**H/I.**
Dar. 17—18/12/56.**N/C.**
Dar. 2/11/59. *Not repaired.*

BOILERS:
　410.
　444 *(ex5024)* 10/8/29.
　658 *(new)* 20/6/31.
　800 *(ex5128)* 9/2/35.
　411 *(exD9 6033)* 21/11/36.
　291 *(exD9 6016)* 16/7/38.
　796 *(ex5030)* 27/7/40.
　3856 *(new)* 7/11/42.
　3850 *(ex5373)* 24/6/44.
　3854 *(ex5411)* 10/8/46.
　3851 *(ex9813)* 10/4/48.
　796 *(ex69812)* 11/4/50.
　796 reno.22353 16/9/50.
22391 *(ex69804)* 15/5/52.
22042 *(new)* 27/11/54.

SHEDS:
Neasden.
Grantham 16/5/54.

RENUMBERED:
5154 14/11/25.
9827 27/1/46.

69827 10/4/48.

CONDEMNED: 2/11/59.
Cut up at Darlington.

5156

Gorton.

To traffic 16/6/1923.

REPAIRS:
Gor. 27/6—5/9/25.**G.**
Gor. 19—26/9/25.**L.**
Gor. 6/8—8/10/27.**G.**
Gor. 22/6—24/8/29.**G.**
Gor. 26/9—31/10/31.**G.**
Gor. 27/5—1/7/33.**G.**
Gor. 21/4—26/5/34.**G.**
Gor. 14/9—12/10/35.**G.**
Fountain lubrication to
axleboxes.
Gor. 22/5—12/6/37.**G.**
Gor. 24/9—22/10/38.**G.**
Gor. 17/8—7/9/40.**G.**
Gor. 14/9—10/10/42.**G.**
Gor. 15—25/9/43.**G.**
Gor. 5—30/9/44.**L.**
Gor. 16/6—4/8/45.**G.**
Gor. 14/12/46—1/2/47.**G.**
New frames & cylinders.
Gor. 5/6—3/7/48.**G.**
Gor. ?—?/8/48.**N/C.**
Modified Hudd ATC fitted.
Dar. 25/5—30/6/50.**G.**
Dar. 11/1—13/2/52.**G.**
Dar. 25/2—5/3/52.**N/C.**
Dar. 15/2—18/3/55.**G.**
Dar. 20—31/3/55.**N/C.**
Gor. 24—27/10/56.*Weigh.*
Gor. 9/1—9/2/57.**C/L.**
Derailment damage.
Gor. 10—13/2/57.**N/C.**
Dar. 25/7—21/8/57.**C/L.**

BOILERS:
　411.
　395 *(ex5046)* 24/8/29.
　1420 *(ex5450)* 31/10/31.
　1532 *(ex5023)* 1/7/33.
　713 *(exD9 6028)* 12/10/35.
　395 *(ex5411)* 12/6/37.
　3842 *(exD9 5104)* 22/10/38.
　174 *(exD9 5104)* 7/9/40.
　672 *(exD9 6022)* 10/10/42.
　806 *(exD9 5111)* 4/8/45.
　3850 *(ex9827)* 1/2/47.
　3847 *(exD9 2330)* 3/7/48.
　3846 *(ex69826)* 30/6/50.
22389 *(ex69802)* 13/2/52.
22372 *(ex69807)* 18/3/55.

SHEDS:
Neasden.
Lincoln 15/6/52.
Langwith Jct. 20/9/53.
Lincoln 4/10/53.
Langwith Jct. 15/5/55.
Tuxford 11/12/55.
Colwick 9/7/56.
Gorton 7/10/56.
Colwick 19/5/57.

RENUMBERED:
5156 5/9/25.
9828 27/1/46.
69828 3/7/48.

CONDEMNED: 26/11/58.
Into Dar. for cut up 26/11/58.

5158

Gorton.

To traffic 30/6/1923.

REPAIRS:
Gor. 27/6—19/9/25.**G.**
Gor. 18/6—6/8/27.**G.**
Gor. 2/2—23/3/29.**G.**
Gor. 28/2—4/4/31.**G.**
Gor. 16—30/9/33.**G.**
Gor. 6/4—4/5/35.**G.**
Intensifore removed.
Fountain lubrication to
axleboxes.
Gor. 31/12/36—30/1/37.**G.**
Gor. 14/5—4/6/38.**G.**
Gor. 9/3—6/4/40.**G.**
Gor. 25/5—4/7/42.**G.**
Gor. 13/10—20/11/43.**H.**
Gor. 29/7—12/8/44.**L.**
Gor. 10/3—21/4/45.**G.**
Gor. 28/12/46—8/2/47.**G.**
Gor. 7/8—18/9/48.**G.**
New frames & cylinders.
WPU gear removed.
Dar. 6/2—15/4/50.**G.**
Dar. 16/4—12/5/51.**C/H.**
Dar. 18/4—23/5/52.**G.**
Part 2 built up chimney fitted.
Gor. 1/5—12/6/54.**G.**
Gor. 15—28/6/54.**N/C.**
Gor. 1—2/11/54.*Weigh.*
Gor. 9—12/2/55.*Weigh.*
Dar. 16/8—4/10/56.**C/L.**

BOILERS:
　416.
　390 *(ex5007)* 23/3/29.
　383 *(ex5024)* 30/9/33.
　1826 *(ex5045)* 4/5/35.

WORKS CODES:- Cw - Cowlairs. Dar- Darlington. Don - Doncaster. Ghd - Gateshead. Gor - Gorton. Inv - Inverurie. Str - Stratford. Tux - Tuxford.
REPAIR CODES:- **C/H** - Casual Heavy. **C/L** - Casual Light. **G** - General. **H**- Heavy. **H/I** - Heavy Intermediate. **L** - Light. **L/I** - Light Intermediate. **N/C** - Non-Classified.

27

5158 cont./
   383 *(ex5448)* 30/1/37.
   984 *(ex5128)* 4/6/38.
   947 *(ex5449)* 6/4/40.
   156 *(exD9 6040)* 4/7/42.
   800 *(ex5450)* 21/4/45.
  3853 *(ex9804)* 8/2/47.
  3866 *(ex9802)* 18/9/48.
  3869 *(ex69804)* 15/4/50.
 22386 *(ex69819)* 23/5/52.
 22384 *(ex69819)* 12/6/54.

SHEDS:
Neasden.
Gorton 13/6/54.
Norwich 11/9/55.
Lowestoft 8/1/56.
Immingham 17/2/57.

RENUMBERED:
   158c *at* 20/6/24.
  5158 19/9/25.
  9829 27/1/46.
 69829 18/9/48.

CONDEMNED: 30/5/60.
Cut up at Stratford.

The engines with deep frames were soon altered to bring them into line. Note that the cab front windows were one-piece and did not curve over the shoulder of the firebox.

Ross 'pop' safety valves were fitted to all of them and were of a short muffled type on the original set of boilers.

The original safety valves were gradually replaced by Ross 'pops' of the more usual type, but the muffled variety were still in use when No.9830 came out from repair in May 1946 (*see* photo 73 page XX).

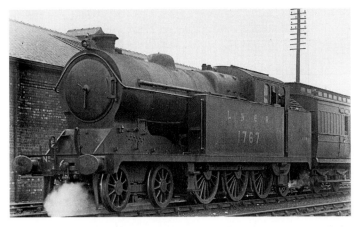

On all thirteen the smokebox door was of GC type with deep hinge and no cross straps, but the fastening was always by two handles. Note frames originally had no lifting holes.

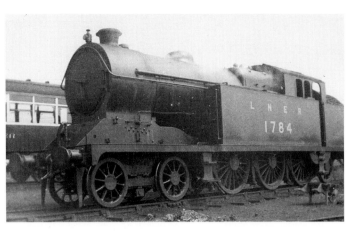

Until the removal of the Westinghouse brake pump in 1932-4, the sandboxes for the leading coupled wheels were fitted under the running plate.

For some reason not discovered, No.1767 in February 1935 was fitted with a NER type door with two straps - it was the only one so altered. Note the vacuum exhaust drain pipe, first fitted to No.1790 in October 1935.

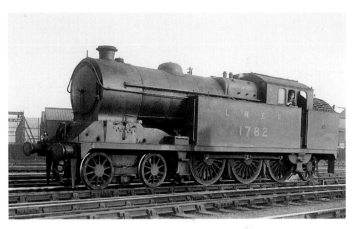

The removal of the brake pump provided space for the leading sandboxes to be placed on the running plate just ahead of the tank on both sides. Most of the class retained the GC style buffers with elongated heads to help prevent buffers locking on tight curves.

By the time No.1767 became No.69837 in May 1948, it had reverted to its original GC type door.

By May 1946 a drain pipe was being fitted on the side of the smokebox to dispose of the condensate from the vacuum ejector exhaust pipe. On this engine, seen at Darlington 16th August 1947, Group Standard buffers and coupling hook had been fitted in June 1936.

1712

Hawthorn Leslie 3616.

To traffic 25/9/1925.

REPAIRS:
Ghd. 27/10—4/11/25.**L.**
Ghd. 1—2/6/26.**L.**
Ghd. 17/9/27—23/1/28.**G.**
Ghd. 19/2—11/4/30.**G.**
Dar. 29/8—5/10/33.**G.**
Westinghouse removed.
Steam brake fitted.
Dar. 14/7—10/9/36.**G.**
Dar. 31/5—11/6/37.**N/C.**
Special bunker fitted.
Dar. 23/1—8/3/39.**G.**
Dar. 7/4—14/5/41.**G.**
Dar. 25/1—2/2/43.**N/C.**
Dar. 7/4—7/5/43.**L.**
Dar. 8/10/43—22/1/44.**G.**
Two new 1⅛ in. part frames.
Dar. 1—25/5/46.**G.**
Dar. 16/8/46. *Weigh.*
Ghd. 29/4—22/5/47.**L.**
Dar. 18/2—7/5/48.**G.**
Dar. 6/9—14/10/49.**G.**
Dar. 17/1—10/2/51.**N/C.**
Dar. 7/8—8/9/51.**G.**
Ghd. 29/1—6/3/52.**C/L.**
Dar. 8—17/1/53.**C/L.**
Dar. 11/7—22/8/53.**G.**
Dar. 11/7—11/8/55.**G.**
Dar. 28/12/56—7/2/57.**H/I.**

BOILERS:
3616.
  152 *(ex1738)* 5/10/33.
  3616 *(ex1784)* 8/3/39.
  3621 *(ex1782)* 14/5/41.
  3616 *(ex1767)* 22/1/44.
  3617 *(ex1750)* 25/5/46.
  3864 *(ex9834)* 7/5/48.
  3857 *(ex69835)* 14/10/49.
  3857 reno.22366 10/2/51.
  22374 *(ex69836)* 8/9/51.
  22371 *(ex69836)* 22/8/53.
  22392 *(ex69815)* 11/8/55.

SHEDS:
Darlington.
Gateshead 22/10/25.
Heaton 21/8/29.
Middlesbrough 31/8/38.
Darlington 20/3/39.
Stratford 8/4/51.
Darlington 20/5/51.
Stockton 13/6/54.
Darlington 19/9/54.
West Hartlepool 15/9/57.
Saltburn 10/11/57.
Middlesbrough 2/2/58.
Thornaby 1/6/58.

RENUMBERED:
9830 25/5/46.
69830 7/5/48.

CONDEMNED: 18/11/58.
Into Dar. for cut up 18/11/58.

1719

Hawthorn Leslie 3617.

To traffic 3/10/1925.

REPAIRS:
Dar. 19—30/10/25.**L.**
Ghd. 29/6—2/7/26.**L.**
Ghd. 30/9—11/11/27.**L.**
Ghd. 31/1—28/3/29.**G.**
Ghd. 16—17/4/29.**L.**
Dar. 19/11/31—15/1/32.**G.**
Westinghouse removed and
steam brake fitted.
Dar. 29/11/33—5/1/34.**G.**
Dar. 5/2—15/3/34.**L.**
Dar. 21/10—29/11/35.**G.**
Dar. 25/1—11/3/38.**G.**
Dar. 8/12/38. *Weigh.*
Dar. 13—21/9/39.**N/C.**
Dar. 29/2—6/4/40.**G.**
Dar. 14/4—15/5/42.**G.**
Dar. 5—9/6/42.**N/C.**
Dar. 5/11/42. *Weigh.*
Dar. 9/5—10/6/44.**G.**
Dar. 17—19/1/46.**N/C.**
Dar. 28/5—20/7/46.**G.**
Dar. 7—10/10/46.**L.**
Dar. 25/3—11/4/47.**L.**
Ghd. 10/8—1/9/47.**L.**
Dar. 6/8—10/9/48.**G.**
Dar. 15/8—16/9/50.**G.**
Dar. 26/2--28/3/52.**G.**
Dar. 3—7/4/52.**N/C.**
Dar. 25/6—10/8/53.**C/L.**
Dar. 15—20/10/53.**N/C.**
Gor. 14/8—2/10/54.**G.**
Dar. 30/8/56. *Weigh.*
Dar. 4/2—8/3/57.**H/I.**

BOILERS:
3617.
  3619 *(ex1750)* 5/1/34.
  3628 *(ex1790)* 29/11/35.
  3617 *(ex1790)* 11/3/38.
  3624 *(ex1790)* 6/4/40.
  3619 *(ex1784)* 15/5/42.
  3622 *(ex1738)* 10/6/44.
  3625 *(ex9832)* 20/7/46.
  3871 *(new)* 10/9/48.
  22354 *(ex69834)* 16/9/50.
  22385 *(ex69833)* 28/3/52.
  22366 *(ex spare)* 2/10/54.

SHEDS:
Darlington.
Neville Hill 10/10/25.

Darlington ?/3/26.
Gateshead 20/5/26.
Heaton 21/8/29.
Saltburn 26/6/30.
Darlington 21/3/39.
Saltburn 17/7/49.
Darlington 13/6/54.
Stockton 13/2/55.
Darlington 25/9/55.
West Hartlepool 15/9/57.
Saltburn 10/11/57.
Middlesbrough 2/2/58.
Thornaby 1/6/58.

RENUMBERED:
9831 20/7/46.
69831 10/9/48.

CONDEMNED: 27/11/58.
Into Dar. for cut up 27/11/58.

1738

Hawthorn Leslie 3618.

To traffic 22/10/1925.

REPAIRS:
Dar. 4—16/11/25.**L.**
Ghd. 22/2—10/3/26.**L.**
Ghd. 8—10/6/26.**L.**
Dar. 11/1—15/3/29.**G.**
Dar. 29/4—7/5/29.**N/C.**
Dar. 6/8—6/9/29.**N/C.**
Dar. 8/4—16/6/31.**G.**
Dar. 3/5—13/6/33.**G.**
Westinghouse removed & steam
brake fitted.
Dar. 5/11/34—12/1/35.**G.**
Dar. 17—19/1/35.**N/C.**
Dar. 23/1—13/3/35.**N/C.**
Dar. 30/10/35—7/1/36.**L.**
Dar. 15/6—30/7/36.**L.**
Dar. 14/12/36—6/4/37.**G.**
Dar. 6/2—29/3/39.**G.**
Dar. 19/9—2/11/40.**G.**
Dar. 16/6—9/8/41.**G.**
Dar. 8—11/9/41.**N/C.**
Dar. 25—29/11/41.**N/C.**
Dar. 18—26/2/42.**N/C.**
Dar. 5—10/3/42.**N/C.**
Dar. 17/7—4/8/42.**N/C.**
Dar. 28/8—15/9/42.**H.**
Dar. 20/1—4/2/43.**L.**
Dar. 13/3—7/4/44.**G.**
Dar. 2/5/44. *Weigh.*
Dar. 16—20/5/44.**N/C.**
Dar. 6/5—28/8/46.**G.**
Dar. 2—11/9/46.**N/C.**
Dar. 11/6/47. *Weigh.*
Dar. 29/6—27/8/48.**G.**
Dar. 16—21/9/48.**N/C.**
Dar. 3—17/8/49.**C/L.**
Dar. 29/8/49. *Weigh.*
Dar. 11/9—11/10/50.**G.**

Dar. 27/8—20/9/52.**G.**
Dar. 27/8/53. *Weigh.*
Gor. 2/10—20/11/54.**G.**
Dar. 2/3—17/4/56.**C/H.**
After collision.
Dar. 11/2—8/3/57.**G.**
Dar. 11—12/3/57.**N/C.**

BOILERS:
3618.
  152 *(new)* 16/6/31.
  3622 *(ex1766)* 13/6/33.
  3625 *(ex1784)* 12/1/35.
  3622 *(ex1760)* 9/8/41.
  3625 *(ex1756)* 7/4/44.
  3620 *(ex1756)* 28/8/46.
  3865 *(ex9833)* 27/8/48.
  22355 *(ex69831)* 11/10/50.
  22394 *(ex spare)* 20/9/52.
  22385 *(ex69831)* 20/11/54.
  22355 *(ex69834)* 8/3/57.

SHEDS:
Darlington.
Heaton ?/12/25.
Blaydon ?/2/26.
Saltburn 28/5/28.
Darlington 17/4/39.
Stratford 8/4/51.
Darlington 20/5/51.
Hull Botanic Gardens 15/9/57.

RENUMBERED:
9832 17/3/46.
69832 27/8/48.

CONDEMNED: 6/10/58.
Into Dar. for cut up 6/10/58.

1750

Hawthorn Leslie 3619.

To traffic 31/10/1925.

REPAIRS:
Ghd. 26—27/5/26.**L.**
Ghd. 20/7—28/9/28.**G.**
Ghd. 1/5—17/6/30.**G.**
Ghd. 17/8—18/9/31.**L.**
Dar. 19/10—24/11/33.**G.**
Westinghouse removed & steam
brake fitted.
Dar. 29/4—13/6/36.**G.**
Dar. 24/10—29/11/38.**G.**
Dar. 29/12/38—26/1/39.**N/C.**
Dar. 26/4/39. *Weigh.*
Dar. 7/7/39. *Weigh.*
Dar. 24—25/9/40.**N/C.**
Dar. 2/12/40—11/1/41.**G.**
Dar. 2—9/12/42.**N/C.**
Dar. 29/10—4/12/43.**G.**
Dar. 20/7/45. *Weigh.*
Dar. 5/3/46.**N/C.**
Dar. 3/4—11/5/46.**G.**

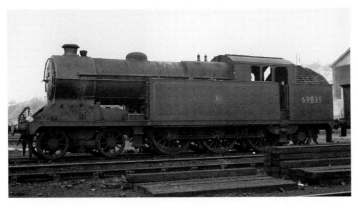

After BR took over, most had the upper lamp iron moved from the top of the smokebox and fixed on the door.

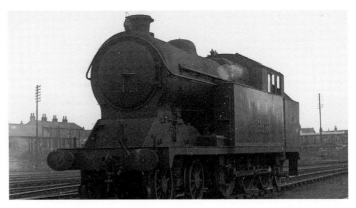

Standard fittings through to BR days were low dome, built-up 'flowerpot' chimney and upper lamp iron on top of the smokebox.

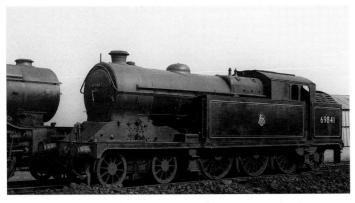

There were cases where the lamp iron alteration was delayed. It had not been made on No.69841 by late 1951. Note Group Standard buffers fitted.

At its last repair in April 1955, Darlington fitted No.69836 with a taller chimney as fitted to Part 1 of the class. The extra height was not a problem as the engine then worked only in the NE Region.

(below) In June 1937, No.1712 (9830) had the outside of its bunker coal rails plated over as an experiment to stop coal dust blowing into the cab when that end was leading.

The outside plating was still in position at least to 1951 but no others were done in this style. Note the 'extra' coal on the cab roof.

Either in August 1953 or August 1955, No.69830 had the bunker plating transferred from the outside to the inside of the coal rails.

The thirteen built in 1925 for NE Area were dual braked as air brakes for train working was then still needed. They had swan neck connections both for Westinghouse and vacuum train brakes.

By April 1955, No.69839 also had plating put behind its coal rails. Unlike the Part 1 engines, those built in 1925 retained the original five rails to withdrawal although they used mechanical coaling plants at some depots.

The Unification of Brakes programme enabled the Westinghouse equipment to be removed. Between January 1932 (No.1719) and August 1934 (No.1782) it was taken off and the brake on the engine changed from air to steam. Note the bracket for the pump still in place.

1750 cont./
Dar. 16—18/5/46.**N/C.**
Ghd. 30/5—28/6/47.**L.**
Dar. 9/4/48. *Weigh.*
Dar. 4/5—4/6/48.**G.**
Dar. 1/4—6/5/50.**G.**
Dar. 17—18/5/50.**N/C.**
Dar. 2/10—2/11/51.**G.**
Dar. 16/9/52. *Weigh.*
Dar. 24/4—1/5/53.**C/L.**
Dar. 3/7—15/8/53.**G.**
Dar. 24/8—5/9/53.**N/C.**
Dar. 7—28/2/55.**N/C.**
Dar. 18/7—17/9/55.**G.**
Dar. 19—22/9/55.**N/C.**
Dar. 22/3/56. *Weigh.*
Dar. 2/5/57. *Not repaired.*

BOILERS:
3619.
3616 *(ex1712)* 24/11/33.
3619 *(ex1719)* 13/6/36.
3628 *(ex1719)* 29/11/38.
3627 *(ex1766)* 11/1/41.
3617 *(ex1766)* 4/12/43.
3865 *(new)* 11/5/46.
3628 *(ex9837)* 4/6/48.
3872 *(ex69840)* 6/5/50.
22380 *(ex69840)* 2/11/51.
22358 *(ex69841)* 15/8/53.
22354 *(ex69841)* 17/9/55.

SHEDS:
Gateshead.
Heaton 21/8/29.
Middlesbrough 24/8/38.
Darlington 20/3/39.
Stratford 8/4/51.
Darlington 13/5/51.

RENUMBERED:
9833 7/7/46.
69833 4/6/48.

CONDEMNED: 27/5/57.
Cut up at Darlington.

1756

Hawthorn Leslie 3620.

To traffic 14/11/1925.

REPAIRS:
Ghd. 14—16/7/26.**L.**
Ghd. 25/4—4/7/29.**G.**
Ghd. 18/11/30—27/1/31.**G.**
Ghd. 10—30/6/32.**N/C.**
Dar. 1/11—4/12/32.**G.**
Westinghouse removed & steam brake fitted.
Dar. 26/10—10/11/34.**G.**
Dar. 15/6—2/10/36.**G.**
Dar. 9—23/10/36.**N/C.**
Dar. 14/4—19/5/39.**G.**

Dar. 31/5—20/6/39.**N/C.**
Dar. 23/6—8/8/41.**G.**
Dar. 2—23/12/42.**N/C.**
Dar. 1/2—3/3/44.**G.**
Dar. 10—31/8/45.**L.**
Dar. 13/3—18/4/46.**G.**
Dar. 25/4—8/5/46.**N/C.**
Dar. 20/10/47. *Weigh.*
Dar. 23/2—9/4/48.**G.**
Dar. 2/10/48—6/1/49.**L.**
Dar. 20/5—4/6/49.**L.**
Dar. 16/9—14/10/49.**L.**
Dar. 15/12/49—9/1/50.**C/L.**
Dar. 18/1—4/2/50.**C/H.**
Dar. 31/5/50. *Weigh.*
Dar. 3/8—29/9/50.**G.**
Dar. 22/1/51. *Weigh.*
Dar. 11/2/52. *Weigh.*
Dar. 14/5—7/6/52.**G.**
Dar. 9—10/6/52.**N/C.**
Dar. 23/6—11/7/52.**N/C.**
Dar. 26/8—3/10/52.**C/H.**
Dar. 20—23/10/52.**N/C.**
Gor. 10/7—4/9/54.**H/I.**
Dar. 1/10—14/11/56.**G.**
Dar. 1/7—6/8/57.**C/L.**

BOILERS:
3620.
3627 *(ex1784)* 4/12/32.
3626 *(ex1784)* 2/10/36.
3620 *(ex1771)* 19/5/39.
3625 *(ex1738)* 8/8/41.
3620 *(ex1771)* 3/3/44.
3864 *(new)* 18/4/46.
152 *(ex9842)* 9/9/48.
3864 *(ex69830)* 4/2/50.
22352 *(ex69829)* 29/9/50.
22354 *(ex69831)* 7/6/52.
22355 *(ex69832)* 3/10/52.
22358 *(ex69833)* 14/11/56.

SHEDS:
Blaydon.
Saltburn 25/5/28.
Middlesbrough 10/5/34.
Saltburn 28/5/35.
Darlington 20/3/39.
Saltburn 13/2/49.
Stockton 13/6/54.
Darlington 19/9/54.
Stockton 13/2/55.
Darlington 25/9/55.
West Hartlepool 15/9/57.
Saltburn 10/11/57.
Middlesbrough 2/2/58.
Thornaby 1/6/58.

RENUMBERED:
9834 7/7/46.
69834 9/4/48.

CONDEMNED: 11/11/58.
Into Dar. for cut up 11/11/58.

1760

Hawthorn Leslie 3621.

To traffic 25/11/1925.

REPAIRS:
Ghd. 28/4—17/5/26.**L.**
Ghd. 30/9—29/12/27.**G.**
Dar. 25/11/29—29/1/30.**G.**
Dar. 2/2—15/3/32.**G.**
Westinghouse removed & steam brake fitted.
Dar. 12/1—19/2/34.**G.**
Dar. 8/5—14/6/35.**G.**
Dar. 18/2—7/4/37.**G.**
Dar. 23/2—13/4/39.**G.**
Dar. 14—26/4/39.**N/C.**
Dar. 10/7—29/8/40.**N/C.**
Dar. 2/4/41. *Weigh.*
Dar. 2/6—19/7/41.**G.**
Dar. 29/7—6/8/41.**N/C.**
Dar. 12—15/8/41.**N/C.**
Dar. 24/5—30/6/43.**G.**
Dar. 27/4—29/5/46.**L.**
Dar. 13/2—17/5/47.**G.**
Dar. 29/5—6/6/47.**N/C.**
Dar. 10/1—13/2/48.**L.**
Dar. 9/3—7/4/49.**G.**
Dar. 14/4—2/5/49.**N/C.**
Dar. 6/12/50—10/1/51.**G.**
Dar. 20/11/52. *Weigh.*
Dar. 8/12/52—17/1/53.**H/I.**
Dar. 23—28/1/53.**N/C.**
Dar. 13/12/54—20/1/55.**G.**
Dar. 22/3—18/4/57.**G.**
Dar. 23—26/4/57.**N/C.**

BOILERS:
3621.
3617 *(ex1719)* 19/2/34.
3623 *(ex1768)* 14/6/35.
3622 *(ex1771)* 7/4/37.
3618 *(ex1767)* 19/7/41.
3857 *(new)* 30/6/43.
3870 *(new)* 7/4/49.
22360 *(ex69841)* 10/1/51.
22394 *(ex69832)* 20/1/55.
22374 *(ex69806)* 18/4/57.

SHEDS:
Darlington.
Blaydon 2/12/25.
Saltburn 25/5/28.
Darlington 10/4/39.
Neasden 7/11/43.
Darlington 27/3/45.
Norwich 28/1/51.
Stratford 8/4/51.
Norwich 13/5/51.
Darlington 5/8/51.
Hull Botanic Gardens 13/6/54.
Stockton 16/6/57.

RENUMBERED:
9835 11/8/46.
ᴇ9835 13/2/48.
69835 7/4/49.

CONDEMNED: 26/11/58.
Into Dar. for cut up 26/11/58.

1766

Hawthorn Leslie 3622.

To traffic 2/12/1925.

REPAIRS:
Dar. 22—23/12/25.**L.**
Dar. 29/4—3/6/26.**L.**
Ghd. 4—30/10/27.**L.**
Dar. 11/11/28—14/2/29.**G.**
Dar. 7/5—4/6/29.**N/C.**
Dar. 9/9—7/10/29.**N/C.**
Dar. 17/2—10/4/31.**G.**
Dar. 1/3—12/4/33.**G.**
Westinghouse removed & steam brake fitted.
Dar. 20—29/5/33.**N/C.**
Dar. 12/9—31/10/34.**L.**
After collision.
Dar. 30/1—3/4/35.**G.**
Dar. 10/9—28/11/36.**G.**
Dar. 8/11—21/12/38.**G.**
Dar. 9/9—16/10/40.**G.**
Dar. 22/10/40. *Weigh.*
Dar. 30/7—27/8/41.**L.**
Dar. 8—21/5/42.**L.**
Dar. 29/7—12/8/42.**N/C.**
Dar. 2/9—9/10/42.**L.**
Dar. 2/7—16/8/43.**G.**
Dar. 4—14/9/43.**N/C.**
Dar. 8—12/1/44.**N/C.**
Dar. 27/2—13/4/45.**G.**
Dar. 7—18/5/45.**N/C.**
Dar. 13/6—13/7/45.**L.**
Dar. 11/3—19/4/47.**G.**
Dar. 30/4—7/5/47.**N/C.**
Ghd. 17/4—14/5/48.**L.**
Dar. 5/1—19/3/49.**G.**
Dar. 29/3—26/4/49.**N/C.**
Dar. 3—14/5/49.**N/C.**
Dar. 31/5—22/6/49.**N/C.**
Dar. 21/3—26/4/51.**G.**
Dar. 7—8/4/52. *Weigh.*
Dar. 15/5—13/6/53.**G.**
Dar. 15—17/6/53.**N/C.**
Dar. 24/3—30/4/55.**G.**
Dar. 20/8/58. *Not repaired.*

BOILERS:
3622.
3624 *(ex1768)* 12/4/33.
3620 *(ex1767)* 3/4/35.
3627 *(ex1756)* 28/11/36.
3617 *(ex1719)* 16/10/40.
3618 *(ex1760)* 16/8/43.
3862 *(new)* 13/4/45.

1766 cont./
22371 *(ex69839)* 26/4/51.
22359 *(ex69839)* 13/6/53.
22389 *(ex69828)* 30/4/55.

SHEDS:
Darlington.
York 14/12/25.
Neville Hill ?/2/26.
Darlington ?/3/26.
Gateshead 20/5/26.
Saltburn 28/5/28.
Darlington 22/3/39.
Middleton-in-Teesdale 20/5/39.
Darlington 11/9/39.
Neasden 29/10/43.
Darlington 13/2/45.
Saltburn 13/2/49.
Darlington 29/1/50.
Norwich 11/2/51.
Darlington 12/8/51.
Hull Botanic Gardens 6/7/52.
Darlington 16/6/57.
Hull Botanic Gardens 15/9/57.

RENUMBERED:
9836 11/8/46.
69836 14/5/48.

CONDEMNED: 25/8/58.
Cut up at Darlington.

1767

Hawthorn Leslie 3623.

To traffic 11/12/1925.

REPAIRS:
Dar. 1—14/9/26.**L.**
Ghd. 18/7—21/9/28.**G.**
Ghd. 6—14/12/28.**N/C.**
Dar. 8/10—6/11/29.**N/C.**
Dar. 11/11—31/12/30.**G.**
Dar. 29/11/32—17/1/33.**G.**
Westinghouse removed & steam brake fitted.
Dar. 18/1—23/2/35.**G.**
Dar. 18—26/3/35.**L.**
Dar. 8/10/36—20/2/37.**G.**
Dar. 23/2—5/3/37.**N/C.**
Dar. 11—14/5/37.**N/C.**
Dar. 22/11/38—24/3/39.**G.**
Dar. 27—28/3/39.**N/C.**
Dar. 28/4—9/6/41.**G.**
Dar. 2—8/3/43.**N/C.**
Dar. 15/11—31/12/43.**G.**
Dar. 10—20/1/44.**N/C.**
Dar. 13/1—5/2/45.**L.**
Dar. 11/12/45.**N/C.**
Dar. 1—25/1/46.**L.**
Dar. 15/5—15/6/46.**G.**
Dar. 24/6—8/7/46.**N/C.**
Dar. 1/5/47. *Weigh.*
Ghd. 9/7—23/8/47.**L.**

Dar. 3/3/48. *Weigh.*
Dar. 3/4—28/5/48.**G.**
Dar. 4—21/6/48.**N/C.**
Dar. 1/9—12/10/49.**C/L.**
Dar. 23/5—8/7/50.**G.**
Dar. 9—25/8/50.**N/C.**
Dar. 5/6/52. *Weigh.*
Dar. 11/6/52. *Weigh.*
Dar. 26/6/52. *Weigh.*
Dar. 22/9—18/10/52.**G.**
Gor. 18/9—23/10/54.**G.**
Dar. 15/1—20/2/58.**G.**

BOILERS:
3623.
3620 *(ex1756)* 17/1/33.
3618 *(ex1771)* 23/2/35.
3616 *(ex1712)* 9/6/41.
3627 *(ex1750)* 31/12/43.
3628 *(ex1782)* 15/6/46.
947 *(ex9840)* 28/5/48.
22350 *(ex69814)* 18/10/52.
22383 *(ex69812)* 23/10/54.
22354 *(ex69833)* 20/2/58.

SHEDS:
York.
Neville Hill ?/2/26.
Gateshead 20/5/26.
Saltburn 28/5/28.
Darlington 10/4/39.
Norwich 18/2/51.
Stratford 8/4/51.
Norwich 20/5/51.
Darlington 1/7/51.
Hull Botanic Gardens 6/7/52.

RENUMBERED:
9837 11/8/46.
69837 28/5/48.

CONDEMNED: 3/12/58.
Into Dar. for cut up 3/12/58.

1768

Hawthorn Leslie 3624.

To traffic 23/12/1925.

REPAIRS:
Ghd. 1—8/7/26.**L.**
Ghd. 26/8—2/9/26.**L.**
Ghd. 3/4—14/6/28.**G.**
Dar. 13/1—3/3/31.**G.**
Ghd. 16/10—16/12/31.**L.**
After collision.
Dar. 15/2—31/3/33.**G.**
Westinghouse removed & steam brake fitted.
Dar. 26/2—23/4/35.**G.**
Dar. 25/3—11/5/37.**G.**
Dar. 13—30/7/37.**N/C.**
Dar. 13/9—23/12/37.**H.**
Dar. 9/2/39. *Weigh.*

Dar. 13—19/9/39.**N/C.**
Dar. 18/3—26/4/40.**G.**
Dar. 13/2/41. *Weigh.*
Dar. 25/4—15/5/41.**G.**
Dar. 2—3/3/42.**N/C.**
Dar. 18/4—23/6/42.**G.**
Dar. 18/8—23/9/44.**G.**
Dar. 15/11/45—17/1/46.**L.**
Dar. 20/11/46—1/2/47.**G.**
Dar. 22/4—9/5/47.**L.**
Dar. 10—20/2/48.**L.**
Dar. 26/1—3/3/49.**G.**
Dar. 29—30/6/50. *Weigh.*
Dar. 23— 25/8/50. *Weigh.*
Dar. 12/12/50—20/1/51.**G.**
Dar. 22—24/1/51.**N/C.**
Dar. 12/8—6/9/52.**G.**
Dar. 8—9/9/52.**N/C.**
Dar. 21/10—4/12/52.**N/C.**
Gor. 18/9—30/10/54.**G.**
Dar. 9—31/1/58.**C/L.**
After collision.

BOILERS:
3624.
3623 *(ex1767)* 31/3/33.
3624 *(ex1766)* 23/4/35.
3623 *(ex1760)* 11/5/37.
3626 *(ex1790)* 23/9/44.
3619 *(ex9842)* 3/3/49.
22361 *(exD9 62307)* 20/1/51.
22352 *(ex69834)* 6/9/52.
22377 *(ex69800)* 30/10/54.

SHEDS:
Heaton.
Blaydon 14/1/26.
Heaton 27/6/28.
Middlesbrough 26/6/30.
Darlington 20/3/39.
Stratford 15/4/51.
Darlington 20/5/51.
Stockton 19/6/55.

RENUMBERED:
9838 11/8/46.
E**9838** 20/2/48.
69838 3/3/49.

CONDEMNED: 5/11/58.
Into Dar. for cut up 5/11/58.

1771

Hawthorn Leslie 3625.

To traffic 8/1/1926.

REPAIRS:
Ghd. 28—30/7/26.**L.**
Ghd. 23/1—27/3/28.**G.**
Ghd. 6/2—28/3/30.**G.**
Dar. 1—11/9/30.**L.**
Dar. 15—24/12/30.**N/C.**
Dar. 24/8—24/10/32.**G.**

Westinghouse removed & steam brake fitted.
Dar. 20/9/33—31/1/34.**L.**
Dar. 12/12/34—14/2/35.**G.**
Dar. 20/5—18/6/35.**L.**
Dar. 13/10/36—28/1/37.**G.**
Dar. 13/4—30/6/38.**H.**
Dar. 22/3—12/5/39.**G.**
Dar. 9/6/39. *Weigh.*
Dar. 7/7—26/8/41.**G.**
Dar. 2—16/7/43.**L.**
Dar. 17/8—3/9/43.**L.**
Dar. 3/1—18/2/44.**G.**
Dar. 29/8/44. *Weigh.*
Dar. 10/5/45. *Weigh.*
Dar. 17/7—1/9/45.**G.**
Dar. 25/3/47. *Weigh.*
Dar. 16/4—19/7/47.**G.**
Dar. 22/7—2/8/47.**N/C.**
Dar. 13/8—1/9/47.**N/C.**
Dar. 22/3—14/4/49.**G.**
Dar. 18/8/49.**L.**
Dar. 5/2—9/3/51.**G.**
Dar. 19—20/3/51.**N/C.**
Dar. 22/11—6/12/51.**C/L.**
Dar. 8/7/52. *Weigh.*
Dar. 14/11—13/12/52.**G.**
Dar. 7/4/53. *Weigh.*
Dar. 8/3—14/4/55.**G.**
Dar. 26—29/4/55.**N/C.**
Dar. 10—18/8/56.**N/C.**
Dar. 7/12/56—11/1/57.**H/I.**
Dar. 16/1/57.**N/C.**

BOILERS:
3625.
3618 *(ex1738)* 24/10/32.
3622 *(ex1738)* 14/2/35.
3620 *(ex1766)* 28/1/37.
152 *(ex1712)* 12/5/39.
3620 *(ex1756)* 26/8/41.
947 *(ex5045)* 18/2/44.
3863 *(new)* 1/9/45.
3874 *(new)* 14/4/49.
22359 *(ex69835)* 9/3/51.
22396 *(ex69837)* 13/12/52.
22352 *(ex69838)* 14/4/55.

SHEDS:
Darlington.
Blaydon 14/1/26.
Heaton 27/6/28.
Middlesbrough 26/6/30.
Darlington 20/3/39.
Stratford 8/4/51.
Darlington 13/5/51.
Stockton 13/6/54.
Darlington 19/9/54.

RENUMBERED:
9839 11/8/46.
69839 14/4/49.

CONDEMNED: 19/9/58.
Into Dar. for cut up 19/9/58.

As these engines often spent almost half their time running bunker first, the Great Central gave due prominence to display of their number at that end.

All ten engines built in 1923 first got Great Central green paint but with L&NER, the first five having full points but the other five lacked them. Their bunker number plates were all the smaller LNER type.

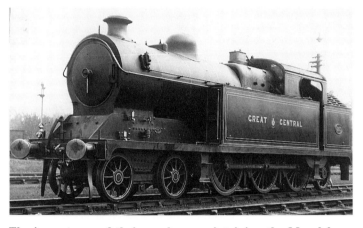

The importance of their work on maintaining the Marylebone commuter traffic qualified them for fully lined out green passenger livery, which all twenty-one wore at Grouping.

No.448, ex paint shop 28th July 1923, lacked the full points but still had the large GC brass number plate on its bunker. Only two of the class, Nos.169 and 452 got the suffix C to their number. They were ex paint shop 3rd October and 29th September 1923 respectively.

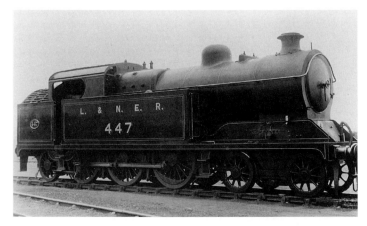

When No.447 was ex paint shop on 21st April 1923 it was still in green with GC style of black and double white lining, and with full points to the new company initials. The large brass number plate continued to be used on the bunker.

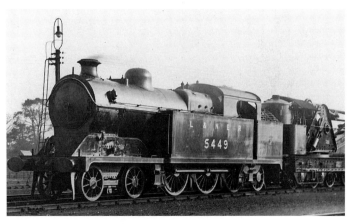

In February 1924 two of the class Nos.5449 (2nd) and 5166 (23rd), acquired their LNER numbers but got L&NER. On the bunker the smaller LNER plate replaced the GC plate.

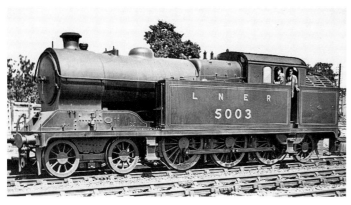

Until May 1925 the green painting continued to appear complete with GC style lining.

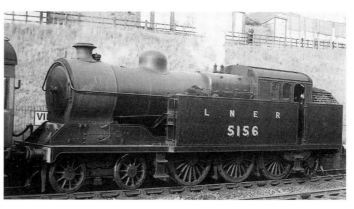

The white patch at the end of the front buffer beam, and only at the end, must have been warning of a tight clearance at some places. As this is a 1936 photograph it is clearly nothing to do with working in the blackout of the 1939-45 war years.

Ex works and paint shop on 30th May 1925, No.5045 was in black, but with the red and white lining which Gorton had used for mixed traffic classes.

From 1942 to 1946 the LNER initials gave way to NE only but the size went up from 7½in. to 12in. letters.

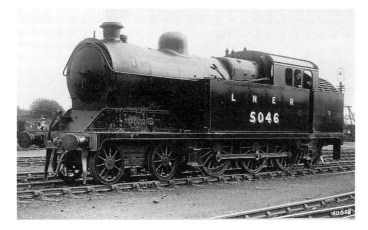

The extra lining which Gorton had put on No.5045 was not continued and that works then had to come into line with the others and use single red lining only. Even so, for some years (this is a 1933 painting) they got a glossier black than the others.

During the war years, only unlined black was used and it was of poor quality and hastily applied. But standard shaded transfers survived.

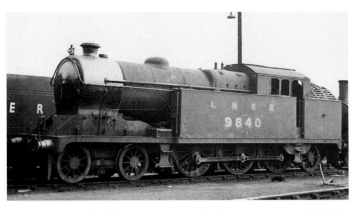

From January 1946 there were two significant changes; LNER in 7½in. letters re-appeared and the complete re-numbering began. Part 2 engines which Darlington maintained also had the date of last general repair put above the number, in this case 4/46. Gorton never followed suit on the Part 1's which were its responsibility.

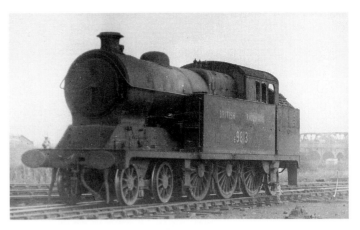

Gorton applied the regional prefix E to only four A5 class, all in 1948: E9813 on 28th February, E9803 and E9816 on 6th March. They had these numbers painted on in yellow unshaded 12in. numerals, in Gill sans but with the LNER modified 6 and 9. They were the last to have their number on the side tanks. The other with the prefix was E9808, ex works 17th January but still with LNER.

It was unusual to find LNER applied in 12in. shaded lettering, but this happened when No.5373 became 9817 at a general repair from which it was ex works 4th May 1946.

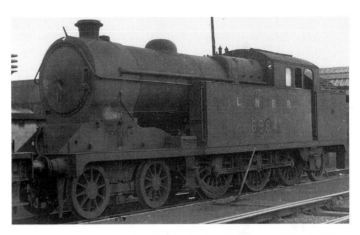

This combination was taken further by Darlington with No.69841 on 7th April 1948 and by Gateshead with No.69836 on the 14th May 1948 (see page 31 top, right). Both got light repairs and were not repainted, the numerals being 12in. painted and unshaded with modified 6 and 9.

This engine did get orthodox style, but only just because when it was ex works on 10th January 1948 the LNER had ceased to exist. During the following week Gorton began putting on BRITISH RAILWAYS.

Early in 1949 all A5 repairs were moved to NE Region, Gorton only giving casual/heavy to 69805 after 69800 and 69806 left there on 5th March 1949. E9803 went to Gateshead 24th March 1949 for a light repair so was not repainted but the E and 12in. numerals were changed to 69803 in 10in. on 29th April 1949 still on the tank.

Beginning with No.69834 on 9th April 1948 and 69840 on 7th May 1948, the number position was moved to the bunker where Darlington used 12in. bold numerals against 9in. light Gill sans lettering, still without any lining.

For some reason Gorton reverted to unlined black for 69820, ex works 9th October 1948, and for 69824, ex works 13th November 1948, and 69805 and 69825 on 5th February 1949 and 29th January 1949 respectively.

On 3rd July Gorton put No.69828 into one of BR's experimental liveries, using red, cream and grey lining to panel the tank and bunker and using 10in. numerals and letters.

Before maintenance was transferred to Darlington, two more Nos.69800 and 69806 were ex works 5th March 1949 after general repair and they too were unlined. Smokebox number plates put on by Gorton had the modified 6 and 9.

Later, in July 1948 it was announced that black with red, cream and grey lining would be standard for some passenger classes and A5 was one of them. No.69829 was ex Gorton on 18th September 1948 in this standard livery and with 6 and 9 in the correct Gill sans style.

From 1949 standard livery was black with red, cream and grey panelling on tank and bunker together with the smaller version of the BR emblem. Only the last few of the smokebox plates put on at Darlington had correct 6 and 9.

1782

Hawthorn Leslie 3626.

To traffic 21/1/1926.

REPAIRS:
Ghd. 29/4—15/6/26.**L.**
Ghd. 15/3—26/5/28.**G.**
Ghd. 21/8—3/9/29.**L.**
Ghd. 29/4—7/6/30.**G.**
Ghd. 12—21/6/30. *Paint.*
Ghd. 9/2—18/3/32.**G.**
Dar. 27/6—6/8/34.**G.**
Westinghouse removed & steam brake fitted.
Dar. 30/6—14/8/36.**G.**
Dar. 24/10—17/12/38.**G.**
Dar. 19/4/40. *Weigh.*
Dar. 22/3—25/4/41.**G.**
Dar. 3—27/4/42.**L.**
Dar. 29/8—22/9/42.**G.**
Dar. 2/12/42—7/1/43.**L.**
After collision.
Dar. 24/7—9/8/43.**L.**
Dar. 22/12/43—11/2/44.**G.**
Dar. 3—27/6/44.**L.**
After collision (bogie damage).
Dar. 14/7/44. *Weigh.*
Dar. 23/2/45. *Weigh.*
Dar. 5/3/45. *Weigh.*
Dar. 15/5/45. *Weigh.*
Dar. 8/3—13/4/46.**G.**
Dar. 17/4/47. *Weigh.*
Dar. 16/5—28/6/47.**L.**
Dar. 8—19/7/47.**L.**
Dar. 22—30/7/47.**N/C.**
Dar. 22/3—7/5/48.**G.**
Dar. 1/11—7/12/49.**G.**
Dar. 26/4/50. *Weigh.*
Dar. 4/7/51. *Weigh.*
Dar. 9/7/51. *Weigh.*
Dar. 13/8—14/9/51.**G.**
Dar. 23/9—23/10/52.**H/I.**
Dar. 20/4—4/5/53.**C/L.**
After collision.
Gor. 5/6—10/7/54.**L/I.**
Dar. 15/3—23/4/56.**G.**
Dar. 30/4—2/5/56.**N/C.**
Dar. 26/5—3/7/56.**N/C.**
Dar. 22/10—11/12/57.**C/H.**
Dar. 1/6/58. *To store.*

BOILERS:
3626.
3621 *(ex1760)* 6/8/34.
3628 *(ex1750)* 25/4/41.
947 *(ex1771)* 13/4/46.
3872 *(new)* 7/5/48.
3863 *(ex9839)* 7/12/49.
22378 *(ex69803)* 14/9/51.
22371 *(ex69830)* 23/4/56.
22359 *(ex69841)* 11/12/57.

SHEDS:
Blaydon.
Heaton 27/6/28.
Middlesbrough 24/8/38.
Darlington 10/4/39.
Norwich 11/2/51.
Stratford 8/4/51.
Norwich 13/5/51.
Darlington 17/6/51.

RENUMBERED:
9840 13/4/46.
69840 7/5/48.

CONDEMNED: 22/9/58.
Cut up at Darlington.

1784

Hawthorn Leslie 3627.

To traffic 10/2/1926.

REPAIRS:
Ghd. 27—28/5/26.**L.**
Dar. 17/9—21/11/28.**G.**
Dar. 25/6—17/7/29.**N/C.**
Dar. 8/8—20/10/30.**G.**
Dar. 4/10—25/11/32.**G.**
Westinghouse removed & steam brake fitted.
Dar. 20—25/9/33. *Clean for Shildon exhibition.*
Dar. 11/10—10/11/34.**N/C.**
Dar. 12/6—30/7/36.**G.**
Dar. 29/11/38—20/1/39.**G.**
Dar. 8/2—2/3/39.**N/C.**
Dar. 7—22/11/40.**L.**
Dar. 30/12/40—10/1/41.**N/C.**
Dar. 28/7—15/10/41.**G.**
Dar. 2—7/7/42.**N/C.**
Dar. 16/7—1/8/42.**N/C.**
Dar. 25/8/43. *Weigh.*
Dar. 9/6—8/7/44.**G.**
Dar. 5/7—24/8/46.**G.**
Dar. 30/8—5/9/46.**N/C.**
Dar. 25/8/47. *Weigh.*
Dar. 7—31/10/47.**L.**
Dar. 4—19/12/47.**L.**
After collision.
Dar. 12/3—7/4/48.**L.**
Dar. 1—29/10/48.**G.**
Dar. 1—12/11/48.**N/C.**
Dar. 13/12/49—24/1/50.**C/L.**
Dar. 17/10—18/11/50.**G.**
Dar. 4/1/51. *Weigh.*
Dar. 10/1—2/2/51.**C/L.**
Dar. 15—19/10/51. *Weigh.*
Dar. 25/10—10/12/51.**C/L.**
Dar. 26/5—18/6/52.**C/H.**
Dar. 14/1—14/2/53.**G.**
Dar. 23—26/2/53.**N/C.**
Dar. 8—29/6/53.**C/L.**
Gor. 8—15/5/54.**C/L.**
Dar. 6/4—9/6/55.**G.**

Dar. 7/9—25/10/56.**C/L.**
Dar. 18/4—23/5/57.**G.**
Dar. 24/9—17/10/57.**C/L.**
Dar. 1/6/58. *To store.*

BOILERS:
3627.
3625 *(ex1771)* 25/11/32.
3626 *(ex1782)* 10/11/34.
3616 *(ex1750)* 30/7/36.
3619 *(ex1750)* 20/1/39.
152 *(ex1771)* 15/10/41.
3619 *(ex1719)* 8/7/44.
3616 *(ex1712)* 24/8/46.
3873 *(new)* 29/10/48.
22358 *(ex69832)* 18/11/50.
22354 *(ex69834)* 14/2/53.
22359 *(ex69836)* 9/6/55.
22385 *(ex69832)* 23/5/57.

SHEDS:
Gateshead.
Saltburn 28/5/28.
Darlington 17/4/39.
Stratford 15/4/51.
Darlington 8/7/51.
Stockton 13/6/54.
Darlington 19/9/54.

RENUMBERED:
9841 27/1/46.
69841 7/4/48.

CONDEMNED: 23/9/58.
Cut up at Darlington.

1790

Hawthorn Leslie 3628.

To traffic 31/3/1926.

REPAIRS:
Dar. 7—16/4/26.**L.**
Ghd. 26/8—22/10/26.**L.**
Dar. 21/10—21/12/29.**G.**
Dar. 8/12/30—29/1/31.**L.**
Dar. 16/9—7/10/31.**N/C.**
Dar. 24/2—18/4/32.**G.**
Westinghouse removed and steam brake fitted.
Dar. 2—8/9/32.**N/C.**
Dar. 27/1—17/3/34.**G.**
Dar. 10/9—14/10/35.**G.**
Dar. 1/4—14/5/37.**G.**
Dar. 9/8/37. *Weigh.*
Dar. 23/6/38. *Weigh.*
Dar. 13/3—12/4/39.**N/C.**
Dar. 5—9/5/39. *Weigh.*
Dar. 30/10—1/12/39.**G.**
Dar. 1/5—10/7/42.**G.**
Dar. 7/4—15/5/43.**L.**
Dar. 10/5—6/9/44.**G.**
Dar. 28/11/45. *Weigh.*
Dar. 16/7—7/9/46.**G.**

Ghd. 11/9—6/10/47.**L.**
Dar. 5/11/47. *Weigh.*
Dar. 19/11—23/12/48.**G.**
Dar. 13—22/1/49.**N/C.**
Ghd. 27/4—18/5/49.**C/L.**
Dar. 15/8—2/9/49.**C/L.**
Dar. 5/5—14/6/50.**C/L.**
Dar. 22/6/50. *Weigh.*
Dar. 24/6—1/7/50.**N/C.**
Dar. 20/12/50—27/1/51.**H/I.**
Dar. 28/3—3/4/51.**C/L.**
Dar. 21—26/11/51.**C/L.**
Dar. 4—28/6/52.**G.**
Dar. 30/6—17/7/52.**N/C.**
Dar. 5/8—1/9/52.**N/C.**
Gor. 18/9—30/10/54.**G.**
Into store at Saltburn shed 10/11/57.

BOILERS:
3628.
3617 *(ex1760)* 14/10/35.
3624 *(ex1768)* 14/5/37.
3626 *(ex1756)* 1/12/39.
152 *(ex1784)* 6/9/44.
3619 *(ex9841)* 7/9/46.
3616 *(ex9841)* 23/12/48.
3616 reno.22363 27/1/51.
22353 *(ex69827)* 28/6/52.
22040 *(new)* 30/10/54.

SHEDS:
Blaydon.
Saltburn 25/5/28.
Darlington 10/4/39.
Saltburn 2/1/49.
Norwich 25/2/51.
Neasden 11/3/51.
Stratford 8/4/51.
Neasden 13/5/51.
Darlington 1/7/51.
Stockton 19/6/54.
West Hartlepool 15/9/57.
Saltburn 10/11/57.
Middlesbrough 2/2/58.
Thornaby 1/6/58.

RENUMBERED:
9842 7/7/46.
69842 23/12/48.

CONDEMNED: 29/10/58.
Cut up at Darlington.

Those repainted from April 1957 to the end of May 1958, of which there were seventeen: 69800, 69801, 69802, 69805, 69806, 69811, 69812, 69814, 69817, 69818, 69819, 69820, 69824, 69835, 69837, 69840 and 69841, got the second emblem.

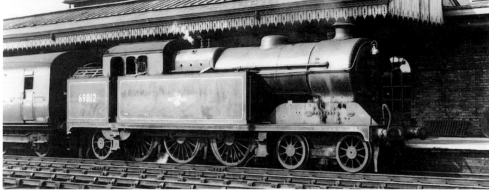

On the right hand side this emblem had the lion facing forward to the right and this was wrong in heraldry. None of the class had major repair after 30th May 1958 so were not corrected in this respect.

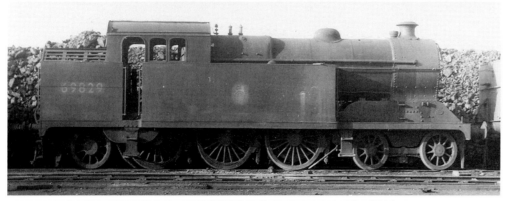

No.69829 at Neasden 9th December 1951 is not without lining - it is simply dirty. A short bit of lining can just be seen above the rear coupled wheels.

A5/1 No.69804, one of the original GC engines, dumped at North Road scrapyard, Darlington in May 1958. Withdrawn on the 7th April, its last shed had been Colwick and prior to that it had been shedded at various depots in Lincolnshire, but most of its working life was spent at Neasden shed operating the commuter trains from Marylebone until ousted by the new Thompson L1's in 1950.

No.5088 was one which stayed at Neasden until BR days and is here at High Wycombe, probably going to Princes Risborough on the line which the GCR shared with the Great Western from Northolt Junction to Aylesbury South Junction.

Here, sometime in 1925, Neasden shedded No.5451 is definitely off GCR lines which they owned or shared because it is on a goods train in the Metropolitan line station at Paddington.

No.5129 had two spells away from Neasden, in 1923 going to Annesley but after being in works 3rd November 1923 to 15th March 1924, to get cab windows and LNER painting, it was at Bradford from 25th March 1924 before going back to Neasden on 21st April. Its second spell began on 20th November 1924 with a transfer to Ardsley which took it into Leeds (Central) as seen here. On 7th May 1928 it moved to King's Cross shed and back to Neasden 18th November 1929.

(above) **In October 1917 two spare boilers were built and put on Nos.688 and 689. These had Ross 'pop' safety valves with their base enclosed in a small casing.**

(left) **None of the class were fitted with superheater until 1937 when Nos.689, 693 and 695 got new Diagram 63C boilers. This type of boiler was also put on No.687 in 1943 and on 9796 (692) in 1946. The last mentioned had previously carried a Diagram 63B superheated boiler.**

Three more, Nos.686, 688 and 692 were superheated, 692 in 1939 and the other two in 1944 but these had Diagram 63B boilers on which the dome was 1ft 9in. further back. Note that no inverted T strap was fitted (*see* page 47). A vacuum exhaust drain pipe was first fitted to No.694 in November 1935 (*see* page 44, centre), No.692 was fitted later that month.

CLASS A 6

686

Gateshead 84.

To traffic 12/1907.

REPAIRS:
Dar. ?/?—?/1/18.**G.**
Dar. 10/4—23/6/23.**G.**
Dar. 7—10/11/24.**L.**
Dar. 4/2—9/7/25.**G.**
Dar. 6/3—19/4/28.**G.**
Dar. 12—28/6/29.**N/C.**
Dar. 11/4—29/5/31.**G.**
Dar. 28/3—10/5/34.**G.**
Dar. 7/4—1/6/38.**G.**
Dar. 4/6—6/7/38.**N/C.**
After derailment.
Dar. 10/8—26/9/39.**L.**
Dar. 15/9—10/10/42.**N/C.**
Dar. 19—30/8/43.**L.**
Dar. 2/4—27/5/44.**G.**
Superheated boiler and
T strap fitted.
Dar. 30—31/8/44. *Weigh.*
Dar. 13/4/47. *Not repaired.*

BOILERS:
G648.
G655 *(ex689)* 1/18.
G803 *(exT1 1353)* 23/6/23.
D1984 *(new)* 19/4/28.
D1791 *(exT1 1659)* 10/5/34.
  3359 *(new)* 27/5/44 *(63B).*

SHEDS:
Neville Hill.
Whitby 23/6/23.
Hull Dairycoates 1/11/37.
Whitby 6/38.
Malton 10/2/40.
Neville Hill 11/7/42.
Starbeck 12/3/45.

RENUMBERED:
9790 24/11/46.

CONDEMNED: 7/6/47.
Cut up at Darlington.

687

Gateshead 85.

To traffic 12/1907.

REPAIRS:
Dar. ?/?—?/4/19.**G.**
Dar. 13/3—30/5/23.**G.**
Dar. 4/12/24—28/2/25.**G.**

Dar. 5/10/27—9/1/28.**G.**
Dar. 13/2—28/3/29.**N/C.**
Dar. 5—29/4/29.**N/C.**
Dar. 10/2—27/3/30.**G.**
Dar. 25/4—3/6/32.**G.**
Dar. 6—16/9/32.**N/C.**
Dar. 6/2—16/3/35.**G.**
Dar. 27/11/39—5/1/40.**G.**
Dar.27/3—27/5/43.**G.**
Superheated boiler, G.S.
buffers & T Strap fitted.
Dar. 23/8—18/9/43.**L.**
Dar. 1/11—6/12/44.**L.**
Dar. 10/5—6/9/47.**G.**
Dar. 17—24/9/47.**N/C.**
Dar. 21/9/49—18/4/50.**C/H.**
Dar. 15/8/51. *Not Repaired.*

BOILERS:
G649.
G665 *(ex693)* ?/4/19.
D1625 *(new)* 28/2/25.
D1787 *(exT1 1657)* 16/3/35.
D1625 *(exT1 1660)* 5/1/40.
  2823 *(ex695)* 27/5/43 *(63C).*
  3359 *(ex9790)* 18/4/50 *(63B).*

SHEDS:
Saltburn.
Middlesbrough 12/10/33.
West Auckland 4/12/39.
Darlington 28/2/42.
Northallerton 21/8/43.
Starbeck 5/3/45.
Hull Botanic Gardens 11/2/51.

RENUMBERED:
9791 5/1/47.
69791 18/4/50.

CONDEMNED: 16/8/51.
Cut up at Darlington.

688

Gateshead 86.

To traffic 12/1907.

REPAIRS:
Dar. ?/?—?/10/17.**G.**
Dar. 20/2—17/5/23.**G.**
Dar. 15/3—30/7/26.**G.**
Dar. 1/1—7/3/28.**L.**
Dar. 4/12/28—13/2/29.**G.**
Dar. 30/10—30/12/31.**G.**
Dar. 11/10—5/11/34.**G.**
Dar. 25/4—10/6/38.**G.**
Dar. 6/2—10/3/42.**G.**
Dar. 20—28/9/43.*Weigh.*

Dar. 23/11—10/12/43.**L.**
Dar. 14—19/1/44.*Weigh.*
Dar. 24/2—13/3/44.**L.**
Dar. 25—30/3/44.**N/C.**
Dar. 15/11—23/12/44.**G.**
Superheater boiler and
T strap fitted.
Dar. 2/5—7/6/47.**G.**
Downs sanding fitted.
Dar. 20—30/6/47.**N/C.**
Dar. 22/11/48. *Not repaired.*

BOILERS:
G654.
D490 *(new)* ?/10/17.
D1786 *(exT1 1656)* 5/11/34.
D2037 *(exT1 1659)* 10/3/42.
  3362 *(new)* 23/12/44 *(63B).*
  3046 *(ex9796)* 7/6/47 *(63B).*

SHEDS:
Whitby
Neville Hill 14/11/23.
Whitby 13/2/24
Hull Dairycoates 2/11/37.
Whitby ?/6/38.
Malton 10/2/40.
Scarborough 4/6/41.
Starbeck 12/3/45.
Whitby 5/10/47.
Starbeck 30/5/48.

RENUMBERED:
9792 15/9/46.

CONDEMNED: 20/12/48.
Cut up at Darlington.

689

Gateshead 87.

To traffic 1/1908.

REPAIRS:
Dar. ?/?—10/17.**G.**
Dar. 4/1—6/4/23.**G.**
Dar. 17/12/25—26/3/26.**G.**
Dar. 11/5—29/6/28.**G.**
Dar. 19/3—11/4/29.**N/C.**
Dar. 1/2—22/3/32.**L.**
Dar. 26/5—3/8/32.**G.**
Dar. 2/6—12/8/37.**G.**
Superheated boiler and
G.S Buffers fitted.
Dar. 19/12/38—18/1/39.**N/C.**
Dar. 21/4—30/5/41.**G.**
Dar. 29/9—13/10/43.**L.**
Dar. 8/6—1/8/44.**G.**
T strap fitted.

Dar. 20/9—16/10/44.**L.**
Dar. 20/10—9/11/44.**L.**
Dar. 29/5—12/7/47.**G.**
Downs sanding fitted.
Dar. 28/1—12/2/49.**C/L.**
After collision.
Ghd. 28/7—2/9/49.**L/I.**
Ghd. 20—23/11/49.**N/C.**
Dar. 17/4—10/5/50.**C/L.**

BOILERS:
G655.
D489 *(new)* ?/10/17.
  2824 *(new)* 12/8/37 *(63C).*
  3064 *(new)* 30/5/41 *(63B).*
  3043 *(ex692)* 1/8/44 *(63B).*

SHEDS:
Whitby.
Neville Hill 2/2/28.
Whitby ?/6/28.
Scarborough 22/8/34.
Starbeck 12/3/45.
Hull Botanic Gardens 11/2/51.

RENUMBERED:
9793 3/11/46.
69793 12/2/49.

CONDEMNED: 9/4/51.
Cut up at Darlington.

690

Gateshead 88.

To traffic 2/1908.

REPAIRS:
Dar. ?/?—?/7/20.**G**
Dar. ?/?—?/11/22.**G.**
Dar. 10/3—16/7/25.**G.**
Dar. 26/10—24/2/27.**G.**
Dar. 28/1—27/3/29.**G.**
Dar. 14/4—29/5/31.**G.**
Dar. 7/11—23/12/33.**G.**
Dar. 4—11/1/34.**N/C.**
Dar. 2—23/8/34.**L.**
Dar. 4/5—19/6/36.**L.**
Dar. 19/11/36—26/1/37.**H.**
Dar. 30/3—25/5/38.**G.**
Dar. 8/10—24/11/42.**G.**
Dar. 17/8/43.**N/C.**
Dar. 30/12/43—6/1/44. **N/C.**
Dar. 3/1—23/2/46.**G.**
Downs sanding & T strap fitted.
Dar. 2—5/3/46.**N/C..**
Dar. 11/11—21/12/48.**G.**
Dar. 15/8/51. *Not Repaired.*

(above) **Nos.687, 689, 693 and 695 with Diagram 63C boiler all changed later to Diagram 63B boiler. No.689 was changed in May 1941 and still no inverted T strap was fitted. No.692 (by then 69796) regained a Diagram 63B boiler in 1950.**

(left) **The other three, Nos.690, 691 and 694, were never superheated, and retained the Diagram 61 boiler, but did change to boilers built in 1922 or later which had Ross 'pop' safety valves from new. Note the drain pipe to vacuum ejector exhaust; No.694 was the first so fitted.**

The original smokebox door was of small diameter with flat flange and six A6's kept this type to withdrawal. Its original fastening was by wheel and handle.

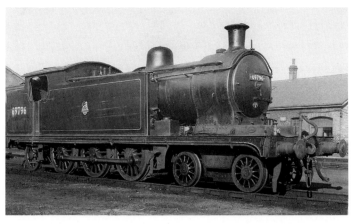

In June 1948 No.69798 was fitted with a larger diameter door which had a pressed joint ring for more effective sealing (*see* page 50). The only others so changed were Nos.691 (April 1945), 69794 (December 1948), and 69796 (June 1950).

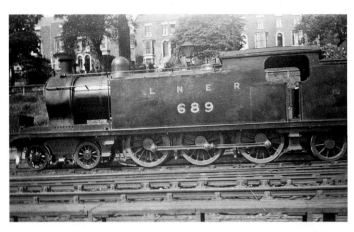

Until the second half of the 1930's, the sandboxes were below the running plate, behind the footsteps.

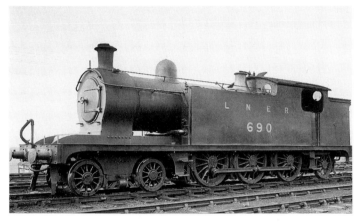

Until at least 1931 some still carried the copper equalising pipe at the base of the side tanks. All except No.686 were recorded as fitted with Raven fog signalling apparatus but the striker does not show in any photograph.

The removal of the tank equalising pipe enabled the box to be placed on the running plate where it was more easily serviced, and all were altered. No.691 being the first in July 1934 and No.686 being the last in June 1938.

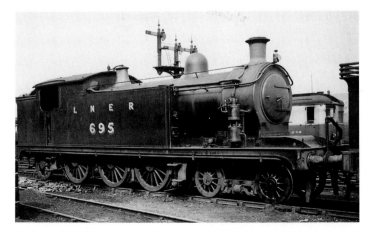

By August 1932 removal of these equalising pipes had begun and all duly lost them.

Between February 1946 and September 1947, five Nos.9792, 9793, 9794, 9796 and 9797 were fitted with Downs' sanding which involved a larger box. This contained a small diameter steam pipe in a coil with the object of keeping the sand dry and free-flowing. The other five retained the smaller box and normal sanding applied by steam.

690 cont./
BOILERS:
  G658.
  G666 *(ex694)* 7/20
D1345 *(new)* 11/22.
D1989 *(ex693)* 26/1/37.
D1787 *(exT1 1657)* 23/2/46.

SHEDS:
Saltburn.
Middlesbrough 12/10/33.
Hull Dairycoates 28/10/37.
Middlesbrough 6/38.
West Auckland 1/1/40.
Stockton 2/12/41.
Darlington 18/5/42.
Northallerton 25/1/43.
Darlington 21/8/43.
Neville Hill 8/1/44.
Starbeck 12/3/45.
Neville Hill 13/4/47.
Starbeck 5/10/47.

RENUMBERED:
  9794 12/10/46.
69794 21/12/48.

CONDEMNED: 15/8/51.
Cut up at Darlington.

691

Gateshead 89.

To traffic 3/1908.

REPAIRS:
Dar. ?/?—4/18.**G.**
Dar. ?/?—3/20 **G.**
Dar. 20/11/22—7/3/23.**G.**
Dar. 24/9/25—25/2/26.**G.**
Dar. 18/5—24/6/26.**L.**
Dar. 11/5—29/6/28.**G.**
Dar. 24/5—12/6/29.**N/C.**
Dar. 28/2—17/4/31.**G.**
Dar. 6/6—14/7/34.**G.**
Dar. 30/8—6/10/34.**N/C.**
Dar. 3/1—12/2/36.**L.**
Dar. 30/11/37—10/2/38.**G.**
Dar. 27/5—29/7/42.**G.**
Dar. 18/1—5/2/43.**L.**
Dar. 3—9/9/43 *Weigh.*
Dar. 2/3—14/4/45.**G.**
Pressed joint ring and
T strap fitted.
Dar. 11/12/47—16/1/48.**G.**
Dar. 10/7—13/8/48.**L.**
Dar. 4/7/50. *Not repaired.*

BOILERS:
  G661.

G654 *(ex688)* 4/18.
  G651 *(ex687)* 3/20.
D1354 *(new)* 7/3/23.
D1630 *(exT1 1359)* 14/7/34.
D2036 *(exT1 1359)* 10/2/38.
D2037 *(ex688)* 14/4/45.
  2372 *(exT1 9918)* 16/1/48.

SHEDS:
Whitby.
Neville Hill 5/2/28.
Whitby 23/6/28.
Malton 10/2/40.
Scarborough 6/10/41.
Starbeck 12/3/45.
Hull Botanic Gardens 13/4/47.

RENUMBERED:
  9795 14/7/46.
69795 13/8/48.

CONDEMNED: 17/7/50.
Cut up at Darlington.

692

Gateshead 90.

To traffic 3/1908.

REPAIRS:
Dar. ?/?—?/10/18.**G.**
Dar. ?/?—?/12/21.**G.**
Dar. 19/3—31/5/24.**G.**
Dar. 7/7—30/11/26.**G.**
Dar. 21—25/2/27 .**L**
Dar. 14/1—11/2/29.**N/C.**
Dar. 2/7—10/9/29.**G.**
Dar. 15/1—3/3/32.**G.**
Dar. 6/9—24/11/33.**H.**
Dar. 10/10—29/11/35.**G.**
Dar. 1/3—27/7/39.**G.**
Superheated boiler and
G.S.Buffers fitted.
Dar. 7—11/8/43. *Weigh.*
Dar. 12/5—17/6/44.**G.**
T strap fitted.
Dar. 19/9—26/10/46.**G.**
Downs sanding fitted.
Dar. 4—25/3/49.**L.**
Dar. 15/5—22/6/50.**G.**
Dar. 5—13/7/50.**N/C.**

BOILERS:
  G663
  G676 *(ex695)* 10/18.
D1343 *(new)* 12/21.
D1360 *(ex694)* 29/11/35.
  3043 *(new)* 27/7/39 *(63B).*
  3046 *(exA8 2143)* 17/6/44
(63B).

2824 *(ex695)* 26/10/46 *(63C).*
3064 *(ex9797)* 22/6/50 *(63B).*

SHEDS:
Whitby.
Malton 1/24.
Whitby 9/6/24.
Heaton 24/3/37.
Whitby 2/5/37.
Malton 21/5/40.
Neville Hill 5/3/42.
Malton 31/7/43.
Starbeck 12/3/45.
Hull Botanic Gardens 13/4/47.

RENUMBERED:
  9796 14/7/46.
69796 25/3/49.

CONDEMNED: 30/3/53
Into Dar.for cut up 31/3/53.

693

Gateshead 91.

To traffic 3/1908.

REPAIRS:
Dar. ?/?—?/8/18.**G.**
Dar. ?/?—?/2/21.**G.**
Dar. 2/12/22—21/3/23.**G.**
Dar. 28/4—31/8/25.**G.**
Dar. 14/5—6/7/28.**G.**
Dar. 23/4—10/5/29.**N/C.**
Dar. 7/9—22/10/31.**G.**
Dar. 11/8—25/9/33.**H.**
Dar. 17—27/10/33.**N/C.**
Dar. 28/9/36—7/1/37.**G.**
Superheated boiler and
G.S. Buffers fitted.
Dar. 11/6—1/7/37.**N/C.**
Dar. 1—11/11/38.**N/C.**
Dar. 9/4—7/5/40.**L.**
Dar. 20/1—1/3/41.**G.**
Dar. 18—24/8/43.**N/C.**
Dar. 26/6—26/8/44.**G.**
T strap fitted.
Dar. 1—22/9/45.**L**
Dar. 24/6—19/9/47.**G.**
Downs sanding fitted.
Dar. 22/6—9/8/49.**G.**
Dar. 24/8/51. *Not repaired.*

BOILERS:
  G665.
  G648 *(ex686)* 8/18.
  G804 *(exT1 1354)* 2/21.
D1989 *(new)* 6/7/28.
  2821 *(new)* 7/1/37 *(63C).*
  3064 *(ex689)* 26/8/44 *(63B).*

3046 *(ex9792)* 9/8/49 *(63B).*

SHEDS:
Scarborough
Whitby 27/6/34.
Middlesbrough 22/8/34.
Heaton 24/3/37.
Middlesbrough 2/5/37.
West Auckland 1/1/40.
Darlington 28/2/42.
West Auckland 24/10/44.
Starbeck 5/3/45.

RENUMBERED:
  9797 14/7/46.
69797 9/8/49.

CONDEMNED: 24/8/51.
Cut up at Darlington.

694

Gateshead 92.

To traffic 4/1908.

REPAIRS:
Dar. ?/?—4/19.**G.**
Dar. 17/3—30/5/23.**G.**
Dar. 20/3—6/5/25.**G.**
Dar. 7—27/5/25.**L.**
Dar. 2/6—19/11/26.**G.**
Dar. 15/1—12/3/29.**G.**
Dar. 5/2—30/3/32.**G.**
Dar. 31/10—17/11/32.**N/C.**
Dar. 24/9—1/11/35.**G.**
Dar. 28/2—6/4/40.**G.**
G.S buffers fitted.
Dar. 14/1—27/2/41.**H.**
Dar. 22/9—8/10/43.**L.**
Dar. 1/12/43—27/1/44.**G.**
Dar. 22/4—4/6/48.**G.**
Dar. 6—26/8/48.**L.**
T strap fitted.

BOILERS:
  G666.
  G663 *(ex692)* 4/19.
D1360 *(new)* 30/5/23.
D1793 *(exT1 1660)* 1/11/35.
D1343 *(exT1 1351)* 6/4/40.
D1624 *(exT1 1658)* 27/1/44.
D1982 *(exT1 9916)* 4/6/48.

SHEDS:
Starbeck.
Scarborough *by* 12/23.
Hull Botanic Gardens 17/5/35.
Scarborough 30/5/35.
Malton 5/8/40.
Neville Hill 31/7/43.

WORKS CODES:- Cw - Cowlairs. Dar- Darlington. Don - Doncaster. Ghd - Gateshead. Gor - Gorton. Inv - Inverurie. Str - Stratford. Tux - Tuxford.
REPAIR CODES:- **C/H** - Casual Heavy. **C/L** - Casual Light. **G** - General. **H**- Heavy. **H/I** - Heavy Intermediate. **L** - Light. **L/I** - Light Intermediate. **N/C** - Non-Classified.

46

694 cont./
West Auckland 8/1/44.
Darlington 8/10/45.
Hull Botanic Gardens 5/7/47.

RENUMBERED:
9798 7/7/46.
69798 4/6/48.

CONDEMNED: 6/2/51.
Cut up at Darlington.

695

Gateshead 93.

To traffic 4/1908.

REPAIRS:
Dar. ?/?—?/7/18.**G.**
Dar. 18/9—30/11/23.**G.**
Dar. 29/4—21/8/25.**G.**
Dar. 11/10/27—11/1/28.**G.**
Dar. 29/7—12/8/29.**N/C.**
Dar. 20/5—22/8/30.**G.**
Dar. 21/6—2/8/32.**G.**
Dar. 1/10/36—12/1/37.**G.**
Superheated boiler fitted.
Dar. 8/6—1/7/37.**N/C.**
Dar. 30/11—14/12/38.**N/C.**
Dar. 29/10—5/12/41.**G.**
Dar. 25/8—14/9/43.**L.**
Dar. 29/8—7/10/44.**G.**
T strap fitted.
Ghd. 7/12/46—18/1/47.**L.**
Dar. 30/10/47—9/1/48.**G.**
Dar. 22/12/49. *Not repaired.*

BOILERS:
G676.
G661 *(ex691)* 7/18.
D1338 *(new)* 30/11/23.
  2823 *(new)*12/1/37 *(63C).*
  2824 *(ex689)* 5/12/41 *(63C).*
  2821 *(ex693)* 7/10/44 *(63C).*
  3359 *(ex9790)* 9/1/48 *(63B).*

SHEDS:
Malton.
Whitby 1/12/23.
Starbeck 12/3/45.
Whitby 15/8/48.
Starbeck 31/10/48.

RENUMBERED:
9799 14/7/46.

CONDEMNED: 6/2/50.
Cut up at Darlington.

Replacement boilers were to Diagram 63B and had their safety valves mounted directly on the firebox without any casing around their base. Note that the chimney is one of those without a windjabber.

From May 1943 when Diagram 63C and 63B boilers were put on they were surmounted by an inverted T-strap connecting the tanks. Note lifting holes were now provided and the chimney was one with a windjabber. Tank fixing alterations on other classes were made between December 1933 and August 1937, but on A6 class the T-straps were only put on much later.

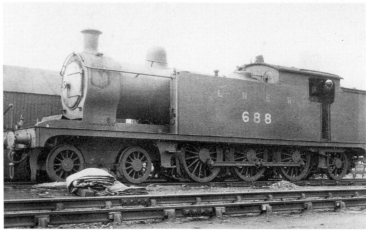

In line with North Eastern practice, the smokebox door fastening was a wheel and handle, which were still to be seen to April 1938.

The change to twin handles had even begun before Grouping as shown by this view of No.691.

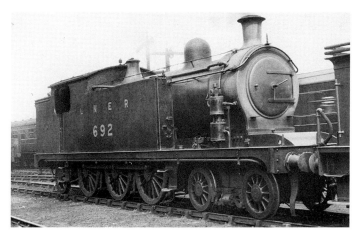

The buffers originally had oval heads to a solid spindle in a taper shank which had a circular flange, they were mounted on a wood sandwich bufferbeam which all kept.

At Grouping all ten were Westinghouse air braked on the engine and for the train brakes. Note N.E.R. style figures still used on the front bufferbeam at 6th April 1923 repair.

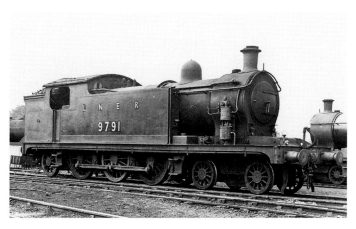

Five of the class Nos.9791, 9793, 9796, 9797 and 9798 were changed to Group Standard buffers and drawhook, both of which were fixed by square flang. No.693 (9797) was the first to get them in January 1937.

Between February and September 1929 all had vacuum ejector added for train braking. Brakes on the bogie wheels were then still fitted.

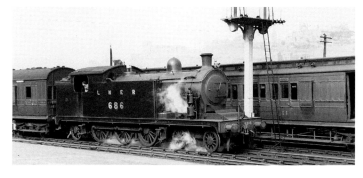

During the middle 1930's the bogie brakes were discarded and taken off.

Of the others, at least five Nos.9790, 9792, 9794, 9795 and 9799, retained the N.E. type although No.9799 did end up with a change to a circular head on one side.

Beginning with No.686 in May 1944, the Westinghouse brake equipment was taken off and the engine was then steam braked, but still with vacuum for train brakes. Only No.9791 did not have the change and retained it to withdrawal in August 1951.

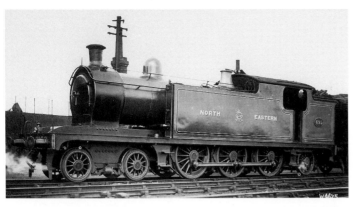

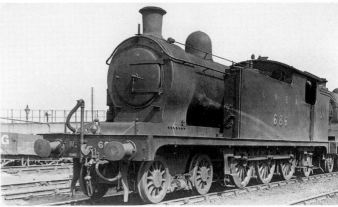

Because the North Eastern regarded the class as passenger engines they had the lined green livery with 24in. wide brass number plate. This photograph shows a Darlington painting as they lined the buffer beam ends whereas Gateshead left them plain. No.691 was the last in this painting - it went to Darlington with it on 24th September 1925 preceded only on 28th April 1925 by No.693. These two actually kept the N.E.R. green livery at their first LNER shopping, No.691 was ex works 7th March 1923 and No.693 on 21st March 1923.

Although they continued to have red lining through the 1930's it became increasingly difficult to discern.

From July 1942 to January 1946 only NE in 12in. letters was used to show ownership and all were so treated. No.9790 still carried NE when withdrawn in June 1947, the first of the class to be condemned.

The LNER never accorded them green livery and within its first six months put five into black with single red lining and those all got L.& N.E.R. on the tanks (see page 45, top right). The large brass number plate on the bunker was replaced by the 8⅝in. cast iron type. Although the area suffix was in use from September 1923 to February 1924, only one A6 No.695ᴅ acquired it and that on 30th November 1923.

No.690 regained 7½in. LNER when ex works 23rd February 1946 after a general repair. It was changed to 9794 on 12th October of that year.

The other four went straight to the established standard livery - LNER on black, red lined painting. No.692 got it 31st May 1924, 690 on 16th Julk 1925, 691 on 25th February 1926 and 693 on 31st August 1925.

In June 1947 No.9792 was the first of the class to get yellow painted and unshaded characters in Gill sans style although with the LNER modified 9. The others to get this style were 9793 (7/47), 9791 (9/47), 9795 and 9799 both January 1948.

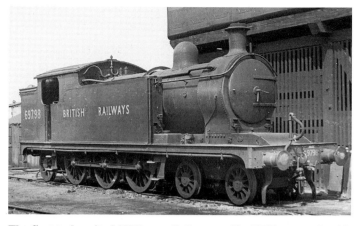

When No.9796 was ex Darlington on 25th March 1949 from a light repair it got its BR number but the shaded LNER was retained. Note that the correct 6 and 9 were used but no smokebox number plate was put on, although it did have a shed allocation plate.

The first to lose its LNER appellation was No.69798, ex works 4th June 1948 in unlined black and with its number moved from tank to bunker. It got 12in. numerals, the only one to do so, but both 6 and 9 were not in true Gill sans style, either on the bunker or buffer beam.

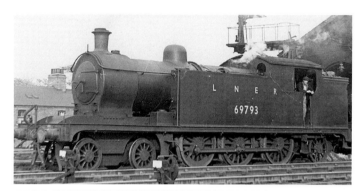

(left) No.9793 was officially recorded as to BR 69793 on 12th February 1949, and this 30th May 1949 photograph shows it had been patched to its new number at a light repair at Darlington.

(below) Only two got this style of 10in. number and letters and they were still on black without lining. No.69797 was ex Darlington 9th August 1949 with correct 6 and 9 both on plate and bunker. No.69794 was out on 21st December 1948 with correct 6 and 9 on the plate.

(below) At York shed yard in April 1923, No.689 is on its way back to Whitby shed from a general repair at Darlington works. It was the first A6 to be changed from NER green with black and white lining to black and single red lining with L.&N.E.R.

Here in April 1937 No.693 is passing Argyle Street signal box on its way from Newbiggin to Newcastle. From 24th March to 2nd May 1937 No.693, and 692, worked from Heaton shed to cover the absence at works of the twin-car Sentinel PHENOMENA, often used on that service.

Most A6 pictures were taken at Whitby but here Whitby shedded 689 is seen at Scarborough station, and before March 1929 because it has only Westinghouse brake.

Although much of their work from March 1945 was done from Starbeck, no less than five were at Hull Botanic Gardens shed when withdrawn. Starbeck sent 9795 and 9796 there on 13th April 1947 and then 9798 on 5th July 1947. As 69795 that one was withdrawn 17th July 1950 and then 69798 on 6th February 1951. Nos.69791 and 69793 were sent to Hull 11th February 1951 as replacements. Here 69791 is about to leave Paragon for Hornsea. By 24th August 1951 only No.69796 was not withdrawn and it continued in service until 30th March 1953 being used on transfer trips between the yards at Dairycoates and Paragon station. Its demise meant the end of Class A6.

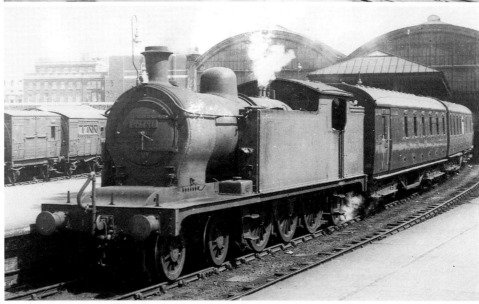

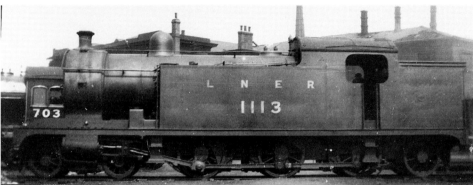

(above) Five of the other seven had Schmidt superheater put in between November 1918 and November 1922. Their smokebox was extended and a handwheel controlled steam circulating valve on the side of the smokebox provided protection for the elements. Nos.1113, 1185, 1190, 1193 and 1195 got these five boilers. Two more were similarly treated by the LNER and put on 1182 (March 1923) and 1114 (September 1924).

(second from top) In 1916 Darlington built two spare boilers which served 1175 (May 1919 to October 1936), also 1126 (July 1917 to August 1931), 1113 (February 1933 to August 1940), and 1190 (January 1941 to July 1943).

(left) In July 1927 Darlington built three more saturated boilers which were put on Nos.1170, 1176 and 1192 and although interchanging did take place, this was not until May 1941, and then only between these three engines.

Between December 1927 and September 1930, Darlington built three batches of boilers, each of five, with Schmidt superheater. They too had a casing round the base of the safety valves but their 'pops' were taller than on the 1916 and July 1927 boilers.

1113

Darlington.

To traffic 10/1910.

REPAIRS:
Dar. ?/?—?/4/20.**G.**
Dar. ?/?—?/5/22.**G.**
Superheated boiler fitted.
Dar. 11/4—28/6/24.**G.**
Dar. 31/8—19/11/25.**G.**
Dar. 1/11/27—31/1/28.**G.**
Dar. 6/10—26/11/30.**G.**
Dar. 22/12/32—1/2/33.**G.**
In store at Darlington paint shop 1/2/33—21/6/35.
Dar. 29/8—3/10/40.**G.**
Dar. 4/5—7/7/43.**G.**
Dar. 1—29/6/46.**G.**
Dar. 2/6—2/7/48.**G.**
Dar. 7/6—8/7/50.**G.**
Rebuil to Part 1.
Dar. 26/7—17/8/50.**N/C.**
Dar. 17/4—9/5/52.**G.**

BOILERS:
G910.
G939 *(ex1182)* 4/20.
G927 *(ex1185)* 5/22.
D2048 *(new)* 31/1/28.
D611 *(ex spare)* 1/2/33.
D2049 *(ex1190)* 3/10/40.
2200 *(ex9783)* 29/6/46.
2492 *(ex9788)* 2/7/48.
3364 *(exT1 69914)* 8/7/50 *(63B)*.
24732 *(ex69771)* 9/5/52 *(63B)*.

SHEDS:
York.
Hull Dairycoates 22/6/37.
Starbeck 22/10/44.
Hull Dairycoates 12/3/45.

RENUMBERED:
9770 27/1/46.
69770 2/7/48.

CONDEMNED: 13/10/54.
Cut up at Darlington.

1114

Darlington.

To traffic 11/1910.

REPAIRS:
Dar. ?/?—?/10/17.**G.**
Dar.3/6—16/9/24.**G.**
Superheated boiler fitted.
Dar. 3/5—15/9/26.**G.**
Dar. 2/10—21/11/28.**G.**
Dar. 24/6—17/8/31.**G.**
Dar. 10/4—16/5/34.**G.**
Dar. 9/2—12/3/37.**G.**
Dar. 23/4—21/5/40.**G.**
Dar. 31/7—28/8/40.**N/C.**
Dar. 28/10—21/11/42.**L.**
Dar. 14/11—9/12/44.**G.**
Dar. 3—29/6/46.**L.**
Dar. 6/5—10/6/48.**G.**
Rebuilt to Part 1.
Dar. 11/10—16/11/50.**C/L.**
Dar. 1/1—1/2/52.**G.**
Dar. 12—20/2/52.**N/C.**
Dar. 25/2—4/3/52.**N/C.**

BOILERS:
G912.
G943 *(ex1190)* 10/17.
G920 *(ex1170)* 16/9/24.
D2049 *(new)* 21/11/28.
2378 *(ex1129)* 16/5/34.
2495 *(ex1182)* 12/3/37.
2055 *(ex1129)* 9/12/44.
3850 *(new)* 10/6/48 *(63B)*.
24731 *(exT1 69914)* 1/2/52 *(63B)*.

SHEDS:
Thirsk.
Starbeck 10/3/24.
Hull Dairycoates 14/1/38.
Cudworth 6/7/40.
Hull Dairycoates 12/3/50.
Hull Springhead 3/10/54.

RENUMBERED:
9771 10/3/46.
69771 10/6/48.

CONDEMNED: 9/11/54.
Cut up at Darlington.

1126

Darlington.

To traffic 11/1910.

REPAIRS:
Dar. ?/?—?/7/17.**G.**
Superheated boiler fitted.
Dar. 10/11/23—20/2/24.**G.**
Dar. 22/9/27—18/1/28.**G.**
Dar. 31/8—10/10/31.**G.**
Dar. 22/8—29/9/34.**G.**
Dar. 6/12—12/1/39.**G.**
Dar. 10/2—13/3/41.**G.**
Dar. 25/3—1/5/43.**G.**
Dar. 14/2—10/3/45.**G.**
Dar. 30/6—16/8/47.**G.**
Dar. 1—19/2/49.**C/L.**
Dar. 23/2—2/3/49.**N/C.**
Dar. 25/10—18/11/49.**G.**
Dar. 13/9—18/10/51.**H/I.**
Dar. 2/3—21/4/52.**C/H.**
Dar. 3/2—6/3/54. **G.**
Dar. 8—10/3/54. **N/C.**
Dar. 16—25/3/54. **N/C.**

BOILERS:
G915.
D611 *(new)* 7/17.
2381 *(new)* 16/10/31.
2195 *(ex1181)* 29/9/34.
D2055 *(ex1129)* 12/1/39.
2204 *(ex1182)* 13/3/41.
2382 *(ex1191)* 1/5/43.
D2054 *(ex9789)* 16/8/47.
2378 *(ex9773)* 18/11/49.
2378 reno.24362 18/10/51.

SHEDS:
Hull Dairycoates.
York 1/6/40.
Hull Dairycoates 28/7/46.
Hull Springhead 27/11/55.

RENUMBERED:
9772 24/2/46.
69772 19/2/49.

CONDEMNED: 16/12/57.
Cut up at Darlington.

1129

Darlington.

To traffic 12/1910.

REPAIRS:
Dar. ?/?—11/2/20.**G.**
Dar. 16/7—21/9/23.**G.**
Dar. 16/5—17/7/28.**G.**
Dar. 25/3—3/10/30.**G.**
Superheated boiler fitted.
Dar. 9/8—8/9/33.**G.**
Dar. 29/2—21/4/36.**G.**
Dar. 17/10—21/11/38.**G.**
Dar. 14/7—1/9/41.**G.**
Dar. 11—29/4/44.**L.**
Dar. 29/9—2/11/44.**G.**
Dar. 23/11—28/12/46.**G.**
Dar. 11—17/1/47.**N/C.**
Dar. 16/2—12/3/49.**G.**
Dar. 4/12/50—5/1/51.**C/L.**
Dar. 15/6—16/7/51.**G.**
Rebuilt to Part 1.

BOILERS:
G917.
G946 *(ex1136)* 21/9/23.
G938 *(ex1181)* 17/7/28.
2378 *(new)* 3/10/30.
D2054 *(ex1183)* 8/9/33.
D2055 *(ex1193)* 21/4/36.
2381 *(ex1190)* 21/11/38.
D2055 *(ex1126)* 1/9/41.
2197 *(ex1183)* 2/11/44.
2378 *(ex9774)* 28/12/46.
2197 *(ex9776)* 12/3/49.
24709 *(ex69788)* 16/7/51 *(63B)*.

SHEDS:
Shildon
York 19/3/25.
Shildon 23/5/25.
Ardsley 30/10/25.
Shildon 1/9/26.
Doncaster 21/10/26.
Immingham 3/5/39.
Doncaster 6/6/39.
Northwich 17/7/39.
Doncaster 11/8/39.
Starbeck 23/6/43.
Hull Dairycoates 12/3/45.

RENUMBERED:
9773 17/2/46.
69773 12/3/49.

CONDEMNED: 23/3/55.
Cut up at Darlington.

1136

Darlington.

To traffic 12/1910.

REPAIRS:
Dar. ?/?—?/10/19.**G.**
Dar. ?/?—?/12/21.**G.**
Dar. 28/3— 11/6/23.**G.**

WORKS CODES:- Cw - Cowlairs. Dar- Darlington. Don - Doncaster. Ghd - Gateshead. Gor - Gorton. Inv - Inverurie. Str - Stratford. Tux - Tuxford.
REPAIR CODES:- **C/H** - Casual Heavy. **C/L** - Casual Light. **G** - General. **H**- Heavy. **H/I** - Heavy Intermediate. **L** - Light. **L/I** - Light Intermediate. **N/C** - Non-Classified.

53

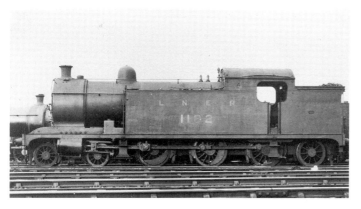

The last two boilers to Diagram 55 were built in March/April 1933 and were put on No.1182 in January 1934 and on No.1136 in September 1935. They had Robinson superheater, Gresley anti-vacuum valve, also footstep injector. No casing was provided around the base of the safety valves.

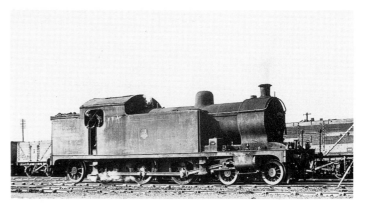

From March 1951 to June 1953 No.69786 was fitted with one of the only five boilers to Diagram 63C, on which the dome was in the forward position.

From September 1943 on No.1190, Diagram 63B boilers were used for replacement. They were 4ft 9in. diameter, had the dome 1ft 9in. further back, and had a single whistle mounted over an isolating valve. Eventually fifteen engines carried Diagram 63B boilers and were reclassified A7/1.

Two remained unsuperheated through to withdrawal, Nos.1176 (69778) and 1192 (69787). Of these, 69778 was the only one of the class to keep the Diagram 55 boiler, which was 5ft 6in. diameter (*see* picture left, bottom).

In August 1951, one of the three engines which were never superheated required a replacement boiler and a new 63B boiler without superheater was put on. A shorter chimney was also then put on No.69787.

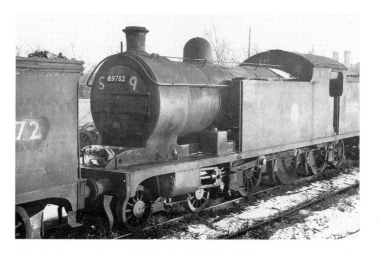

After being superheated in March 1923, No.69782 carried a succession of 5ft 6in. Diagram 55 boilers with superheater until it went to Darlington on 21st December 1953. When it came out on 22nd January 1954 it was without a superheater but still with a Diagram 55 boiler, which it retained to withdrawal on 16th December 1957, as seen here in the scrap yard at Darlington in January 1958.

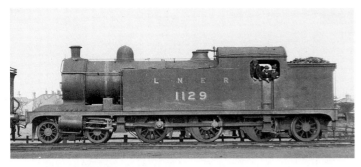

In accordance with North Eastern practice, Raven fog signalling apparatus was fitted, and the striker for it can be seen just ahead of the rear coupled wheels. As No.1129 was shedded at Doncaster from 21st October 1926, the apparatus was redundant from then on.

In January 1935, No.1179 was fitted with vacuum ejector for operating passenger train brakes and was used between Newcastle and Blackhill. Screw couplings replaced the three-link type and connections for train heating were fitted at both ends, it did not however get Group Standard buffers. This extra equipment was taken off in May 1943 when 1179 reverted to steam brake.

The original smokebox doors had a flat flange, widely spaced straps, with wheel and handle fastening. The wheel survived to July 1935 on No.1195 but all changed to two handles.

Of the superheated engines all except No.69784 got a door with a pressed joint ring. No.69784 was the only superheated engine to get a shorter chimney.

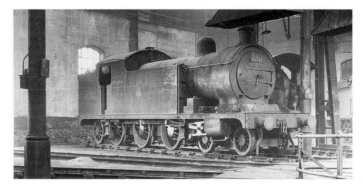

In BR days the three without superheater were Nos.69778, 69782 and 69787 of which No.69778 (1176) was never superheated, 69782 (1182) lost its superheater from January 1954, and 69787 (1192) was never superheated but acquired a Diagram 63B boiler in August 1951 (*see* page 54, bottom left). The other two retained Diagram 55 boiler, as did No.69772, 69777 and 69789 but which were superheated. Those with 5ft 6in. boiler had flat door with the straps much closer together so the number plate was fitted above the top strap.

(*above*) No.69788 appears to be the only A7 to carry a chimney with windjabber and this was only fitted after Nationalisation.

(*left*) Beginning with No.1181 on 7th February 1944, a larger, more dished door with pressed joint ring was introduced.

1136 cont./
Dar. 24/4—21/6/28.**G.**
Dar. 18/4—24/5/32.**G.**
Superheated boiler fitted.
Dar. 12/8—26/9/35.**G.**
Dar. 10/8—16/9/39.**G.**
Dar. 9—28/5/41.**L.**
Dar. 20/5—30/6/42.**H/I.**
Dar. 6—31/7/42.**N/C.**
Dar. 5/4—4/5/44.**G.**
Dar. 1/10—9/11/46.**G.**
Dar. 14/4—19/5/50.**G.**
Rebuilt to Part 1.
Dar. 21/5—2/7/53.**H/I.**
Dar. 18/8/54. *Not repaired.*

BOILERS:
G920.
G942 *(ex1185)* 10/19.
G946 *(ex1192)* 12/21.
G933 *(ex1182)* 11/6/23.
G943 *(ex1114)* 21/6/28.
2382 *(new)* 24/5/32.
2492 *(new)* 26/9/35.
2195 *(ex1126)* 16/9/39.
2378 *(ex1181)* 4/5/44.
2050 *(ex9777)* 9/11/46.
3988 *(new)* 19/5/50 *(63B).*
3988 reno.24747 2/7/53.

SHEDS:
Selby.
Hull Springhead 16/5/25.
Malton 14/6/27.
Neville Hill 3/10/33.
Starbeck 16/10/39.
Hull Springhead 12/3/45.

RENUMBERED:
9774 23/3/46.
69774 19/5/50.

CONDEMNED: 23/8/54.
Cut up at Darlington.

1170

Darlington.

To traffic 12/1910.

REPAIRS:
Dar. ?/?—?/11/19.**G.**
Dar. 1/2—22/4/24.**G.**
Dar. 16/4—16/7/25.**G.**
Dar. 4/8—26/10/27.**G.**
Dar. 22/10—18/12/28.**G.**
Dar. 17/6—19/8/29.**G.**
Dar. 4/11—22/12/32.**G.**
Dar. 27/4—11/6/38.**G.**
Dar. 17/10—20/11/40.**G.**
Dar. 24/3—29/5/43.**G.**
Dar. 6/10—17/11/45.**G.**
*Superheated boiler fitted
and rebuilt to Part 1.*

Dar. 23/1—27/2/48.**G.**
Dar. 12/10—5/11/49.**C/L.**
Dar. 16/8—23/9/50.**G.**

BOILERS:
G923.
G920 *(ex1136)* 11/19.
G917 *(ex1129)* 22/4/24.
D1977 *(new)* 26/10/27.
3365 *(new)* 17/11/45 *(63B).*
3854 *(new)* 27/2/48 *(63B).*
3854 reno.24683 23/9/50.

SHEDS:
Starbeck.
Hull Dairycoates 12/9/32.

RENUMBERED:
9775 31/3/46.
ᴇ**9775** 27/2/48.
69775 5/11/49.

CONDEMNED: 4/4/52.
Cut up at Darlington.

1174

Darlington.

To traffic 1/1911.

REPAIRS:
Dar. 10/1—5/2/24.**L.**
Dar. 5/6—6/9/24.**G.**
Dar. 29/10/29—3/1/30.**G.**
Superheated boiler fitted.
Dar. 29/6—12/8/32.**G.**
Dar. 12—29/8/32.**N/C.**
Dar. 8/5—12/6/34.**G.**
Dar. 1/3—6/4/37.**G.**
Dar. 29/8—7/10/39.**G.**
Dar. 20/5—27/6/42.**H/I.**
Dar. 6—28/7/42.**N/C.**
Dar. 19/4—13/5/44.**G.**
Dar. 23/8—9/9/44.**L.**
Dar. 18/2—29/3/47.**G.**
Dar. 15/10—5/11/48.**G.**
Dar. 8/11/48.**N/C.**
Dar. 11/12/51—18/1/52.**G.**
Rebuilt to Part 1.

BOILERS:
G925.
2200 *(new)* 3/1/30.
D2049 *(ex1114)* 12/6/34.
2378 *(ex1114)* 6/4/37.
2492 *(ex1136)* 7/10/39.
2195 *(ex1136)* 13/5/44.
2197 *(ex9773)* 29/3/47.
2381 *(ex9781)* 5/11/48.
24727 *(exA6 69797)* 18/1/52
(63B).

SHEDS:
Shildon.
Bullcroft Jct. 23/1/25.
York 3/3/30.
Starbeck 21/10/39.
Hull Springhead 12/3/45.
Hull Dairycoates 21/3/54.
Hull Springhead 2/5/54.

RENUMBERED:
9776 10/3/46.
69776 5/11/48.

CONDEMNED: 14/6/54.
Cut up at Darlington.

1175

Darlington.

To traffic 1/1911.

REPAIRS:
Dar. ?/?—?/5/19.**G.**
Superheated boiler fitted.
Dar. 23/3—16/6/23.**G.**
Dar. 3/11/26—25/2/27.**G.**
Dar. 9/7—10/9/29.**G.**
Dar. 1/6—7/7/32.**G.**
Dar. 13/10—22/12/36.**G.**
Dar. 29/5—22/6/40.**G.**
Dar. 14/8—26/9/42.**G.**
Dar. 9/8—2/9/44.**G.**
Dar. 7/9—18/10/46.**G.**
Dar. 5—8/11/46.**N/C.**
Dar. 20—27/11/46.**N/C.**
Dar. 10/9—1/10/48.**G.**
Dar. 18/9—14/10/50.**G.**
Dar. 16—17/10/50.**N/C.**
Dar. 1/5/52. *Not repaired.*

BOILERS:
G927.
D623 *(new)* 5/19.
2380 *(ex1185)* 22/12/36.
D2050 *(ex1183)* 22/6/40.
2200 *(ex1181)* 26/9/42.
D2050 *(ex1180)* 2/9/44.
D2049 *(ex9770)* 18/10/46.
2380 *(ex9782)* 1/10/48.
24361 *(ex69782)* 14/10/50.

SHED:
Hull Dairycoates.

RENUMBERED:
9777 23/3/46.
69777 1/10/48.

CONDEMNED: 12/5/52.
Cut up at Darlington.

1176

Darlington.

To traffic 2/1911.

REPAIRS:
Dar. ?/?—?/3/21.**G.**
Dar. 26/4—14/7/23.**G.**
Dar. 21/1—8/5/25.**G.**
Dar. 26/1—16/2/26.**L.**
Dar. 23/5—14/9/27.**G.**
Dar. 20/9—15/11/29.**G.**
Dar. 2/11—18/12/31.**G.**
Dar. 16/7—10/9/34.**L.**
Dar. 11—18/9/34.**N/C.**
Dar. 18/6—15/8/35.**G.**
Dar. 20/7—9/9/38.**G.**
Dar. 10/4—24/6/41.**G.**
Dar. 2—25/9/41.**L.**
Dar. 10/2—10/3/44.**G.**
Dar. 5/10—17/11/45.**G.**
Dar. 5/12/47—16/1/48.**G.**
Dar. 10/11/49—6/1/50.**G.**
Dar. 16/1—16/2/52.**G.**
Dar. 18—21/2/52.**N/C.**

BOILERS:
G930.
G910 *(ex1113)* 3/21.
D1976 *(new)* 14/9/27.
D1978 *(ex1192)* 24/6/41.
D1976 *(ex1192)* 16/1/48.
D1977 *(ex9787)* 6/1/50.
24363 *(ex69787)* 16/2/52.

SHEDS:
Thirsk.
Neville Hill 12/12/27.
Starbeck 25/9/29.
West Hartlepool 27/9/38.
Newport 10/4/39.
York 24/6/39.
Hull Dairycoates 28/7/46.
Hull Springhead 3/10/54.

RENUMBERED:
9778 10/2/46.
69778 6/1/50.

CONDEMNED: 3/5/55.
Cut up at Darlington.

1179

Darlington.

To traffic 2/1911.

REPAIRS:
Dar. ?/?—?/5/19.**G.**
Dar. 11/7—27/8/23.**G.**
Dar. 22/10/25—11/2/26.**G.**
Dar. 27/11/28—27/2/29.**G.**
Superheated boiler fitted.

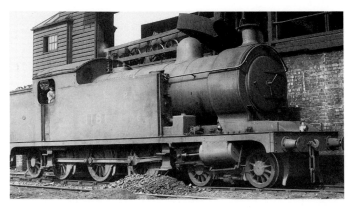

All had sandwich buffer beam at both ends and buffers with circular head and flange spindle was solid in a tapered shank. Normal whistle gear was a pair of bell shaped on a mounting on front of the cab. Note absence of lifting holes on the front end of the frames; they were put in from 1932.

When No.1170 got a Diagram 63B boiler on 17th November 1945, it was the first A7 to be fitted with Downs' sanding apparatus. This involved fitting larger sandboxes to house the steam heating coil which kept the sand dry. Another six are known to have had this sanding equipment fitted: 9785 (3/47), 69784 (5/48), 69779 (12/49), 69780 (1/50), 69774 (5/50) and 69770 (7/50). Note the paint date 11/45 applied just over the 7 of the engine number.

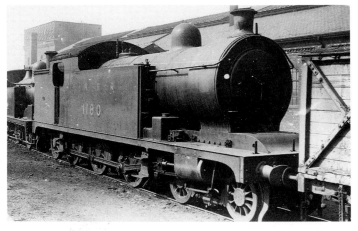

The only buffer change on the majority was to elliptical heads to help prevent locking on tight curves. This began in North Eastern days. On some, the larger bell shaped whistle was changed to an organ pipe.

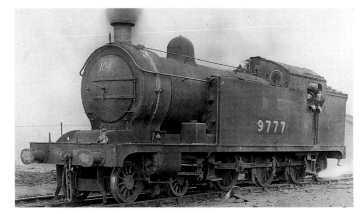

Prior to 1923 the leading sandboxes were shallow and had a level top (*see* page 58 top, right). From then on they were given increased capacity as shown and some had this type to withdrawal. With Diagram 55 boiler, blower control was external, its control rod being very prominent. Note the single whistle but still on the double mounting.

Four are known to have been fitted with Group Standard buffers and hook:- 1192 (17/6/39), 1183 (15/6/40), 1182 (3/1/41) and 9772 (16/8/47). New whistle gear was fitted from 28th July 1940 beginning with 1185, the same mounting being used but only a single bell shape was carried. On 63B boilers the single whistle was mounted over an isolating valve.

Diagram 63B boilers had internal control for the blower so the prominent rod then disappeared but Diagram 55 boilers retained it through to withdrawal in December 1957 (*see* page 54 bottom, right). Note elliptical number plate moved from bunker to sandbox on this and 69784 (*see* page 55 top, right). The normal place was on the frame, below the smokebox (*see* page 55 bottom, right).

Brakes on the bogie wheels were not original equipment but were fitted from July 1913. Until October 1935 the brake blocks were applied to the rear of the leading coupled wheels. Beginning with 1180 on 17th October 1935, they were moved to a position in front of these wheels and, to suit them, the sandpipes had to be lengthened (*see* page 52 bottom).

From 1917 - No.1126 was altered in July - there was only a small number plate on the bunker, but large shaded transfer numbers, between the company's initials were put on the tank sides.

When No.9780 was ex works 13th March 1946, the bogie brakes had been removed and all then lost them. No.9787 which was ex works 8th February 1946 still had them.

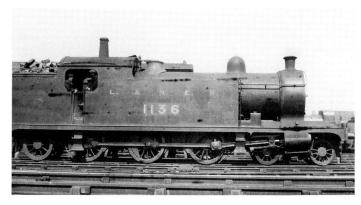

The first four painted after Grouping got L. & N. E. R. in almost the same style as before. They were 1180 (7th March), 1182 (28th March), 1136 (11th June) and 1175 (16th June), all 1923. Note alteration to front sandbox capacity.

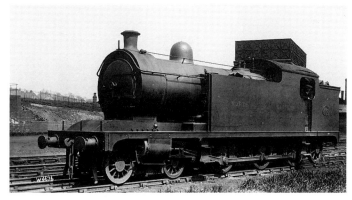

Although always painted black, until 1917 onwards they had the 24in. wide brass number plate on the bunker with company name and large crest applied by transfers on the tank sides.

In July 1923 the initials became LNER and 1176 (14th July), 1192 (15th August) and 1179 (27th August) were so treated before the area suffix was introduced and used for six months. In A7 class it was put on 1129D (21st September 1923), 1193D (8th December 1923) and 1126D (20th February 1924).

1179 cont./
Dar. 29/9/31—4/11/31.**G**.
Dar.19/11/34—19/1/35.**G**.
Vacuum brake fitted.
Dar. 25/1—24/2/40.**G**.
Dar. 19/5—24/6/43.**G**.
Dar. 12/9—13/10/45.**G**.
Dar. 5/11—7/12/45.**L**.
Dar. 12/2—11/3/48.**G**.
Dar. 4/11—8/12/49.**G**.
Rebuilt to Part 1.
Ghd. 28/5—6/7/51.**C/L**.
Dar. 26/6—9/9/52.**G**.

BOILERS:
G933.
G915 *(ex1190)* 5/19.
 2197 *(new)* 27/2/29.
 2379 *(ex1193)* 24/2/40.
 2204 *(ex1126)* 24/6/43.
 2198 *(ex1185)* 13/10/45.
 2379 *(ex9780)* 11/3/48.
 3971 *(new)* 8/12/49 *(63B)*.
 3971 reno. 24715 6/7/51.

SHEDS:
Stockton.
Thirsk 18/2/27.
Starbeck 12/12/27.
Hull Dairycoates 12/9/32.
Gateshead 6/6/35.
Hull Dairycoates 23/10/37.

RENUMBERED:
 9779 17/2/46.
 E9779 11/3/48.
 69779 8/12/49.

CONDEMNED: 30/11/54.
Cut up at Darlington.

1180

Darlington.

To traffic 2/1911.

REPAIRS:
Dar. 11/10/22—7/3/23.**G**.
Dar. 28/12/27—13/4/28.**G**.
Dar. 7/5—14/6/28.**L**.
Dar. 30/9—12/12/30.**G**.
Superheated boiler fitted.
Dar. 1/5—13/6/33.**G**.
Dar. 17/9—17/10/35.**G**.
Dar. 8/5—1/6/40.**G**.
Dar. 19/9—17/10/42.**G**.
Dar. 28/6—5/8/44.**G**.
Dar. 7/2—13/3/46.**G**.
Dar. 29/12/47—30/1/48.**G**.
Dar. 7/12/49—18/1/50.**G**.
Rebuilt to Part 1.
Dar. 23/6—7/8/53.**C/H**.

BOILERS:
G937.
 2379 *(new)* 12/12/30.
 2198 *(ex1195)* 17/10/35.
 2197 *(ex1179)* 1/6/40.
D2050 *(ex1175)* 17/10/42.
 2492 *(ex1174)* 5/8/44.
 2379 *(ex1182)* 13/3/46.
 2382 *(ex9772)* 30/1/48.
 3358 *(ex9785)* 18/1/50 *(63B)*.

SHEDS:
Shildon.
Percy Main 8/3/23.
Shildon *by* 12/23.
Neville Hill 20/1/25.
Starbeck 18/1/37.
West Hartlepool 28/9/38.
York 10/4/39.
Hull Dairycoates 28/7/46.
Hull Springhead 17/6/51.

RENUMBERED:
 9780 3/2/46.
 E9780 30/1/48.
 69780 18/1/50.

CONDEMNED: 15/11/54.
Cut up at Darlington.

1181

Darlington.

To traffic 3/1911.

REPAIRS:
Ghd. 16/7—7/10/25.**G**.
Ghd. 10/10/28—4/3/29.**G**.
Superheated boiler fitted.
Dar. 17/8—20/9/34.**G**.
Dar. 16/8—18/9/39.**G**.
Dar. 6/8—26/9/40.**H**.
Dar. 5/1—6/2/42.**G**.
Dar. 11/1—7/2/44.**G**.
Dar. 7/4—10/5/45.**L**.
Dar. 27/3—4/5/46.**G**.
Dar. 16/4—14/6/47.**L**.
Dar. 1/7—20/8/48.**G**.
Dar. 13/3—17/4/50.**C/L**.
Dar. 21/3—24/4/51.**G**.
Rebuilt to Part 1.
Dar. 20/1—13/2/54.**H/I**.
Dar. 15—16/2/54.**N/C**.

BOILERS:
G938.
 G944 *(ex spare)* 7/10/25.
 2195 *(new)* 4/3/29.
 2200 *(ex1174)* 20/9/34.
 2378 *(ex1193)* 6/2/42.
D2048 *(ex1195)* 7/2/44.
 2381 *(ex1193)* 4/5/46.
 2200 *(ex9770)* 20/8/48.
 24757 *(new)* 24/4/51 *(63B)*.

SHEDS:
West Hartlepool.
Newport 27/5/37.
Stockton 16/10/39.
Hull Dairycoates 15/2/53.
Hull Springhead 3/10/54.

RENUMBERED:
 9781 10/2/46.
 69781 20/8/48.

CONDEMNED: 23/11/56.
Cut up at Darlington.

1182

Darlington.

To traffic 3/1911.

REPAIRS:
Dar. ?/?—?/11/19.**G**.
Dar. 9/11/22—28/3/23.**G**.
Superheated boiler fitted.
Dar. 15/7—8/10/24.**G**.
Dar. 6/1—20/4/27.**G**.
Dar. 28/8—27/10/30.**G**.
Dar. 27/11/33—5/1/34.**G**.
Dar. 12/12/36—3/2/37.**G**.
Dar. 23/5—4/8/38.**H**.
Dar. 28/11/40—3/1/41.**G**.
Dar. 19/6—27/7/43.**G**.
Dar. 17/1—21/2/46.**G**.
Dar. 23/6—16/7/48.**G**.
Ghd. 14/12/49—6/2/50.**C/L**.
Dar. 21/8—16/9/50.**G**.
Dar. 25/1—21/2/52.**C/H**.
Dar. 28/2—13/3/52.**N/C**.
Dar. 21/12/53—22/1/54.**G**.
Dar. 27/1—8/2/54.**N/C**.

BOILERS:
G939.
 G933 *(ex1179)* 11/19.
 G940 *(ex1183)* 28/3/23.
 2495 *(new)* 5/1/34.
 2204 *(ex1191)* 3/2/37.
D2054 *(ex1191)* 3/1/41.
 2379 *(ex1179)* 27/7/43.
 2380 *(ex1191)* 21/2/46.
 2495 *(ex9784)* 16/7/48.
 24360 *(ex69770)* 16/9/50.
 24361 *(ex69777)* 22/1/54.

SHEDS:
Starbeck.
West Hartlepool 28/9/38.
Hull Dairycoates 8/6/39.
Tyne Dock 6/3/55.
Hull Springhead 16/12/56.

RENUMBERED:
 9782 21/2/46.
 69782 16/7/48.

CONDEMNED: 16/12/57.
Cut up at Darlington.

1183

Darlington.

To traffic 3/1911.

REPAIRS:
Dar. 6/9/22—17/1/23.**G**.
Dar. 6/6—13/6/24.**L**.
Dar. 1/4—30/7/26.**G**.
Dar. 17/10—30/11/28.**G**.
Superheated boiler fitted.
Dar. 10/11—31/12/30.**G**.
Dar. 9/3—26/4/33.**G**.
Dar. 2/4—11/5/35.**G**.
Dar. 25/5—15/6/40.**G**.
Dar. 30/10—3/12/42.**G**.
Dar. 5—29/9/44.**G**.
Dar. 14/5—7/6/46.**G**.
Dar. 5/3—23/4/48.**G**.
Rebuilt to Part 1.
Dar. 26/9—15/11/49.**C/H**.
Dar. 27/2—29/3/51.**G**.
Dar. 2—6/4/51.**N/C**.
Dar. 26/4—26/5/51.**N/C**.
Dar. 5—30/1/54.**G**.
Dar. 1—2/2/54.**N/C**.
Dar. 17/12/56. *Not repaired.*

BOILERS:
G940.
 G952 *(ex1195)* 17/1/23.
D2054 *(new)* 30/11/28.
D2048 *(ex1113)* 26/4/33.
D2050 *(ex1190)* 11/5/35.
 2198 *(ex1180)* 15/6/40.
 2197 *(ex1180)* 3/12/42.
 2200 *(ex1175)* 29/9/44.
D2048 *(ex9781)* 7/6/46.
 3365 *(ex9775)* 23/4/48 *(63B)*.
 24706 *(ex69786)* 29/3/51
(63B).
 24699 *(ex69788)* 30/1/54
(63B).

SHEDS:
Shildon.
Neville Hill 20/1/25.
York 10/4/39.
Hull Dairycoates 28/7/46.
Hull Springhead 14/9/52.

RENUMBERED:
 9783 10/2/46.
 69783 23/4/48.

CONDEMNED: 17/12/56.
Cut up at Darlington.

1185

Darlington.

To traffic 4/1911.

REPAIRS:
Dar. ?/?—?/5/19.**G.**
Dar. ?/?—?/3/22.**G.**
Superheated boiler fitted.
Dar. 5/11/24—7/2/25.**G.**
Dar. 30/3—13/7/27.**G.**
Dar. 30/11/28—15/1/29.**L.**
Dar. 27/1—3/4/30.**G.**
Dar. 5/1—23/2/51.**G.**
Dar. 1/5—15/6/33.**G.**
Dar. 14/11/35—9/1/36.**G.**
Dar. 27/6—28/7/40.**G.**
Dar. 6/1—13/2/43.**G.**
Dar. 28/6—11/8/45.**G.**
Dar. 10/4—21/5/48.**G.**
Rebuilt to Part 1.
Dar. 26/11/48—23/2/49.**C/H.**
Ghd. 2/5—14/6/50.**C/L.**
Dar. 4/4—4/5/51.**G.**
Dar. 13/7—9/8/51.**C/L.**
Dar. 29/10—30/11/53.**C/H.**

BOILERS:
G942.
G927 *(ex1175)* 5/19.
G942 *(ex1136)* 3/22.
2380 *(new)* 23/2/31.
2382 *(ex1136)* 9/1/36.
2380 *(ex1175)* 28/7/40.
2198 *(ex1183)* 13/2/43.
2495 *(ex1114)* 11/8/45.
3867 *(new)* 21/5/48 *(63B).*
3867 reno.24711 4/5/51.

SHEDS:
Starbeck.
Neville Hill *by* 8/24.
Hull Dairycoates 10/4/39.
Hull Springhead 2/9/51.

RENUMBERED:
9784 17/2/46.
69784 21/5/48.

CONDEMNED: 5/3/56.
Cut up at Darlington.

1190

Darlington.

To traffic 4/1911.

REPAIRS:
Dar. ?/?—?/9/17.**G.**
Dar. ?/?—?/11/18.**G.**
Superheated boiler fitted.
Dar. 15/1—10/4/24.**G.**
Dar. 1/7—16/9/25.**G.**
Dar. 1—16/4/26.**L.**
Dar. 31/8—16/11/28.**G.**
Dar. 23/11/31—19/1/32.**G.**
Dar. 11/12/34—6/2/35.**G.**
Sanding altered.
Dar. 20/12/37—16/2/38.**G.**
Dar. 28/7/40—7/1/41.**G.**
Don. 23/7—7/8/42.**L.**
Dar. 30/7—18/9/43.**G.**
Rebuilt to Part 1.
Dar. 23/2—25/3/44.**L.**
After collision.
Dar. 29/1—15/3/47.**G.**
Dar. 12/9—8/10/49.**G.**
Dar. 23/4—17/5/52.**L/I.**

BOILERS:
G943.
G915 *(ex1126)* 9/17.
G912 *(ex1114)* 11/18.
D2050 *(new)* 16/11/28.
2381 *(ex1126)* 6/2/35.
D2049 *(ex1174)* 16/2/38.
D611 *(ex1113)* 7/1/41.
3358 *(new)* 18/9/43 *(63B).*
3987 *(new)* 8/10/49 *(63B).*
3987 reno.24737 17/5/52.

SHEDS:
Stockton.
Ardsley 26/2/26.
Stockton 1/9/26.
Doncaster 21/10/26.
Frodingham 8/10/41.
Starbeck 23/6/43.
Hull Springhead 12/3/45.

RENUMBERED:
9785 14/4/46.
69785 8/10/49.

CONDEMNED: 17/11/55.
Cut up at Darlington.

1191

Darlington.

To traffic 5/1911.

REPAIRS:
Dar. ?/?—?/8/21.**G.**
Ghd. 7/9/25—16/1/26.**G.**
Dar. 19/2—12/4/30.**G.**
Superheated boiler fitted.
Dar. 11/5—9/6/36.**L.**
Dar. 18/11/36—14/1/37.**G.**
Dar. 8/4—21/5/37.**H.**
Dar. 1—30/8/40.**G.**
Dar. 18/3—19/4/43.**G.**
Dar. 19/12/45—26/1/46.**G.**
Dar. 27/2—16/4/48.**G.**
Rebuilt to Part 1.
Dar. 31/1—2/3/51.**G.**
Dar. 17/6—18/7/53.**G.**

BOILERS:
G944.
G930 *(ex1176)* 8/21.
2204 *(new)* 12/4/30.
D2054 *(ex1129)* 14/1/37.
2382 *(ex1185)* 30/8/40.
2380 *(ex1185)* 19/4/43.
2204 *(ex1179)* 26/1/46.
3863 *(new)* 16/4/48 *(63B).*
24693 *(exA8 69889)* 2/3/51
(63C).
24746 *(exA6 69796)* 18/7/53
(63B).

SHEDS:
West Hartlepool.
Newport 27/5/37.
West Hartlepool 27/9/38.
Hull Dairycoates 10/6/39.
Hull Springhead 25/3/56.

RENUMBERED:
9786 14/4/46.
69786 16/4/48.

CONDEMNED: 16/12/57.
Cut up at Darlington.

1192

Darlington.

To traffic 5/1911.

REPAIRS:
Dar. ?/?—?/4/21.**G.**
Dar. 9/6—15/8/23.**G.**
Dar. 15/1—29/4/25.**G.**
Dar. 25/7—21/10/27.**G.**
Dar. 9/10/30—6/2/31.**G.**
Dar. 1/9—10/10/33.**G.**
Dar. 22/8—25/9/34.**L.**
Dar. 18/8—3/10/36.**G.**
Dar. 2/5—17/6/39.**G.**
Dar. 8/5—10/6/40.**H.**
Dar. 15/4—17/5/41.**G.**
Dar. 18/8—20/9/43.**G.**
Dar. 24/7—15/8/44.**L.**
Dar. 3—30/1/45.**L.**
After collision.
Dar. 3/1—8/2/46.**G.**
Dar. 25/6—6/8/46.**L.**
Dar. 28/8—24/9/47.**G.**
Ghd.16/5—21/6/50.**C/L.**
Dar. 9/7—18/8/51.**G.**
Rebuilt to Part 1 (saturated).
Dar. 4/9/51. *Weigh.*
Dar. 7/8/54. *Not repaired.*

BOILERS:
G946.
G947 *(ex1193)* 4/21.
D1978 *(new)* 21/10/27.
D1976 *(ex1176)* 17/5/41.
D1977 *(ex1170)* 8/2/46.
D1978 *(ex9778)* 24/9/48.
24753 *(new)* 18/8/51 *(63B sat.)*

SHEDS:
York.
Stockton 1/4/40.
Hull Dairycoates 15/2/53.
Hull Springhead 10/5/53.

RENUMBERED:
9787 19/5/46.
69787 24/9/48.

CONDEMNED: 9/8/54.
Cut up at Darlington.

1193

Darlington.

To traffic 5/1911.

REPAIRS:
Dar. ?/?—?/9/20.**G.**
Superheater boiler fitted.
Dar. 4/9—8/12/23.**G.**
Dar. 15/3—29/7/26.**G.**
Dar. 29/2—10/5/28.**G.**
Dar. 18/11/29—8/1/30.**G.**
Dar. 15/8—18/9/33.**G.**
Dar. 4/2—20/3/36.**G.**
Dar. 29/8—17/10/39.**G.**
Dar. 30/9—31/10/41.**G.**
Dar. 1/2—2/3/44.**G.**
Dar. 9/3—13/4/46.**G.**
Dar. 27/4—7/5/46.**N/C.**
Dar. 18/5—2/7/48.**G.**
Rebuilt to Part 1.
Dar. 6/3—12/4/51.**G.**
Dar. 17/4—16/5/53.**G.**

BOILERS:
G947.
G923 *(ex1170)* 9/20.
D2055 *(new)* 10/5/28.
2379 *(ex1180)* 20/3/36.
2378 *(ex1174)* 17/10/39.
2381 *(ex1129)* 31/10/41.
2492 *(ex9780)* 13/4/46.
3893 *(new)* 2/7/48 *(63B).*
24699 *(ex69783)* 12/4/51 *(63B).*
24766 *(new)* 16/5/53 *(63B).*

SHEDS:
Starbeck.
York. 4/5/34.
Hull Dairycoates 28/7/46.
Hull Springhead 16/10/55.

RENUMBERED:
9788 14/7/46.
69788 2/7/48.

CONDEMNED: 21/11/55.
Cut up at Darlington.

1195

Darlington.

To traffic 6/1911.

REPAIRS:
Dar. ?/?—?/11/22.**G**.
Superheated boiler fitted.
Dar. 25/2—22/6/26.**G**.
Dar. 28/12/27—25/2/28.**G**.
Dar. 9/4—30/5/29.**G**.
Dar. 11/8—22/9/31.**G**.
Dar. 10/7—22/8/35.**G**.
Dar. 6/9—21/10/39.**G**.
Dar. 10/12/43—8/1/44.**G**.
Dar. 7/5—21/6/47.**G**.

BOILERS:
G952.
 G939 *(ex1113)* 11/22.
 2198 *(new)* 30/5/29.
D2048 *(ex1183)* 22/8/35.
D2054 *(ex1182)* 8/1/44.
 2195 *(ex9776)* 21/6/47.

SHEDS:
Shildon.
York 20/3/25.
Ardsley 30/10/25.
York 22/2/26.
Neville Hill 1/27.
Hull Dairycoates 12/9/32.
Cudworth 6/7/40.
Hull Springhead 16/10/49.

RENUMBERED:
9789 14/4/46.

CONDEMNED: 28/5/51.
Into Dar. for cut up 28/5/51.

Until 1932 North Eastern Area works continued to put Class Y on the buffer beam and only then changed to A7.

From March 1924 the class had single red lining put on and No.1129 on 17th July 1928 probably was the first to have just plain black which was then used through to withdrawal (*see* page 55 top, left).

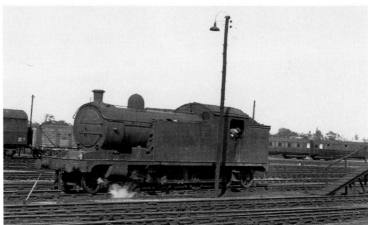

From July 1942 LNER in 7½in. letters was superseded by just NE but in 12in. letters. No.1175 on 26th September 1942 would be the first A7 and all duly carried it with the original number (*see* page 57 top, right).

In January 1946 the reversion to LNER took place and re-numbering began. Only three regained LNER with their original numbering, all in 1946: 1191 (26th January to 14th April), 1192 (8th February to 19th May) and 1193 (13th April to 14th July). No.1192 changed to 9787 by patching on Sunday 19th May.

By the beginning of 1947 Darlington had changed from shaded transfers to yellow painted letters and numbers in Gill sans style but with modified 6 and 9.

From the beginning of July 1948, bunker numbers changed to 10in. to match the lettering but the next three still had the wrong 6 and 9. They were 69770 (2nd July), 69788 (2nd July) and 69782 (16th July). These were also fitted with a number plate on the smokebox which had wrong 6 and 9, No.69781 (20th August) had the wrong 6 and 9 on the number plate but they were correct on the bunker. Tank lettering was also applied to 69787 (24th September 1948), 69777 (1st October 1948), 69776 (5th November 1948), 69772 (19th February 1949), 69784 (23rd February 1949) and 69773 (12th March 1949).

The first BRITISH RAILWAYS style had 10in. letters but 12in. numbers and until mid-March 1948 a regional prefix to the number applied. Three A7 class got this: E9780 (30th January), E9775 (27th February) and E9779 (11th March), on bunker and buffer beam.

At some time in their LNER career, of the twenty engines, all except Nos.1181 and 1192 worked from Hull sheds. Nos.1136, 1174 and 1190 were at Springhead and the other fifteen at Dairycoates. Here, on 21st April 1936, No.1126 is just east of Hessle on the Dairycoates duty hauling regular trains of chalk from Hessle quarry to the cement works at Wilmington, Hull. This was a job it shared with No.1175 whose only shed was Hull Dairycoates.

The next four shopped had similar style except that a regional number 6 took the place of the E and Darlington continued to use 12in. numbers. These were 69786 (16th April), 69783 (23rd April), 69784 (21st May) and 69771 (10th June), all 1948.

Until 21st October 1926, No.1129 was at Shildon except for brief workings at York, 19th March to 23 May 1925, and then at Ardsley 30th October 1925 to 1st September 1926. From 21st October 1926 it worked as shed pilot at Doncaster until 23rd June 1943 (as seen here) but they too also sent it out twice for brief periods. Immingham had it 3rd May to 6th June 1939 and then from 17th July to 11th August 1939 it was at Northwich banking trains of hopper wagons to the ICI sidings at Greenbank. It went to Starbeck 23rd June 1943 and then to Dairycoates on 12th March 1945.

CLASS A 8

2143

Darlington - Rebuilt
from Class H1.

To traffic 5/12/1933.

REPAIRS:
Dar. 1/4—22/6/35.**G.**
Dar. 13/9—29/10/37.**G.**
Dar. 10—26/11/37.**N/C.**
Dar. 30/11—15/12/37.**N/C.**
Dar. 3—14/1/38.**N/C.**
Dar. 23/2—31/3/38.**N/C.**
Dar. 18/11—30/12/39.**G.**
Dar. 26/6—4/8/42.**G.**
Dar. 11/1—4/2/44.**L.**
Dar. 29/4—27/5/44.**G.**
Dar. 28/8—28/9/46.**G.**
Ghd. 15—30/9/47.**L.**
Dar. 10/8—17/9/49.**G.**
Positive lub. drive fitted.
Dar. 9/9—1/10/49.**N/C.**
Dar. 9—14/7/51.**C/L.**
Dar. 19/2—20/3/52.**H/I.**
Dar. 4—30/5/53.**C/H.**
Dar. 3/1—3/2/55.**G.**
Dar. 14—24/2/55.**N/C.**
Dar. 7—11/3/55.**N/C.**
Dar. 29/7—24/8/57.**G.**
Dar. 26—28/8/57.**N/C.**
Dar. 9—12/9/57.**N/C.**

BOILERS:
D1091 (63).
D1063 *(exH1 2157)* 22/6/35 (63).
D1106 *(ex2154)* 29/10/37 (63).
  3059 *(new)* 30/12/39 (63B).
  3046 *(ex2160)* 4/8/42 (63B).
  2827 *(ex1528)* 27/5/44 (63C).
  3367 *(ex1519)* 28/9/46 (63B).
  3984 *(new)* 17/9/49 (63B).
  3984 reno.24717 14/7/51.
24710 *(ex69883)* 3/2/55 (63B).
24737 *(ex spare)* 24/8/57 (63B).

SHEDS:
Middlesbrough.
Blaydon 18/1/39.
Sunderland 31/10/41.

RENUMBERED:
  9850 28/9/46.
69850 17/9/49.

CONDEMNED: 21/6/60.
Into Dar. for cut up 21/6/60.

2144

Darlington - Rebuilt
from Class H1.

To traffic 26/3/1935.

REPAIRS:
Dar. 17/8—1/10/37.**G.**
Dar. 6/6—20/7/39.**G.**
Dar. 29/11/40—21/1/41.**L**
Dar. 22/7—2/9/41.**G.**
Dar. 8—13/9/41.**N/C.**
Dar. 20/5—11/6/43.**L.**
Dar. 11/8—16/9/44.**G.**
Dar. 28/1—14/2/46.**L.**
Dar. 8/11—6/12/46.**L.**
Dar. 3/10—7/11/47.**G.**
Dar. 11—14/11/47.**N/C.**
Ghd. 26/10—15/12/49.**C/L.**
Dar. 30/1—23/2/51.**G.**
Positive lub. drive fitted.
Dar. 5—9/3/51.**N/C.**
Dar. 30/5/52.*Weigh.*
Dar. 12/2—27/6/53.**H/I.**
Dar. 29/6—3/7/53.**N/C.**
Dar. 24/6—23/7/55.**G.**
Dar. 25—29/7/55.**N/C.**
Dar. 20/11—11/12/56.**C/H.**
Dar. 15—28/1/57.**C/L.**
After collision.

BOILERS:
D1282 (63).
  2373 *(ex2150)* 1/10/37 (63).
  2375 *(ex1327)* 2/9/41 (63).
D1251 *(ex1525)* 16/9/44 (63).
  3050 *(ex9894)* 7/11/47 (63B).
24755 *(new)* 23/2/51 (63B).
24758 *(ex69879)* 23/7/55 (63B).

SHEDS:
Gateshead.
Tyne Dock 9/7/38.
Gateshead 17/9/38.
Sunderland 14/11/38.
Blaydon 18/1/39.
West Auckland 28/5/50.

RENUMBERED:
  9851 20/10/46.
69851 15/12/49.

CONDEMNED: 11/11/58.
Into Dar. for cut up 11/11/58.

2145

Darlington - Rebuilt
from Class H1.

To traffic 29/2/1936.

REPAIRS:
Dar. 8/11/38—18/1/39.**G.**
Dar. 26/1—6/2/39.**N/C.**
Dar. 24/7—4/8/39.**N/C.**
Dar. 14—31/5/41.**L.**
Dar. 27/4—27/5/43.**G.**
Dar. 14/11—9/12/44.**L.**
Dar. 31/10—8/12/45.**G.**
Dar. 9/4—27/8/48.**G.**
Dar. 1/1—3/2/51.**G.**
Positive lub. drive fitted.
Dar. 25/11—24/12/53.**G.**
Dar. 5—6/1/54.**N/C.**
Ghd. 12/7—3/8/55.**C/L.**
Ghd. 21/11—23/12/55.**C/L.**
Dar. 26/6—13/8/56.**G.**
Dar. 23/11—6/12/56.**C/L.**
Dar. 11—27/2/57.**C/L.**
Dar. 12/6—3/7/57.**C/L.**
Dar. 2—23/8/57.**C/L.**

BOILERS:
  2664 *(new)* 29/2/36 (63A).
  2458 *(ex1528)* 18/1/39 (63A).
D1316 *(ex2149)* 27/5/43 (63).
  3374 *(new)* 8/12/45 (63B).
24697 *(ex69867)* 3/2/51 (63B).
24756 *(ex69876)* 24/12/53 (63B).
24740 *(ex69880)* 13/8/56 (63B).

SHEDS:
Heaton.
Stockton 4/7/38.
Starbeck 28/2/40.
Whitby 12/3/45.
West Hartlepool 4/6/50.
Stockton 6/7/52.
Middlesbrough 5/10/52.
Saltburn 19/9/54.
Sunderland 15/9/57.

RENUMBERED:
  9852 20/10/46.
69852 27/8/48.

CONDEMNED: 4/11/59.
Into Dar. for cut up 15/11/59.

2146

Darlington - Rebuilt
from Class H1.

To traffic 9/5/1935.

REPAIRS:
Dar. 22/9—11/11/37.**G.**
Dar. 18/11—19/12/39.**G.**
Dar. 17/2—1/4/42.**G.**
Dar. 10—17/7/42.**N/C.**
Dar. 5/7—26/8/44.**G.**
Dar. 28/12/46—8/2/47.**G.**
Positive lub. drive fitted.
Dar. 11—18/2/47.**N/C.**
Dar. 5/8—2/9/49.**G.**
Dar. 27/11—29/12/51.**G.**
Dar. 2/3—3/4/54.**G.**
Dar. 6/11—6/12/56.**G.**

BOILERS:
  2455 (63A).
  3056 *(new)* 19/12/39 (63B).
  3031 *(ex1530)* 1/4/42 (63B).
  3361 *(new)* 26/8/44 (63B).
  3065 *(ex9860)* 8/2/47 (63B).
  3036 *(ex9871)* 2/9/49 (63B).
24726 *(exA6 69793)* 29/12/51
(63B).
24695 *(ex69893)* 3/4/54 (63B).
24736 *(ex69859)* 6/12/56 (63B).

SHEDS:
Gateshead.
Blaydon 17/1/39.
Sunderland 30/5/48.

RENUMBERED:
  9853 20/10/46.
69853 2/9/49.

CONDEMNED: 25/1/60.
Into Dar. for cut up 13/2/60.

2147

Darlington - Rebuilt
from Class H1.

To traffic 31/8/1933.

REPAIRS:
Dar. 31/5—5/7/35.**G.**
Dar. 9—19/7/35.**L.**
Dar. 30/8—24/9/35.**H.**
Dar. 30/9—13/12/35.**N/C.**

WORKS CODES:- Cw - Cowlairs. Dar- Darlington. Don - Doncaster. Ghd - Gateshead. Gor - Gorton. Inv - Inverurie. Str - Stratford. Tux - Tuxford.
REPAIR CODES:- **C/H** - Casual Heavy. **C/L** - Casual Light. **G** - General. **H** - Heavy. **H/I** - Heavy Intermediate. **L** - Light. **L/I** - Light Intermediate. **N/C** - Non-Classified.

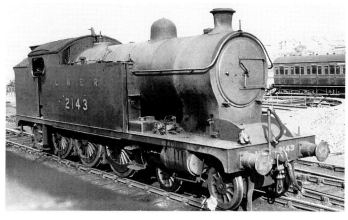

The changes produced such a more effective engine that another six were rebuilt in 1933: Nos.1518, 1525, 1528, 2143, 2147 and 2155. During 1934 fourteen more changed from Class H1 to A8, these were Nos.1327, 1328, 1329, 1330, 1500, 1501, 1519, 1522, 1524, 1529, 1531, 2149, 2153 and 2159.

Diagram 63 boilers had three ring barrels and Schmidt type superheater but as used on Class A8 they all had the valve on the side of the smokebox replaced by a Gresley anti-vacuum valve.

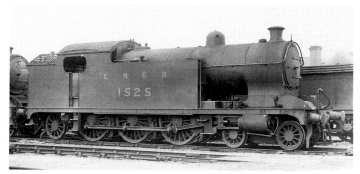

A further twelve were rebuilt in 1935, their numbers being: 1326, 1520, 1521, 1523, 1530, 2144, 2146, 2150, 2154, 2156, 2157 and 2158. The remaining twelve, Nos.1499, 1502, 1503, 1517, 1526, 1527, 2145, 2148, 2151, 2152, 2160 and 2161, were converted during 1936.

In 1929 this boiler design had been changed to Dia.63A which had a single plate barrel and Robinson superheater. Five were built in 1930 and fourteen from 1932 to 1935. They could be distinguished from Dia.63 only by the shorter appearance of the safety valves. Only 2143, 2144 and 2151 never carried one of these nineteen Dia.63A boilers.

(below) Only three months after completion of re-building, re-boilering began using a Diagram 63C boiler on No.1579 in November 1936. This boiler was the same diameter as the 63 and 63A type but had closer cladding. No.2154 was next in October 1937. Although only five boilers were built to Diagram 63C, due to interchange they found their way on to a total of sixteen Class A8 engines. No.69855 (2148) was withdrawn with one, in January 1960.

Only five 63C boilers were built before it was re-designed as 63B with the dome 1ft 9in. to the rear. As with the 63C, the cladding was no longer made the same diameter as the smokebox at 5ft 8¼in., and an inverted T-strap behind the dome gave mutual support to the tanks. No.1530, on 8th June 1939, was the first to get 63B with 2160 being fitted on 4th August. By the time of withdrawal the whole class had the Diagram 63B boiler except for 69855, but even this engine had carried one from February 1953 to October 1956.

Diagram 63 and 63A boilers had this larger door as the standard. When used on H1 class, fastening had been by wheel and handle but all A8 class had two handles.

Standard chimney for the A8 class did not have a windjabber nor had it been used on H1 class, but one A8 was so fitted, probably from December 1936 to November 1938.

The same type of door was also used on Diagram 63B boilers until 1945 but was then slowly superseded by a new design of door.

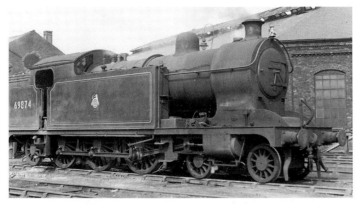

The unusual small diameter smokebox door with flat flange continued in use at least to 1955 (*see* also photo 17 pageXX). This is also a 63C boiler which No.69874 had from August 1950 to November 1952, and which then went to 69892. This door was peculiar to the Diagram 63C boiler.

On 8th December 1945, No.2145 was the first A8 to get a smokebox door with pressed joint ring to improve air tightness, and ultimately all got this type of door.

2147 cont./
Dar. 8/11—24/12/37.**G.**
Dar. 3/10—4/11/39.**G.**
Dar. 19/7/40.*Weigh.*
Dar. 9/9—9/10/40.**L.**
Dar. 15/12/42—21/1/43.**G.**
Dar. 18/9—19/10/44.**L.**
Dar. 14/11—15/12/45.**G.**
Ghd. 9—23/1/47.**L.**
Dar. 21/1—18/6/48.**G.**
Ghd. 4—25/2/49.**C/L.**
Dar. 16/5—8/6/50.**C/L.**
Dar. 13/2—15/3/51.**G.**
Positive lub. drive fitted.
Dar. 9/7—3/9/52.**C/H.**
Dar. 8—20/6/53.**C/L.**
After collision.
Dar. 1—31/12/53.**G.**
Dar. 29/8—28/9/56.**G.**

BOILERS:
D1316 (63).
D1301 *(exH1 2158)* 5/7/35 (63).
D1208 *(ex1521)* 24/12/37 (63).
115 *(ex1329)* 4/11/39 (63A).
114 *(ex1525)* 21/1/43 (63A).
2377 *(ex1521)* 15/12/45 (63).
24703 *(ex69893)* 15/3/51 (63B).
24724 *(ex69870)* 31/12/53 (63B).
24709 *(exA7 69773)* 28/9/56 (63B).

SHEDS:
Whitby 31/8/33
Neville Hill 11/10/33
Darlington 27/6/34
Middlesbrough 20/3/39
West Auckland 1/1/40
Middlesbrough 14/2/42
Hull Botanic Gardens 12/1/46
Middlesbrough 27/6/48
Hull Botanic Gardens 4/6/50
Middlesbrough 19/11/50
Sunderland 15/9/57

RENUMBERED:
9854 10/2/46.
69854 18/6/48.

CONDEMNED: 10/5/60.
Into Dar. for cut up 10/5/60.

2148

Darlington - Rebuilt
from Class H1.

To traffic 26/3/1936.

REPAIRS:
Dar. 20/6—4/8/38.**G.**
Dar. 5/8—10/10/39.**L.**
Dar. 20/6—18/7/40.**G.**
Dar. 19/11—18/12/43.**G.**

Dar. 19/12/44—6/2/45.**L.**
Dar. 17/6—20/7/46.**G.**
Dar. 18/9—22/10/48.**G.**
Dar. 11—24/11/48.**N/C.**
Dar. 19/9—21/10/50.**G.**
Positive lub. drive fitted.
Dar. 30/1/52.*Weigh.*
Dar. 3—24/3/52.**N/C.**
Dar. 4/8/52—14/2/53.**G.**
Dar. 16—19/2/53.**N/C.**
Dar. 2—15/7/53.**L.**
Dar. 15/10—19/11/54.**C/L.**
Dar. 28/2—26/3/55.**G.**
Dar. 28—30/3/55.**N/C.**
Dar. 3—15/12/55.**C/L.**
After collision.
Dar. 12/10—16/11/56.**G.**
Dar. 11—27/3/57.**C/L.**
After collision.

BOILERS:
2467 (63A).
2377 *(ex2152)* 4/8/38 (63).
D1282 *(ex1501)* 18/7/40 (63).
113 *(ex1327)* 18/12/43 (63A).
2457 *(ex1327)* 20/7/46 (63A).
2664 *(ex9868)* 22/10/48 (63A).
24687 *(ex69878)* 21/10/50 (63A).
24742 *(ex69877)* 14/2/53 (63B).
24730 *(ex69888)* 26/3/55 (63B).
24693 *(ex69884)* 16/11/56 (63C).

SHEDS:
Neville Hill.
Hull Botanic Gardens 13/10/42.
Saltburn 19/8/51.
Sunderland 15/9/57.

RENUMBERED:
9855 20/7/46.
69855 22/10/48.

CONDEMNED: 25/1/60.
Into Dar. for cut up 25/1/60.

2149

Darlington - Rebuilt
from Class H1.

To traffic 7/9/1934.

REPAIRS:
Dar. 6/10/36—21/1/37.**G.**
Dar. 5/7—12/8/39.**G.**
Dar. 4—9/9/39.**N/C.**
Dar. 26/3—3/5/43.**G.**
Dar. 20/9—25/10/63.**H.**
Dar. 17/11—21/12/45.**G.**
Dar. 12/2—25/3/48.**G.**
Dar. 6/2—1/4/50.**G.**
Positive lub. drive fitted.
Dar. 10/3—3/4/52.**G.**
Dar. 15/2—13/3/54.**G.**

Dar. 15—17/3/54.**N/C.**
Dar. 22/3—1/4/54.**N/C.**
Dar. 12/1—10/2/56.**G.**

BOILERS:
D1219 *(exH1 1524)* (63).
D1316 *(ex1519)* 21/1/37 (63).
2468 *(ex1531)* 3/5/43 (63A).
2661 *(ex1527)* 21/12/45 (63A).
3056 *(ex9867)* 25/3/48 (63B).
2821 *(ex9886)* 1/4/50 (63C).
24723 *(ex69865)* 3/4/52 (63B).
24703 *(ex69854)* 13/3/54 (63B).
24752 *(ex69887)* 10/2/56 (63B).

SHEDS:
Blaydon.
Heaton 17/3/36.
Gateshead 17/9/38.
Sunderland 17/11/38.
Whitby 12/5/46.
West Auckland 29/9/46.

RENUMBERED:
9856 3/11/46.
ᴇ9856 28/3/48.
69856 1/4/50.

CONDEMNED: 2/12/59.
Into Dar. for cut up 2/12/59.

2150

Darlington - Rebuilt
from Class H1.

To traffic 14/6/1935.

REPAIRS:
Dar. 8/6—10/8/37.**G.**
Dar. 12—24/8/37.**N/C.**
Dar. 30/12/39—1/2/40.**G.**
Dar. 3—29/11/41.**L.**
Dar. 26/10—2/12/42.**G.**
Dar. 28/3—25/4/44.**L.**
Dar. 19/3—11/8/45.**G.**
Ghd. 21/11—6/12/46.**L.**
Ghd. 1/1—23/3/48.**L.**
After collision.
Dar. 3/6—9/7/48.**G.**
Dar. 20/3—21/4/51.**G.**
Positive lub. drive fitted.
Dar. 11/9—10/10/53.**G.**
Dar. 12—13/10/53.**N/C.**
Dar. 12/8—23/9/54.**C/H.**
Dar. 4/10—7/11/56.**L/I.**
Dar. 22/11—6/12/57.**N/C.**

BOILERS:
2373 (63).
D1267 *(ex2157)* 10/8/37 (63).
D1251 *(ex1328)* 1/2/40 (63).
2453 *(ex1503)* 2/12/42 (63A).
117 *(ex1531)* 11/8/45 (63A).

3898 *(new)* 9/7/48 (63B).
24708 *(ex69862)* 21/4/51 (63B).
24685 *(ex69884)* 10/10/53 (63B).

SHEDS:
Middlesbrough 14/6/35.
Blaydon 17/1/39.
Sunderland 7/11/48.

RENUMBERED:
9857 27/10/46.
69857 9/7/48.

CONDEMNED: 5/2/60.
Into Dar. for cut up 5/2/60.

2151

Darlington - Rebuilt
from Class H1.

To traffic 11/6/1936.

REPAIRS:
Dar. 5/10—15/12/38.**G.**
Dar. 17/9—30/10/41.**G.**
Dar. 7/11—9/12/44.**G.**
Dar. 17—26/4/47.**G.**
Ghd. 25/8—10/9/48.**L.**
Dar. 8/6—8/7/49.**G.**
Positive lub. drive fitted.
Dar. 11—13/7/49.**N/C.**
Ghd. 26/9—9/11/49.**C/L.**
Dar. 24/9—20/10/51.**G.**
Dar. 22—24/10/51.**N/C.**
Dar. 15/12/53—16/1/54.**G.**
Dar. 25—30/1/54.**N/C.**
Dar. 28/2—30/3/57.**G.**
Ghd. 10/7—16/8/57.**C/L.**
After collision.

BOILERS:
D1254 *(exH1 1526)* (63).
3067 *(new)* 30/10/41 (63B).
3031 *(ex2146)* 9/12/44 (63B).
3059 *(ex9865)* 26/4/47 (63B).
3048 *(ex69860)* 8/7/49 (63B).
24713 *(ex69881)* 20/10/51 (63B).
24697 *(ex69852)* 16/1/54 (63B).
24686 *(ex69877)* 30/3/57 (63B).

SHEDS:
Middlesbrough 11/6/36.
Blaydon 17/1/39.
Hull Botanic Gardens 28/3/40.
Middlesbrough 12/1/46.
Whitby 30/5/48.
Neville Hill 29/6/54.
Hull Botanic Gardens 10/6/56.
Middlesbrough 16/6/57.
Sunderland 15/9/57.

RENUMBERED:
9858 20/10/46.
69858 10/9/48.

2151 cont./
CONDEMNED: 10/5/60.
Into Dar. for cut up 10/5/60.

2152

Darlington - Rebuilt
from Class H1.

To traffic 13/3/1936.

REPAIRS:
Dar. 8/3—29/4/38.**G.**
Dar. 30/4—9/5/38.**N/C.**
Dar. 28/5—20/6/40.**G.**
Dar. 9—22/7/41.**N/C.**
Dar. 31/12/43—29/1/44.**G.**
Dar. 18/12/46—1/2/47.**G.**
Positive lub. drive fitted.
Dar. 3/5/48.Weigh.
Dar. 31/5—1/7/49.**G.**
Dar. 3—29/9/51.**G.**
Dar. 8—10/10/51.**N/C.**
Dar. 15—19/10/51.**N/C.**
Dar. 23/9—28/10/54.**G.**
Dar. 19/9--23/10/56.**G.**
Dar. 21/5—12/6/57.**C/L.**

BOILERS:
2377 (63).
D1293 (ex1518) 29/4/38 (63).
2659 (ex1503) 20/6/40 (63A).
D1102 (ex1326) 29/1/44 (63).
2376 (ex9888) 1/2/47 (63).
2468 (ex9869) 1/7/49 (63A).
24716 (ex69882) 29/9/51 (63A).
24736 (ex69889) 28/10/54 (63A).
24756 (ex69852) 23/10/56 (63B).

SHEDS:
Blaydon.
Middlesbrough 29/5/36.
Hull Botanic Gardens 4/6/50.
Middlesbrough 19/11/50.
Stockton 21/6/53.
Middlesbrough 20/9/53.
Saltburn 13/6/54.
Sunderland 15/9/57.

RENUMBERED:
9859 20/10/46.
69859 1/7/49.

CONDEMNED: 8/2/60.
Into Dar. for cut up 8/2/60.

2153

Darlington - Rebuilt
from Class H1.

To traffic 8/8/1934.

REPAIRS:
Dar. 13—17/8/34.**L.**

Dar. 7/2—18/3/36.**G.**
Dar. 17/1—19/2/38.**G.**
Dar. 22/2—4/4/38.**N/C.**
Dar. 1/9—14/10/39.**G.**
Dar. 25/1—27/2/40.**H.**
Dar. 24/9—6/11/43.**G.**
Dar. 26/11/46—11/1/47.**G.**
Ghd. 16/8—3/9/48.**L.**
Dar. 19/5—17/6/49.**G.**
Positive lub. drive fitted.
Dar. 28/6—8/7/49.**N/C.**
Dar. 22/11—15/12/51.**G.**
Dar. 27/12/51—11/1/52.**N/C.**
Dar. 10/3—22/5/54.**G.**
Dar. 27/12/56—1/2/57.**G.**
Dar. 9—13/2/57.**N/C.**

BOILERS:
D1067 (exH1 2159) (63).
2453 (ex1330) 18/3/36 (63A).
D1274 (ex1329) 19/2/38 (63).
3048 (new) 14/10/39 (63B).
3065 (ex1520) 6/11/43 (63B).
3048 (ex9871) 11/1/47 (63B).
2827 (ex9876) 17/6/49 (63C).
24728 (exA6 69791) 15/12/51 (63B).
24713 (ex69858) 22/5/54 (63B).
24695 (ex69853) 1/2/57 (63B).

SHEDS:
Darlington 8/8/34.
Middlesbrough 20/3/39.
Hull Botanic Gardens 23/5/42.
Middlesbrough 29/4/46.
Whitby 30/5/48.
Hull Botanic Gardens 25/9/55.
Middlesbrough 16/6/57.
Thornaby 1/6/58.

RENUMBERED:
9860 15/9/46.
69860 3/9/48.

CONDEMNED: 14/6/60.
Into Dar. for cut up 14/6/60.

2154

Darlington - Rebuilt
from Class H1.

To traffic 23/8/1935.

REPAIRS:
Dar. 31/8—19/10/37.**G.**
Dar. 6—19/10/38.**N/C.**
Dar. 17/10—17/11/39.**G.**
Dar. 22/12/39—23/1/40.**N/C.**
Dar. 3—31/5/43.**G.**
Dar. 3—14/3/44.**N/C.**
Dar. 7/2—10/3/45.**G.**
Dar. 19/12/45—5/2/46.**L.**
Dar. 16/6—14/7/47.**G.**
Dar. 24/7—19/8/47.**N/C.**

Dar. 16—24/9/47.**N/C.**
Dar. 1—22/10/47.**N/C.**
Dar. 4/4—6/5/50.**G.**
Positive lub. drive fitted.
Dar. 8—11/5/50.**N/C.**
Dar. 30/10—8/12/51.**G.**
Dar. 14/7—14/8/54.**H/I.**
Dar. 13/7—29/8/56.**C/H.**
Dar. 21/2—1/4/58.**G.**

BOILERS:
D1106 (63).
2822 (new) 19/10/37 (63C).
3369 (new) 31/5/43 (63B).
3362 (exA6 9792) 14/7/47 (63B).
3986 (new) 6/5/50 (63B).
3986 reno.24729 8/12/51.
24747 (ex69878) 1/4/58 (63B).

SHEDS:
Gateshead.
Sunderland 18/1/39.
Consett 5/8/46.
Sunderland 20/1/47.
Whitby 4/6/50.
Selby 21/10/51.
Whitby 11/5/52.
Malton 3/6/56.

RENUMBERED:
9861 6/12/46.
69861 6/5/50.

CONDEMNED: 20/6/60.
Into Dar. for cut up 20/6/60.

2155

Darlington - Rebuilt
from Class H1.

To traffic 15/1/1933.

REPAIRS:
Dar. 20/7—24/8/33.**L.**
Dar. 13/3—4/5/35.**G.**
Dar. 28/2—24/6/36.**H.**
Dar. 30/11/38.Weigh.
Dar. 7/2—20/4/39.**G.**
Dar. 19/5—1/6/39.**N/C.**
Dar. 21/4—6/6/42.**G.**
Dar. 11/5—11/7/45.**G.**
Dar. 29/3—23/4/46.**L.**
Ghd. 24/11—7/12/46.**L.**
Dar. 7/10—5/11/48.**G.**
Dar. 28/2—6/4/51.**G.**
Positive lub. drive fitted.
Dar. 10—13/4/51.**N/C.**
Dar. 29/3—1/5/54.**G.**
Dar. 3—4/5/54.**N/C.**
Dar. 7—14/5/54.**N/C.**
Dar. 16/11—12/12/56.**C/L.**

BOILERS:
2D/689 (63A).

2D/689 reno. 114 4/5/35.
D1287 (ex1524) 24/6/36 (63).
2456 (ex1523) 20/4/39 (63A).
2453 (ex2150) 11/7/45 (63A).
3905 (new) 5/11/48 (63B).
24705 (ex69851) 6/4/51 (63B).
24768 (new) 1/5/54 (63B).

SHEDS:
Heaton.
Darlington 19/6/34.
Whitby 22/8/34.
Neville Hill 28/3/42.
West Hartlepool 7/11/42.
West Auckland 20/6/45.
West Hartlepool 26/11/45.
Stockton 6/7/52.
Middlesbrough 5/10/52.
Stockton 21/6/53.
Middlesbrough 20/9/53.
Sunderland 15/9/57.

RENUMBERED:
9862 11/8/46.
69862 5/11/48.

CONDEMNED: 30/7/58.
Into Dar. for cut up 30/7/58.

2156

Darlington - Rebuilt
from Class H1.

To traffic 5/9/1935.

REPAIRS:
Dar. 24/5—7/7/38.**G.**
Dar. 24/3—15/4/41.**N/C.**
Dar. 8/12/41—12/2/42.**G.**
Dar. 7—14/7/42.**N/C.**
Dar. 28/7—12/8/42.**N/C.**
Dar. 25/1—2/3/45.**G.**
Dar. 6/9—7/11/47.**G.**
Dar. 19/1—25/3/50.**G.**
Positive lub. drive fitted.
Dar. 17—20/4/50.**N/C.**
Dar. 28/1—28/2/53.**H/I.**
Dar. 20/5—30/6/55.**C/L.**
Dar. 10/9—8/10/55.**G.**
Dar. 7/3—25/4/57.**C/H.**

BOILERS:
2466 (63A).
D1301 (ex2147) 7/7/38 (63).
D1293 (ex1526) 2/3/45 (63).
D1219 (ex9878) 7/11/47 (63).
3973 (new) 25/3/50 (63B).
3973 reno. 24743 28/2/53.
24760 (ex69894) 8/10/55 (63B).

SHEDS:
Blaydon.
Gateshead 30/9/35.

The new type of door was also fitted in conjunction with Diagram 63A boilers.

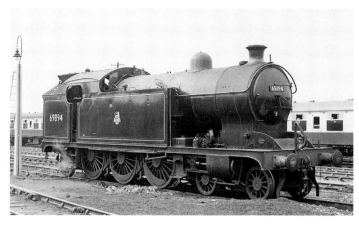

The cab window replacement was a long process and No.69894 still had the two-piece type until it went to works on 13th June 1957.

Only one of the five Diagram 63C boilers had a smokebox with small diameter door. This was boiler No.2824 (later 24741) used on A8 69874 (August 1950 to November 1952) and 69892 (January 1953 to December 1954). The other three 63C boilers which were used on A8 class had large diameter door with pressed joint ring.

Even at that late date, (the first A8 was withdrawn only four months later) No.69894 was ex works 12th July 1957 fitted with one-piece windows.

Until June 1939 the cab front windows were in two parts, and the outer part could be opened. Beginning with No.2161 on 15th June 1939 one-piece windows were put on in replacement as needed.

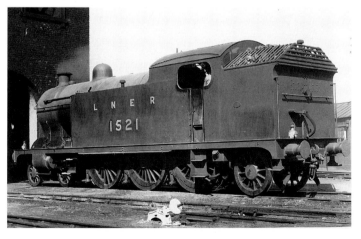

Until June 1945 the rear of the bunker had only a single step to provide access to the top although there was good handrail provision.

Starting with No.1524 on 7th June 1945, an additional step was fitted just below the flare of the rear sheet. No.2145 was so fitted on 8th December 1945 and by the end of the LNER all but three had been fitted with the extra step.

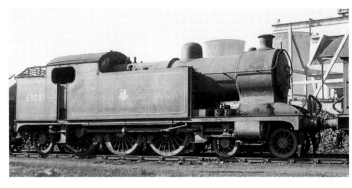

The seventeen built from June 1921 to May 1922 did not have horizontal rails but had a cage with sloping sides. It had been found that with the open bunker, coal could be piled up which then obscured the rear windows and interfered with forward vision when working bunker leading. It had been the intention to change all the earlier engines to a cage but only nineteen were done although No.2153 (*see page 82 top, left*) did get a vent pipe to suit a cage which it never acquired.

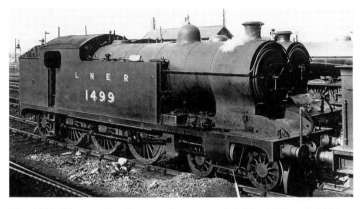

The 1938 Diagram Book alterations recorded Nos.1499 and 2144 as equipped with 'bogie having side supports'. No further information seems to have been recorded on this fitting or mention made in the Special Fittings Register. No.1499 received its special bogie on 5th April 1929 when H1 class.

Between 2162's rebuilding in June 1931, and the early rebuilding of the rest of the class, two other factors affected A8 class. The ten H1/A8 engines shedded at Leeds Neville Hill and Starbeck sheds were to be fitted with a hopper top to the coal bunker to suit the mechanical coaling plants just erected at those two sheds. Three had them fitted whilst still H1 class, the other seven, Nos.1326, 1500, 1518, 1528, 1531, 2143 and 2147, at the time they were rebuilt to A8.

The twenty built in 1913/14 and the eight built during May and June of 1920, Nos.2143 to 2162, and 1517 to 1520, 1523, 1528, 1529, 1531, originally had just an open bunker top with three coal rails around it. Nine of them were never altered and kept just three rails to withdrawal. They were: 2153, 2154, 2157, 2159, 2160, 1517, 1519, 1523 and 1529.

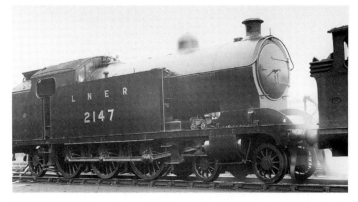

No.2147, fitted 31st August 1933, went to Whitby ex works and only back to Leeds on 11th October 1933, whilst No.1518 went to Middlesbrough when rebuilt instead of back to Leeds. These two A8's proved to be the answer to working the coast line trains which had grown beyond the capability of the A6 class normally on the job. So, concurrently with the fitting of the hopper, Leeds and Starbeck lost eight of their A8's to coast line sheds which had no real need for a hopper bunker top.

2156 cont./
Stockton 16/7/38.
West Auckland 10/6/40.
West Hartlepool 1/2/43.
Sunderland 6/7/52.

RENUMBERED:
9863 17/11/46.
69863 25/3/50.

CONDEMNED: 3/11/58.
Into Dar. for cut up 3/11/58.

2157

Darlington - Rebuilt
from Class H1.

To traffic 27/6/1935.

REPAIRS:
Dar. 7/6—26/7/37.**G.**
Dar. 16/10/37.*Weigh.*
Dar. 15/4—28/5/41.**G.**
Dar. 9/7—19/7/41.**N/C.**
Dar. 2/7—18/8/42.**L.**
Dar. 24/8 –2/9/42.**N/C.**
Dar. 4/8—9/9/44.**G.**
Dar. 21/10/46—18/1/47.**G.**
Ghd. 29/6—13/7/48.**L.**
Dar. 8/6—12/7/49.**G.**
Positive lub. drive fitted.
Dar. 2/2—10/3/50.**C/L.**
Dar. 16/4—12/5/51.**C/L.**
Dar. 16/10—10/11/51.**G.**
Dar. 12—13/11/51.**N/C.**
Dar. 19—23/11/51.**N/C.**
Dar. 25/3—24/4/54.**G.**
Dar. 26—30/4/54.**N/C.**

BOILERS:
D1267 *(ex1525)* 27/6/35 (63).
D1219 *(ex2149)* 26/7/37 (63).
2374 *(ex1329)* 9/9/44 (63).
2659 *(ex9892)* 12/7/49 (63A).
2659 *reno.* 24712 12/5/51.
24721 *(ex69859)* 10/11/51 (63A).
24723 *(ex69856)* 24/4/54 (63B).

SHEDS:
Stockton 27/6/35.
West Hartlepool 28/2/42.
Whitby 4/6/50.

RENUMBERED:
9864 26/10/46.
69864 13/7/48.

CONDEMNED: 29/10/58.
Into Dar. for cut up 12/1/59.

2158

Darlington - Rebuilt
from Class H1.

To traffic 24/5/1935.

REPAIRS:
Dar. 22/1—11/3/37.**G.**
Dar. 6/5/37.*Weigh.*
Dar. 6/7—23/8/39.**G.**
Dar. 6/12/39—18/1/40.**L.**
After collision.
Dar. 25/8—1/10/40.**L.**
Dar. 9/2—20/3/42.**G.**
Dar. 12/8—14/9/44.**G.**
Dar. 18/1—15/2/47.**G.**
Positive lub. drive fitted.
Dar. 4—7/3/47.**N/C.**
Ghd. 21/5—4/6/48.**L.**
Dar. 18/3—23/4/49.**G.**
Dar. 25—26/4/49.**N/C.**
Dar. 22/11—1/12/49.**C/L.**
Dar. 26—31/1/51.**C/L.**
Dar. 19/9—20/10/51.**G.**
Dar. 23—26/10/51.**N/C.**
Dar. 5—8/8/53.**C/L.**
Dar. 25/5—24/6/54.**G.**
Dar. 15/4/58. *Not repaired.*

BOILERS:
2662 *(new)* (63A)
2465 *(ex2160)* 23/8/39 (63A).
3050 *(new)* 20/3/42 (63B).
3059 *(ex1330)* 14/9/44 (63B).
3361 *(ex9853)* 15/2/47 (63B).
3066 *(ex9889)* 23/4/49 (63B).
24720 *(ex69883)* 20/10/51 (63B).
24683 *(ex69872)* 24/6/54 (63B).

SHEDS:
Gateshead.
Middlesbrough 25/5/35.
Blaydon 16/1/39.
Whitby 30/5/48.

RENUMBERED:
9865 18/8/46.
69865 4/6/48.

CONDEMNED: 21/4/58.
Cut up at Darlington.

2159

Darlington - Rebuilt
from Class H1.

To traffic 30/8/1934.

REPAIRS:
Dar. 2—6/9/34.**N/C.**
Dar. 20/5—18/7/36.**G.**
Dar. 28—29/7/36.**N/C.**
Dar. 29/6—25/8/38.**G.**
Dar. 30/8—9/9/38.**N/C.**
Dar. 5/9—17/10/40.**G.**
Dar. 9/9—15/10/41.**L.**
Dar. 29/12/43—15/2/44.**G.**
Dar. 22/8—4/10/46.**G.**
Dar. 4/11—5/12/47.**L.**
Dar. 12/5—11/6/48.**G.**
Dar. 22—29/6/48.**N/C.**
Dar. 8—31/3/50.**C/L.**
Dar. 19/2—24/3/51.**G.**
Positive lub. drive fitted.
Dar. 20/5/52.*Weigh.*
Dar. 6/8—3/9/53.**L/I.**
Dar. 23—30/11/54.**C/L.**
Dar. 15—18/2/55.**C/L.**
Dar. 6/6—13/7/55.**C/L.**
Dar. 14/3—17/4/56.**G.**

BOILERS:
D1022 *(exH1 2153)* (63).
D1103 *(ex1522)* 25/8/38 (63).
2466 *(ex1522)* 17/10/40 (63A).
2659 *(ex2152)* 15/2/44 (63A).
2463 *(ex1328)* 4/10/46 (63A).
2456 *(ex9890)* 11/6/48 (63A).
24700 *(ex69873)* 24/3/51 (63B).
24755 *(ex69851)* 17/4/56 (63B).

SHEDS:
Darlington 30/8/34.
Hull Botanic Gardens 8/9/36.
Middlesbrough 11/7/48.
Hull Botanic Gardens 4/6/50.
Middlesbrough 19/11/50.
Saltburn 19/9/54.
Middlesbrough 2/2/58.
Thornaby 1/6/58.

RENUMBERED:
9866 4/10/46.
69866 11/6/48.

CONDEMNED: 18/11/58.
Into Dar. for cut up 18/11/58.

2160

Darlington - Rebuilt
from Class H1.

To traffic 14/7/1936.

REPAIRS:
Dar. 6—20/9/37.**N/C.**
Dar. 5/10/38.*Weigh.*
Dar. 21/6—4/8/39.**G.**

Dar. 8/6/42—18/7/42.**G.**
Dar. 3/11—15/12/43.**L.**
Dar. 19/6—15/9/45.**G.**
Ghd. 6—22/11/46.**L.**
Dar. 13/1—20/2/48.**G.**
Ghd. 30/8—14/10/49.**C/L.**
Dar. 31/10—25/11/50.**G.**
Positive lub. drive fitted.
Dar. 27—29/11/50.**N/C.**
Dar. 6—13/8/52.**N/C.**
Dar. 27/11—29/12/52.**C/H.**
Dar. 9/9—6/10/54.**G.**
Dar. 5/6/56.*Weigh.*

BOILERS:
2465 (63A).
3046 *(new)* 4/8/39 (63B).
3056 *(ex2146)* 18/7/42 (63B).
3069 *(ex9886)* 20/2/48 (63B).
24689 *(ex69884)* 25/11/50 (63B).
24764 *(new)* 6/10/54 (63B).

SHEDS:
Hull Botanic Gardens 14/7/36.
Stockton 4/7/38.
Hull Botanic Gardens 12/10/38.
Selby 17/7/49.
Scarborough 1/7/51.
Selby 21/10/51.
Scarborough 8/6/52.
Hull Botanic Gardens 9/1/55.
Scarborough 29/5/55.

RENUMBERED:
9867 10/2/46.
E9867 20/2/48.
69867 14/10/49.

CONDEMNED: 23/12/59.
Into Dar. for cut up 23/12/59.

2161

Darlington - Rebuilt
from Class H1.

To traffic 23/1/1936.

REPAIRS:
Dar. 22/2—15/6/39.**G.**
Dar. 21/7—7/9/39.**L.**
Dar. 24/8—1/10/42.**G.**
Dar. 10/2/43.*Weigh.*
Dar. 21/12/43.*Weigh.*
Dar. 27/4—25/5/44.**L.**
Dar. 31/10—27/11/44.**L.**
Dar. 19/2—30/3/46.**G.**
Ghd. 24/6—12/7/47.**L.**
Dar. 5/7—20/8/48.**G.**
Dar. 15—24/9/48.**N/C.**
Dar. 13/9—13/10/50.**G.**

2161 cont./
Positive lub. drive fitted.
Dar. 10/10—6/11/52.**G**.
Dar. 3—26/6/53.**C/H**.
Dar. 25/3—30/4/55.**G**.
Dar. 2—3/5/55.**N/C**.
Dar. 9—13/5/55.**N/C**.
Ghd. 16/9—7/10/55.**C/L**.
After collision.

BOILERS:
2457 (63A).
3036 *(new)* 15/6/39 (63B).
3040 *(ex1330)* 1/10/42 (63B).
2664 *(ex1500)* 30/3/46 (63A).
3904 *(new)* 20/8/48 (63B).
3904 reno.24686 13/10/50.
24739 *(ex69875)* 6/11/52 (63B).
24735 *(ex69874)* 30/4/55 (63B).

SHEDS:
Gateshead 23/1/36.
Middlesbrough 20/3/39.
West Hartlepool 20/5/41.
Middlesbrough 1/4/44.
Hull Botanic Gardens 29/4/46.
Saltburn 13/4/47.
West Auckland 2/1/49.

RENUMBERED:
9868 30/3/46.
69868 20/8/48.

CONDEMNED: 7/11/57.
Into Dar. for cut up 7/11/57.

2162

Darlington - Rebuilt
from Class H1.

To traffic 30/6/1931.

REPAIRS:
Dar. 13/7—6/8/31.**N/C**.
Dar. 24/8/31.**N/C**.
Dar. 1—11/7/32.**N/C**.
Dar. 17/8—15/9/33.**G**.
Dar. 2—8/8/34.**N/C**.
Dar. 7/9—17/10/34.**L**.
Dar. 25/9—1/11/35.**G**.
Dar. 5/2—25/3/36.**L**.
Dar. 17/8/38.*Weigh.*
Dar. 23/9—18/11/38.**G**.
Dar. 12/4—24/5/41.**G**.
Dar. 15/5—18/6/42.**L**.
Dar. 19/11/43—4/1/44.**G**.
Dar. 11—20/12/44.**N/C**.
Dar. 19/12/45—2/2/46.**G**.
Dar. 1/11—11/12/47.**L**.
Dar. 16/11—18/12/48.**G**.
Dar. 30/12/48—5/1/49.**N/C**.
Dar. 17—22/1/49.**N/C**.
Dar. 27/6—13/7/50.**C/L**.
Dar. 6/4—10/5/51.**G**.

Positive lub. drive fitted.
Dar. 16/12/52.*Weigh.*
Dar. 18/3—25/4/53.**G**.
Dar. 27/4—1/5/53.**N/C**.
Dar. 11/5—10/6/55.**G**.
Dar. 10/5—7/6/57.**H/I**.

BOILERS:
2375 *(new)* 30/6/31 (63).
D1091 *(ex2143)* 1/11/35 (63).
113 *(ex1499)* 18/11/38 (63A).
2664 *(ex1529)* 24/5/41 (63A).
2455 *(ex1328)* 4/1/44 (63A).
2468 *(ex2149)* 2/2/46 (63A).
116 *(ex9891)* 18/12/48 (63A).
24707 *(ex69866)* 10/5/51 (63A).
24688 *(ex69892)* 25/4/53 (63A).
24763 *(new)* 10/6/55 (63B).

SHEDS:
Heaton.
Darlington 16/12/31.
Middlesbrough 8/3/33.
West Auckland 1/1/40.
Middlesbrough 13/4/47.
Saltburn 29/1/50.
Middlesbrough 2/2/58.
Thornaby 1/6/58.

RENUMBERED:
9869 11/8/46.
69869 18/12/48.

CONDEMNED: 13/6/60.
Into Dar. for cut up 13/6/60.

1517

Darlington - Rebuilt
from Class H1.

To traffic 12/8/1936.

REPAIRS:
Dar. 17—26/8/36.**N/C**.
Dar. 15/2—22/6/39.**G**.
Dar. 8/4—4/6/41.**L**.
Dar. 4/1—10/2/43.**G**.
Dar. 15—20/2/43.**N/C**.
Dar. 13/2—14/3/45.**G**.
Dar. 19/6—19/7/47.**G**.
Dar. 22—30/7/47.**N/C**.
Dar. 26/8—2/9/47.**N/C**.
Ghd. 21/9—6/10/48.**L**.
Dar. 29/10—26/11/49.**G**.
Positive lub. drive fitted.
Dar. 3—31/10/51.**H/I**.
Dar. 26/9—1/11/52.**C/L**.
Dar. 25/8—25/9/53.**G**.
Dar. 3/8—16/9/55.**H/I**.
Dar. 30/8—28/9/57.**G**.
Dar. 30/9—2/10/57.**N/C**.

BOILERS:
117 (63A).

115 *(ex2147)* 10/2/43 (63A).
2465 *(ex1499)* 14/3/45 (63A).
115 *(ex9877)* 19/7/47 (63A).
3985 *(new)* 26/11/49 (63B).
3985 reno.24724 31/10/51.
24761 *(new)* 25/9/53 (63B).
24710 *(ex69850)* 28/9/57 (63B).

SHEDS:
Heaton.
Hull Botanic Gardens 23/9/36.
Stockton 27/5/39.
West Auckland 27/5/40.
Sunderland 22/6/58.

RENUMBERED:
9870 11/8/46.
69870 6/10/48.

CONDEMNED: 24/6/60.
Into Dar. for cut up 24/6/60.

1518

Darlington - Rebuilt
from Class H1.

To traffic 18/5/1933.

REPAIRS:
Dar. 4—13/9/33.**N/C**.
Dar. 4—19/1/34.**N/C**.
Dar. 8/6—24/9/34.**H**.
Dar. 2/1—25/2/35.**L**.
Dar. 6/6/35.*Weigh..*
Dar. 26/9/35.*Weigh.*
Dar. 2/3—18/4/36.**G**.
Dar. 21/4—4/5/36.**N/C**.
Dar. 3/9/36.*Weigh..*
Dar. 7/1—11/2/37.**L**.
Dar. 5/2—18/3/38.**G**.
Dar. 22/4—3/5/38.**N/C**.
Dar. 16—26/5/38.**N/C**.
Dar. 15/4—16/5/40.**G**.
Dar. 20—23/5/40.**N/C**.
Dar. 24/6—1/7/41.**N/C**.
Dar. 2/4—5/6/42.**H/I**.
Dar. 25/11/43—8/1/44.**H**.
Dar. 6/11—7/12/46.**G**.
Dar. 26—27/8/48.*Weigh.*
Dar. 15/6—5/8/49.**G**.
Positive lub. drive fitted.
Dar. 11—18/8/49.**N/C**.
Dar. 8—31/5/52.**H/I**.
Dar. 3—20/6/52.**N/C**.
Dar. 14/2—12/3/55.**G**.
Dar. 14—26/3/55.**N/C**.

BOILERS:
1293 (63).
2453 *(ex2153)* 18/3/38 (63A).
3060 *(new)* 16/5/40 (63B).
3048 *(ex2153)* 8/1/44 (63B).
3036 *(ex9876)* 7/12/46 (63B).
3982 *(new)* 5/8/49 (63B).

3982 reno. 24738 31/5/52.
24717 *(ex69850)* 12/3/55 (63B).

SHEDS:
Neville Hill.
Middlesbrough 22/5/33.
Darlington 5/7/34.
Saltburn 17/4/39.
West Hartlepool 16/5/41.
Darlington 2/10/55.

RENUMBERED:
9871 1/4/46.
69871 5/8/49.

CONDEMNED: 7/11/58.
Into Dar. for cut up 7/11/58.

1519

Darlington - Rebuilt
from Class H1.

To traffic 5/9/1934.

REPAIRS:
Dar. 26/8—11/10/35.**G**.
Dar. 23/9—20/11/36.**G**.
Dar. 8/12—9/12/36.**N/C**
Dar. 20/5—22/6/37.**N/C**.
Dar. 11/10—26/11/38.**G**.
Dar. 14/2—28/2/39.**N/C**.
Dar. 2/10—23/10/39.**L**.
Dar. 10/7—22/8/40.**L**.
Dar. 10/2—21/3/41.**G**.
Dar. 21/9—22/10/42.**G**.
Dar. 13—22/1/43.**N/C**.
War damage. Collision with
aircraft at Dinsdale.
Dar. 2—27/6/44.**G**.
Dar. 2/8/44.*Weigh.*
Dar. 17/11—21/12/45.**L**.
Dar. 29/6—30/8/46.**G**.
Dar. 17/12/46.*Weigh.*
Ghd. 1/10—16/10/47.**L**.
Dar. 11/11—17/12/48.**G**.
Dar. 17/8—23/9/50.**G**.
Positive lub. drive fitted.
Dar. 28/9—17/10/50.**N/C**.
Dar. 26/5—28/6/52.**G**.
Dar. 7—9/7/52.**N/C**.
Dar. 21/4—15/5/54.**G**.
Dar. 17—22/5/54.**N/C**.
Dar. 17/2/55.*Weigh.*
Dar. 13/1—8/2/56.**C/L**.
Dar. 2/5—12/6/56.**H/I**.
Dar. 22—26/6/56.**N/C**.

BOILERS:
3D/689 (63A).
D1316 *(ex2147)* 11/10/35 (63).
2827 *(new)* 20/11/36 (63C).
3066 *(new)* 21/3/41 (63B).
3367 *(new)* 27/6/44 (63B).
3040 *(ex2161)* 30/8/46 (63B).

1519 cont./
3908 *(new)* 17/12/48 (63B).
24682 *(ex69875)* 23/9/50 (63A).
24683 *(exA7 69775)* 28/6/52 (63B).
24762 *(new)* 15/5/54 (63B).

SHEDS:
Heaton.
Darlington 8/9/34.
Saltburn 10/4/39.
West Auckland 20/2/49.
Sunderland 15/9/57.

RENUMBERED:
9872 30/8/46.
69872 17/12/48.

CONDEMNED: 16/10/58.
Into Dar. for cut up 16/10/58.

1520

Darlington - Rebuilt
from Class H1.

To traffic 8/4/1935.

REPAIRS:
Dar. 1/2—19/3/37.**G.**
Dar. 18/4—17/5/40.**G.**
Dar. 27/3—15/4/41.**L.**
Dar. 7/6—3/7/43.**G.**
Ghd. 21/11—8/12/44.**L.**
Dar. 11/2—6/4/46.**G.**
Ghd. 9—22/3/47.**L.**
Dar. 28/3—3/4/47.**N/C.**
Dar. 21/6—13/8/48.**G.**
Dar. 17—21/8/48.**N/C.**
Dar. 10/1—10/2/51.**G.**
Positive lub. drive fitted.
Dar. 13/2/51.**N/C.**
Dar. 22/5/51.*Weigh.*
Dar. 2/7/51.*Weigh.*
Dar. 7/1/52.*Weigh.*
Dar. 10/3/52.*Weigh.*
Dar. 16/4—2/5/52.**C/L.**
Dar. 12/5/52.*Weigh.*
Dar. 9/9/52.*Weigh.*
Dar. 4/11/52.*Weigh.*
Dar. 4/2/53.*Weigh.*
Dar. 5/5/53.*Weigh.*
Dar. 10/11/53.*Weigh.*
Dar. 9/12/53—15/1/54.**G.**
Dar. 10/8—14/9/56.**G.**

BOILERS:
2376 (63).
3065 *(new)* 17/5/40 (63B).
2822 *(ex2154)* 3/7/43 (63C).
3060 *(ex1528)* 6/4/46 (63B).

3067 *(ex9884)* 13/8/48 (63B).
24698 *(ex69887)* 10/2/51 (63A).
24707 *(ex69869)* 15/1/54 (63A).
24765 *(new)* 14/9/56 (63B).

SHEDS:
Neville Hill.
Scarborough 22/5/35.
Hull Botanic Gardens 2/12/35.
Middlesbrough 12/9/48.
Hull Botanic Gardens 4/6/50.
Middlesbrough 19/11/50.
West Hartlepool 17/7/55.
Durham 15/9/57.
Sunderland 7/12/58.

RENUMBERED:
9873 6/4/46.
69873 13/8/48.

CONDEMNED: 8/2/60.
Into Dar. for cut up 8/2/60.

1523

Darlington - Rebuilt
from Class H1.

To traffic 25/4/1935.

REPAIRS:
Dar. 15/2—19/5/39.**G.**
Dar. 14/6—17/7/39.**N/C.**
Dar. 20/10—9/11/42.**L.**
Dar. 20/9—21/10/43.**G.**
Dar. 28/11/45—12/1/46.**G.**
Dar. 12/11—12/12/47.**G.**
Dar. 9—20/1/48.**N/C.**
Dar. 12/7—25/8/50.**G.**
Positive lub. drive fitted.
Dar. 3—28/11/52.**G.**
Dar. 9/3—2/4/55.**G.**
Dar. 4—7/4/55.**N/C.**
Dar. 12/9—18/10/57.**G.**
Dar. 12—18/11/57.**N/C.**

BOILERS:
2456 (63A).
2457 *(ex2161)* 19/5/39 (63A).
2458 *(ex2145)* 21/10/43 (63A).
114 *(ex2147)* 12/1/46 (63A).
D1251 *(ex9851)* 12/12/47 (63).
2824 *(exA6 69796)* 25/8/50 (63C).
24735 *(ex69880)* 28/11/52 (63B).
24732 *(exA7 69770)* 2/4/55 (63B).
24711 *(exA7 69784)* 18/10/57 (63B).

SHEDS:
Heaton.
Whitby 22/5/35.

Starbeck 26/2/40.
Sunderland 28/6/43.

RENUMBERED:
9874 7/7/46.
69874 25/8/50.

CONDEMNED: 20/5/60.
Into Dar. for cut up 20/5/60.

1528

Darlington - Rebuilt
from Class H1.

To traffic 3/1/1933.

REPAIRS:
Dar. 13/2—5/4/35.**G.**
Dar. 19/10—24/12/36.**G.**
Dar. 30/12/36—12/1/37.**N/C.**
Dar. 21/11/38—14/3/39.**G.**
Dar. 30/3—20/4/39.**N/C.**
Dar. 25/4—4/5/39.**N/C.**
Dar. 15/9—23/10/41.**G.**
Dar. 31/10—10/11/41.**N/C.**
Dar. 21/1—19/2/44.**G.**
Dar. 23/2—2/3/44.**N/C.**
Dar. 3/5/45.*Weigh.*
Dar. 31/7—3/9/45.**L.**
Dar. 23/1—23/2/46.**G.**
Dar. 6—16/12/46.**L.**
Ghd. 27/3—19/4/47.**L.**
Dar. 13/2—7/4/48.**G.**
Dar. 29/4/48.*Weigh.*
Dar. 22/5—21/6/50.**G.**
Positive lub. drive fitted.
Dar. 14/7—23/8/52.**G.**
Dar. 2/6/54.*Weigh.*
Dar. 20/10—23/11/54.**G.**
Dar. 25/9—2/11/56.**G.**

BOILERS:
2458 *(new)* (63A).
D1313 *(ex1500)* 14/3/39 (63).
2827 *(ex1519)* 23/10/41 (63C).
3060 *(ex1518)* 19/2/44 (63B).
2458 *(ex1523)* 23/2/46 (63A).
3362 *(ex9861)* 21/6/50 (63B).
24690 *(ex69889)* 23/8/52 (63A).
24716 *(ex69859)* 23/11/54 (63A).
24724 *(ex69854)* 2/11/56 (63B).

SHEDS:
Starbeck.
Darlington 29/5/34.
Saltburn 10/4/39.
West Auckland 20/2/49.
Sunderland 22/6/58.

RENUMBERED:
9875 14/7/46.
69875 7/4/48.

CONDEMNED: 20/5/60.
Into Dar. for cut up 20/5/60.

1529

Darlington - Rebuilt
from Class H1.

To traffic 5/5/1934.

REPAIRS:
Dar. 20/5—11/7/36.**G.**
Dar. 7/11—22/12/38.**G.**
Dar. 12—24/1/39.**N/C.**
Dar. 28/6—13/7/40.**L.**
Dar. 7/11—17/12/40.**G.**
Dar. 2—7/7/42.**N/C.**
Dar. 28/12/42—5/2/43.**G.**
Dar. 26/7—2/9/44.**H.**
Dar. 4/12/44.*Weigh.*
Dar. 6/3/45.*Weigh.*
Dar. 1/10/45.*Weigh.*
Dar. 27/10—24/11/45.**L.**
After collision.
Dar. 11/2/46.*Weigh.*
Dar. 25/9—7/11/46.**G.**
Dar. 15—30/11/46.**N/C.**
Dar. 12—21/11/47.**L.**
Dar. 1/12/48—3/1/49.**G.**
Dar. 11/7—18/8/49.**H.**
Dar. 23/2—4/3/50.**C/L.**
Dar. 6/2—10/3/51.**G.**
Positive lub. drive fitted.
Dar. 21/5/51.*Weigh.*
Dar. 3/7/51.*Weigh.*
Dar. 8/1/52.*Weigh.*
Dar. 11/3/52.*Weigh.*
Dar. 5/5/52.*Weigh.*
Dar. 26/8/52.*Weigh.*
Dar. 8—18/10/52.**C/L.**
After collision.
Dar. 5/11/52.*Weigh.*
Dar. 3/2/53.*Weigh.*
Dar. 12/5/53.*Weigh.*
Dar. 19/8—18/9/53.**G.**
Dar. 11/11/53.*Weigh.*
Dar. 17/9/57. *Not repaired.*

BOILERS:
D1251 (63).
D1107 *(ex1328)* 11/7/36 (63).
2664 *(ex2145)* 22/12/38 (63A).
2661 *(ex1525)* 17/12/40 (63A).
3036 *(ex2161)* 5/2/43 (63B).
2827 *(ex2143)* 7/11/46 (63C).
3040 *(ex9872)* 3/1/49 (63B).
24756 *(new)* 10/3/51 (63B).

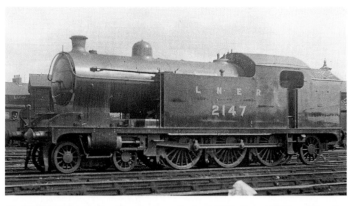

No.2147 left Leeds for Darlington shed on 27th June 1934 and by the 5th August the latter shed had removed the hopper top. No.1518 which was transferred to Darlington from Middlesbrough on 5th July 1934 whilst actually undergoing a heavy repair in Darlington works, had its hopper taken off by the works. No.1500 did not return to Starbeck on rebuilding but went to Darlington who took off the hopper by 27th May 1934, less than twelve days after fitting. No.1531 also went to Darlington shed on rebuilding in February 1934 and had lost its hopper by July.

No.1326 (9892 later) was rebuilt and got a hopper on 4th March 1935. It was transferred to Scarborough from Leeds eight days later but was back at Starbeck from 9th August 1940 to 28th June 1943 where its hopper served its original purpose, and it was one of the four still so fitted when withdrawn 5th November 1958.

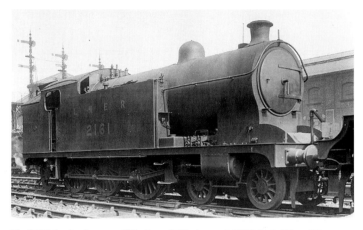

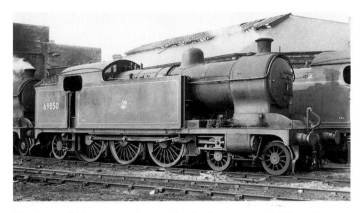

No.2161 had a hopper fitted on 27th August 1933 but did not become an A8 until 23rd January 1936. By then, sufficient A8's were already available for coast line needs, but it did not return to Starbeck when it was rebuilt, being sent to Gateshead shed instead. However, it was one of the four which retained the hopper through to withdrawal as No.69868 in November 1957. No.1528, with a hopper from 13th January 1933 as an A8, did go back to Starbeck until 29th May 1934 when it then went to Darlington to meet coast line requirements and by 29th November 1934 that shed had removed its hopper.

The four which managed to retain the hoppers to withdrawal were: 69850, 69868, 69892 and 69894.

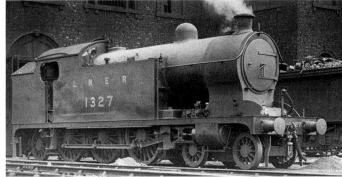

At rebuilding, steel plate buffer beams and Group Standard buffers replaced the sandwich type beam and buffers of NER design. For some years the buffer heads were circular instead of elliptical as they had been on H1 class.

(left) No.9873, as 1520 of H1 class, got its hopper on 21st September 1933 but only became Class A8 on 8th April 1935 when it did return to Leeds although only briefly, because it left for Scarborough on 22nd May 1935 and then moved to Hull Botanic Gardens shed on 2nd December 1935. When transferred to Middlesbrough in November 1950 it still had the hopper, but that shed removed it in the summer of 1954.

During the war there was a gradual return to elliptical heads, although the other parts remained Group Standard.

Evidently the circular hollow spindles could twist in the shanks leading to some curious buffer head positions.

On rebuilding there was no change to the whistles, which continued to be organ pipe on the driver's side and bell shape on the fireman's, although the change of driving position needed the whistles to be transposed.

Not every engine had its whistle type changed over. On this one they remained as they had been when it was a right hand driven engine.

At the front end, heater connection and hose were continued as standard equipment as the engines were required to operate equally well with either end leading. During and immediately after the 1939-45 war fuel restrictions led to carriage heating being curtailed and in many cases the hose was removed although the front end connection was retained. As fuel restrictions eased, it was possible to replace the carriage warming hose at the front end.

Beginning in June 1935 on No.2143, new whistle gear was fitted and there was a gradual change to only a single whistle. On this one, with a Diagram 63A boiler, the twin mounting was retained with the organ pipe discarded. On Diagram 63C boilers (*see* page 64, bottom) a manifold was provided and the single whistle was on the cab front just below the roof. Diagram 63B boilers had their single whistle on the firebox above an isolating valve (*see* page 65 top, left).

1529 cont./
24744 *(ex69890)* 18/9/53 (63B).

SHEDS:
Heaton.
Scarborough 29/5/34.
Starbeck 16/10/34.
Darlington 30/9/35.
Saltburn 10/4/39.
Hull Botanic Gardens 11/6/50.
Middlesbrough 19/11/50.

RENUMBERED:
9876 14/7/46.
69876 3/1/49.

CONDEMNED: 21/10/57.
Cut up at Darlington.

1531

Darlington - Rebuilt
from Class H1.

To traffic 23/2/1934.

REPAIRS:
Dar. 30/7/35.*Weigh.*
Dar. 23/10—6/12/35.**G.**
Dar. 4/10—19/11/37.**G.**
Dar. 22/11—2/12/37.**N/C.**
Dar. 10—21/12/37.**N/C.**
Dar. 23/3—28/4/39.**L.**
Dar. 9/7—22/8/40.**G.**
Dar. 29/1—3/3/43.**G.**
Dar. 18/4—12/6/45.**G.**
Dar. 13/5—14/6/47.**G.**
Dar. 24—30/6/47.**N/C.**
Dar. 29/11/49—4/1/50.**G.**
Positive lub. drive fitted.
Dar. 11/11—6/12/52.**G.**
Dar. 15/12/52—3/1/53.**N/C.**
Dar. 18/12/56—19/1/57.**G.**
Dar. 21—23/1/57.**N/C.**
Dar. 12/3—22/3/57.**C/L.**

BOILERS:
D1103 (63).
  2468 *(ex1501)* 6/12/35 (63A).
  117 *(ex1517)* 3/3/43 (63A).
  115 *(ex1517)* 12/6/45 (63A).
  3031 *(ex9858)* 14/6/47 (63B).
  3367 *(ex9850)* 4/1/50 (63B).
24686 *(ex69868)* 6/12/52 (63B).
24730 *(ex69855)* 19/1/57 (63B).

SHEDS:
Starbeck.
Darlington 3/3/34.
Middlesbrough 10/4/39.
West Auckland 1/1/40.
Hull Botanic Gardens 30/5/48.
Scarborough 4/6/50.
Selby 19/11/50.

Neville Hill 1/7/51.
Selby 21/10/51.
Neville Hill 11/5/52.
Malton 7/6/53.
York 21/10/56.
Malton 3/3/57.
Neville Hill 15/9/57.
Scarborough 8/4/58.

RENUMBERED:
9877 11/8/46.
69877 4/1/50.

CONDEMNED: 30/12/59.
Into Dar. for cut up 30/12/59.

1499

Darlington - Rebuilt
from Class H1.

To traffic 24/6/1936.

REPAIRS:
Dar. 2—15/7/36.**N/C.**
Dar. 27/7—3/8/36.**N/C.**
Dar. 26/8—13/10/36.**L.**
After collision.
Dar. 15/12/36—7/1/37.**L.**
Dar. 30/7—19/8/37.**N/C.**
Dar. 14/9—27/10/38.**G.**
Dar. 6/3—14/4/42.**G.**
Dar. 6/12/44—25/1/45.**G.**
Dar. 22/8—27/9/47.**G.**
Dar. 25/11/49—12/1/50.**C/L.**
Dar. 16/6—1/8/50.**G.**
Positive lub. drive fitted.
Dar. 19/3—12/4/52.**H/I.**
Dar. 15—21/4/52.**N/C.**
Dar. 9—15/7/52.**N/C.**
Dar. 2/3—2/4/55.**G.**
Dar. 12—18/4/55.**N/C.**
Dar. 10/1/57.*Weigh.*
Dar. 14/1—15/2/58.**G.**
Dar. 17—19/2/58.**N/C.**

BOILERS:
  113 (63A).
  2467 *(ex2148)* 27/10/38 (63A).
  2465 *(ex2158)* 14/4/42 (63A).
D1219 *(ex2157)* 25/1/45 (63).
  2662 *(ex9883)* 27/9/47 (63A).
  2466 *(ex69880)* 1/8/50 (63A).
  2466 reno.24734 12/4/52.
24747 *(exA7 69774)* 2/4/55 (63B).
24732 *(ex69874)* 15/2/58 (63B).

SHEDS:
Middlesbrough 24/6/36
Hull Botanic Gardens 4/6/50.
Middlesbrough 19/11/50.
West Hartlepool 8/9/57.
Sunderland 15/9/57.

RENUMBERED:
9878 14/7/46.
69878 12/1/50.

CONDEMNED: 24/6/60.
Into Dar. for cut up 24/6/60.

Because of a clerical blunder
during the compilation of the
Thompson renumbering scheme,
No.**1500/9879** does not follow
the sequence of the 1946
numbering and instead follows
the usual order of construction.
Therefore 1500 will be found
after No.**1326/9892**.

1501

Darlington - Rebuilt
from Class H1.

To traffic 23/1/1934.

REPAIRS:
Dar. 30/9—15/11/35.**G.**
Dar. 25/10—14/12/37.**G.**
Dar. 29/6—1/9/38.**L.**
Dar. 15/5—8/6/40.**G.**
Dar. 11—24/6/40.**N/C.**
Dar. 20/1—25/2/42.**L.**
Dar. 21/3—24/4/44.**G.**
Dar. 27—31/4/46.**L.**
Dar. 4/6—10/10/47.**G.**
Dar. 4/4—5/5/49.**C/L.**
Dar. 7—10/2/50.**C/L.**
Dar. 15—21/3/50.**C/L.**
Dar. 9/5—10/6/50.**G.**
Positive lub. drive fitted.
Dar. 25/8—19/9/52.**G.**
Dar. 9—13/11/54.**C/L.**
Dar. 22/3—4/5/55.**G.**
Dar. 4/4—4/5/57.**G.**
Dar. 24/5—18/6/57.**C/L.**
After collision.

BOILERS:
  2468 *(new)* (63A).
  115 *(ex1519)* 15/11/35 (63A).
D1282 *(ex2144)* 14/12/37 (63).
  2376 *(ex1520)* 8/6/40 (63).
  2466 *(ex2159)* 24/4/44 (63A).
  3031 *(ex9877)* 10/6/50 (63B).
24740 *(ex69858)* 19/9/52 (63B).
24738 *(ex69871)* 4/5/55 (63B).
24697 *(ex69858)* 4/5/57 (63B).

SHEDS:
Heaton.
Darlington 19/6/34.
Middlesbrough 5/7/34.
Whitby 22/8/34.
Neville Hill 24/10/34.
Malton 5/9/40.

Neville Hill 5/3/42.
Middlesbrough 19/10/42.
Whitby 30/5/48.
Middlesbrough 11/7/48.
Hull Botanic Gardens 4/6/50.
Middlesbrough 19/11/50.
Saltburn 13/6/54.
West Hartlepool 10/11/57.

RENUMBERED:
9880 30/8/46.
69880 5/5/49.

CONDEMNED: 23/6/60.
Into Dar. for cut up 23/6/60.

1502

Darlington - Rebuilt
from Class H1.

To traffic 16/4/1936.

REPAIRS:
Dar. 30/11/37—28/1/38.**H.**
Dar. 1/9/38.*Weigh.*
Dar. 22/4—17/6/39.**G.**
Dar. 22/6—3/7/39.**N/C.**
Dar. 18/5—21/6/43.**G.**
Dar. 11—18/6/45.**L.**
Dar. 23/3—2/5/46.**G.**
Dar. 8—16/5/46.**N/C.**
Dar. 27/9—22/10/48.**G.**
Dar. 17/4—3/6/50.**C/H.**
Dar. 5—7/6/50.**N/C.**
Dar. 11—18/5/51.**C/L.**
Dar. 3/7—11/8/51.**G.**
Dar. 25/2/54.*Weigh.*
Dar. 30/9—4/11/54.**H/I.**
Positive lub. drive fitted.
Dar. 5/6/56.*Weigh.*
Dar. 22/5/58. *Not repaired.*

BOILERS:
  2463 (63A).
  116 *(ex1524)* 21/6/43 (63A).
  2822 *(ex1520)* 2/5/46 (63C).
  3060 *(ex9873)* 22/10/48 (63B).
  3060 reno.24713 18/5/51.
24714 *(ex69876)* 11/8/51 (63B).

SHEDS:
Heaton.
Scarborough 6/6/36.
Starbeck 26/2/40.
Scarborough 12/3/45.
Hull Botanic Gardens 9/1/55.
Scarborough 29/5/55.
Neville Hill 9/12/56.
Scarborough 16/6/57.

RENUMBERED:
9881 2/5/46.
69881 22/10/48.

1502 cont./
CONDEMNED: 2/6/58.
Cut up at Darlington.

1503

Darlington - Rebuilt
from Class H1.

To traffic 13/2/1936.

REPAIRS:
Dar. 10/6/36.*Weigh.*
Dar. 2/5—11/6/38.**G.**
Dar. 29/7/38.*Weigh.*
Dar. 30/5/39.*Weigh.*
Dar. 15/8/39.*Weigh.*
Dar. 30/4—31/5/40.**G.**
Dar. 28/7—5/9/42.**G.**
Dar. 7—12/9/42.**N/C.**
Dar. 27/4—25/5/44.**G.**
Dar. 2/2— 2/3/16.**G.**
Dar. 15/6—1/10/48.**G.**
Dar. 4—13/10/48.**N/C.**
Dar. 21—29/10/48.**N/C.**
Dar. 25/5—17/6/50.**C/L.**
Dar. 19—20/6/50.**N/C.**
Dar. 5/6—6/7/51.**G.**
Positive lub. drive fitted.
Dar. 22/1—18/7/53.**C/H.**
Ghd. 7/10—3/11/54.**C/L.**
Dar. 16/3—22/4/55.**G.**

BOILERS:
2659 *(new)* (63A).
2453 *(ex1518)* 31/5/40 (63A).
D1208 *(ex1521)* 5/9/42 (63).
2373 *(ex1500)* 25/5/44 (63).
2455 *(ex2162)* 2/3/46 (63A).
2463 *(ex9866)* 1/10/48 (63A).
24702 *(ex69869)* 6/7/51 (63A).
24706 *(exA7 69783)* 22/4/55
(63B).

SHEDS:
Blaydon.
Darlington 29/5/36.
Saltburn 10/4/39.
Scarborough 17/7/49.
Whitby 1/10/50.
Neville Hill 19/11/50.
Whitby 19/7/53.
Neville Hill 20/9/53.
Whitby 6/6/54.
Neville Hill 19/9/54.
Hull Botanic Gardens 10/6/56.
Middlesbrough 14/7/57.
Thornaby 1/6/58.

RENUMBERED:
9882 15/9/46.
69882 1/10/48.

CONDEMNED: 19/11/58.
Into Dar. for cut up 19/11/58.

1524

Darlington - Rebuilt
from Class H1.

To traffic 9/8/1934.

REPAIRS:
Dar. 24/8—7/9/34.**N/C.**
Dar. 22/4—13/6/36.**G.**
Dar. 24/9/37.*Weigh.*
Dar. 25/4—9/6/38.**G.**
Dar. 9—21/6/38.**N/C.**
Dar. 22/7—5/9/40.**G.**
Dar. 8/3—10/4/43.**G.**
Dar. 2/2—7/6/45.**H.**
Dar. 28/6—12/9/47.**G.**
Dar. 4—27/8/49.**G.**
Positive lub. drive fitted.
Dar. 29/8—2/9/49.**N/C.**
Dar. 17—26/9/49.**N/C.**
Dar. 9—17/11/49.**C/L.**
Dar. 25/7—6/9/51.**G.**
Dar. 10—12/9/51.**N/C.**
Dar. 13/9—16/10/54.**G.**
Dar. 15/1—11/2/57.**C/H.**
Dar. 17/6—2/8/57.**H/I.**
Dar. 12/8—14/8/57.**N/C.**

BOILERS:
D1287 *(exH1 1330)* (63).
114 *(ex2155)* 13/6/36 (63A).
116 *(ex1526)* 5/9/40 (63A).
2662 *(ex1527)* 10/4/43 (63A).
2465 *(ex9870)* 12/9/47 (63A).
3059 *(ex69858)* 27/8/49 (63B).
24710 *(ex69857)* 6/9/51 (63B).
24767 *(new)* 16/10/54 (63B).

SHEDS:
Darlington.
Middleton in Teesdale 16/7/38.
Saltburn 22/3/39.
Stockton 11/6/50.
Middlesbrough 5/10/52.
Northallerton 9/11/52.
Middlesbrough 1/3/53.
Stockton 7/6/53.
Middlesbrough 20/9/53.
West Hartlepool 14/2/54.
Durham 15/9/57.
Sunderland 7/12/58.

RENUMBERED:
9883 15/9/46.
69883 27/8/49.

CONDEMNED: 1/6/60.
Into Dar. for cut up 1/6/60.

1525

Darlington - Rebuilt
from Class H1.

To traffic 14/6/1933.

REPAIRS:
Dar. 20/7—1/8/33.**N/C.**
Dar. 29/3—10/5/35.**G.**
Dar. 6/8—18/9/36.**G.**
Dar. 22/9—6/10/36.**N/C.**
Dar. 7—20/10/36.**N/C.**
Dar. 23/6—17/8/38.**G.**
Dar. 19/8—7/9/38.**N/C.**
Dar. 12—21/9/38.**N/C.**
Dar. 30/9—7/10/38.**N/C.**
Dar. 23/9—31/10/40.**G.**
Dar. 11/11—14/12/42.**G.**
Dar. 31/8/43.*Weigh.*
Dar. 16/6—14/7/44.**G.**
Dar. 3/9/45.*Weigh.*
Dar. 9/1—9/2/46.**G.**
Dar. 16—25/2/46.**N/C.**
Ghd. 21/4—3/5/47.**L.**
Dar. 8/6—16/7/48.**G.**
Dar. 5—13/8/48.**N/C.**
Dar. 28/2—16/3/49.**C/L.**
Ghd. 26/9/49—11/1/50.**C/L.**
Dar. 3/10—2/11/50.**G.**
Positive lub. drive fitted.
Dar. 7—21/5/51.**C/L.**
After collision.
Dar. 18—24/1/52.**C/L.**
Dar. 7/7—16/8/52.**G.**
Dar. 18—27/8/52.**N/C.**
Dar. 7/8—24/9/54.**G.**
Dar. 1—28/10/54.**N/C.**
Dar. 4/9—5/10/56.**G.**

BOILERS:
D1267 (63).
2661 *(new)* 10/5/35 (63A).
114 *(ex1524)* 31/10/40 (63A).
D1251 *(ex2150)* 14/12/42 (63).
D1208 *(ex1503)* 14/7/44 (63).
3067 *(ex spare &2151)* 9/2/46
(63B).
3901 *(new)* 16/7/48 (63B).
24685 *(ex69894)* 2/11/50 (63B).
24682 *(ex69872)* 16/8/52 (63A).
24693 *(ex spare)* 24/9/54 (63C).
24766 *(exA7 69788)* 5/10/56
(63B).

SHEDS:
Darlington.
Middleton in Teesdale 22/3/39.
Saltburn 20/5/39.
West Hartlepool 10/11/57.

RENUMBERED:
9884 5/1/47.
69884 16/7/48.

CONDEMNED: 4/11/58.
Into Dar. for cut up 4/11/58.

1526

Darlington - Rebuilt
from Class H1.

To traffic 20/5/1936.

REPAIRS:
Dar. 24/6—25/7/40.**G.**
Dar. 11/12/44—13/1/45.**G.**
Dar. 10/7—12/9/47.**G.**
Dar. 26/6—23/8/48.**G.**
Dar. 17/4—13/5/50.**G.**
Positive lub. drive fitted.
Dar. 9/4—9/5/53.**H/I.**
Dar. 11—14/5/53.**N/C.**
Dar. 27/6/56.*Weigh.*
Dar. 8—14/2/57.**C/L.**
Dar. 7/5—8/6/57.**G.**

BOILERS:
116 *(exH1 1527)* (63A).
D1293 *(ex2152)* 25/7/40 (63).
2375 *(ex2144)* 13/1/45 (63).
2455 *(ex9882)* 23/8/48 (63A).
3056 *(ex69856)* 13/5/50 (63B).
3056 reno.24745 9/5/53.
24738 *(ex69880)* 8/6/57 (63B).

SHEDS:
Scarborough 20/5/36.
Selby 6/10/41.
Starbeck 8/7/42.
Selby 1/8/42.
Scarborough 12/3/45.
Selby 21/10/51.
Scarborough 8/6/52.
Neville Hill 9/12/56.
Scarborough 16/6/57.
Neville Hill 15/9/57.
Scarborough 8/6/58.

RENUMBERED:
9885 27/10/46.
69885 23/8/48.

CONDEMNED: 20/6/60.
Into Dar. for cut up 20/6/60.

1527

Darlington - Rebuilt
from Class H1.

To traffic 28/5/1936.

REPAIRS:
Dar. 4/8—25/9/39.**G.**
Dar. 20—30/6/42.**N/C.**
Dar. 4/2—13/3/43.**G.**
Dar. 16/11—22/12/44.**L.**
Dar. 6/6—1/12/45.**G.**
Dar. 5—8/12/45.**N/C.**
Ghd. 6—19/12/46.**L.**
Dar. 14/11—24/12/47.**G.**

This 63C boiler had a manifold and whistle similar to that of 2160 (page 65) when new and put on No.2154 in October 1937. But by 1946 as shown here, on sister engine 9881 (ex1502), the whistle had been moved to the firebox and mounted above an isolating valve as on diagram 63B boilers.

This was the original arrangement of fixing the tanks and bunker to the boiler and running plate and it proved inadequate.

When altered to a single whistle on the 63A twin mounting, it was usually the high pitch bellshape which was kept but this shows that at least one retained its organ pipe and until after Nationalisation. The photograph of 69864 on page 68 shows the engine did get a bellshape whistle in 1951, still on a 63A twin mounting but that was after a change of boiler.

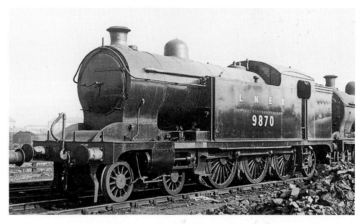

Beginning with No.1500, ex works 29th March 1944, strengthening was provided by fitting a length of angle-iron along the bottom of the tank and also the bunker. The projection of the base of the angle-iron provided a better toe-hold than the original running plate did. This extra fitting was quite independent of the type of boiler which was carried, this one having Diagram 63A.

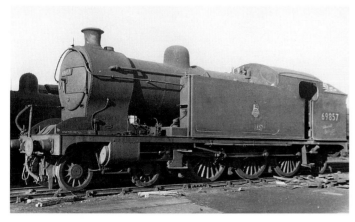

This is the standard whistle on Diagram 63B boiler which the whole class except one carried at withdrawal.

Before the fixing at the base of the tanks was begun, those which got 63C and 63B boilers were fitted with an inverted T-strap connecting the top of the tanks and this was a separate modification.

The standard arrangement on all four boiler diagrams was two washout plugs on the left side. On the Diagram 63 and 63A boilers the cladding had circular plates fixed over them.

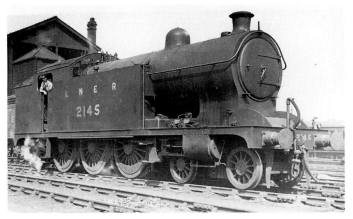

On the right hand side there were three plugs which, in the re-designed 63C and 63B boilers were superseded by handholes.

Class A8 were provided with the same sanding arrangement which was steam operated, and none ever got Downs' sanding equipment. Sand could be applied ahead of the coupled wheels for either direction of running. Note GS buffers were also fitted at the bunker end.

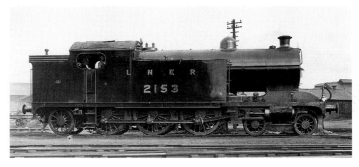

Blower control was always internal, through the boiler as it had been on H1 class, a most unusual NER feature. Note the bunker vent pipe has been extended to suit a cage but No.2153 never got one. Later, this engine had a standard vent pipe for three-rail bunker (*see* page 69 bottom, left).

For main lubrication there were two NER design mechanical lubricators on the right hand running plate and driven off the inside motion. One fed the three cylinders and valves and the other supplied the three coupled axleboxes, on that side of the engine. A similar lubricator on the left hand running plate fed the axleboxes on that side.

Beginning with No.9859 on 1st February 1947, a positive drive for the lubricators was fitted. This was taken from the connecting rod big end on both sides of the engine through linkage. No.9853 (8/2/47) and 9865 (15/2/47) were also fitted similarly, and then no more were done until 69892 out 9th February 1949. By March 1950 a total of thirteen had been so fitted.

(*left*) Front sandboxes were on the running plate ahead of the tank and they were never enlarged as they were on A7 class.

1527 cont./
Dar. 2—8/1/48.**N/C.**
Dar. 10/10/49.*Weigh.*
Dar. 19/12/49—24/1/50.**G.**
Positive lub. drive fitted.
Dar. 17/8—17/9/51.**G.**
Dar. 7/4—14/5/54.**G.**
Dar. 27/3—27/4/57.**G.**

BOILERS:
2374 *(exH1 2151)* (63).
2662 *(ex2158)* 25/9/39 (63A).
2661 *(ex1529)* 13/3/43 (63A).
3069 *(ex1530)* 1/12/45 (63B).
2821 *(exA6 9799)* 24/12/47
(63C).
3983 *(new)* 24/1/50 (63B).
3983 reno.24719 17/9/51.
24726 *(ex69853)* 14/5/54 (63B).
24708 *(ex69893)* 27/4/57 (63B).

SHEDS:
Heaton.
Whitby 29/5/36.
Starbeck 26/2/40.
Scarborough 12/3/45.
West Auckland 29/9/46.
Scarborough 4/6/50.
Hull Botanic Gardens 25/9/55.
Malton 16/2/58.

RENUMBERED:
9886 16/12/46.
69886 24/1/50.

CONDEMNED: 21/6/60.
Into Dar. for cut up 21/6/60.

1327

Darlington - Rebuilt
from Class H1.

To traffic 10/1/1934.

REPAIRS:
Dar. 19/1—8/2/34.**N/C.**
Dar. 29/8/35.*Weigh.*
Dar. 16/10—29/11/35.**G.**
Dar. 31/12/36.*Weigh.*
Dar. 25/1—29/4/38.**G.**
Dar. 30/4—11/5/38.**N/C.**
Dar. 14—19/9/39.**N/C.**
Dar. 16/4—17/5/40.**L.**
Dar. 2/6—1/8/41.**G.**
Dar. 2/11—24/12/43.**G.**
Dar. 5—31/1/44.**L.**
After collision.
Dar. 7—27/9/44.**L.**
Dar. 21/3—27/4/46.**G.**
Dar. 7/5—11/6/48.**G.**

Dar. 15—24/6/48.**N/C.**
Dar. 14/12/50—20/1/51.**G.**
Positive lub. drive fitted.
Dar. 8/1—7/2/53.**H/I.**
Dar. 9—10/2/53.**N/C.**
Dar. 25/4—21/5/55.**G.**
Dar. 23—27/5/55.**N/C.**
Dar. 31/8—27/10/55.**C/L.**
After collision.

BOILERS:
D1310 (63).
2375 *(ex2162)* 29/11/35 (63).
113 *(ex2162)* 1/8/41 (63A).
2457 *(ex1523)* 24/12/43 (63A).
2373 *(ex1503)* 27/4/46 (63).
2661 *(ex9856)* 11/6/48 (63A).
24752 *(new)* 20/1/51 (63B).
24739 *(ex69868)* 21/5/55 (63B).

SHEDS:
Heaton.
Darlington 19/6/34.
Middlesbrough 5/7/34.
Blaydon 30/1/39.
Sunderland 31/10/41.
Blaydon 5/10/47.
Sunderland 15/11/47.
Darlington 10/6/56.

RENUMBERED:
9887 27/4/46.
69887 11/6/48.

CONDEMNED: 16/12/59.
Into Dar. for cut up 16/12/59.

1329

Darlington - Rebuilt
from Class H1.

To traffic 1/5/1934.

REPAIRS:
Dar. 18/6—8/8/36.**G.**
Dar. 22/9/36.*Weigh.*
Dar. 15/11/37—22/1/38.**G.**
Dar. 17/2/39.*Weigh.*
Dar. 13/3/39.*Weigh.*
Dar. 5/9—18/10/39.**G.**
Dar. 20/4/42.*Weigh.*
Dar. 17/7—29/8/42.**L/I.**
Dar. 21—30/10/43.**L.**
Dar. 17/5—17/6/44.**G.**
Dar. 27/10/44.*Weigh.*
Dar. 5/3/45.*Weigh.*
Dar. 20/8/45.*Weigh.*
Dar. 15/1/46.*Weigh.*
Dar. 7/9—12/10/46.**G.**
Ghd. 24/2—2/4/47.**L.**

After collision.
Dar. 9/3—9/4/49.**G.**
Positive lub. drive fitted.
Dar. 26/9—14/10/49.**C/L.**
Dar. 12/9—4/10/51.**C/L.**
Dar. 25/3—23/4/52.**G.**
Dar. 5/6—5/7/52.**C/H.**
Dar. 4/1—4/2/55.**G.**
Dar. 14—16/2/55.**N/C.**

BOILERS:
D1274 *(exH1 1526)* (63).
115 *(ex1501)* 22/1/38 (63A).
2374 *(ex1527)* 18/10/39 (63).
2376 *(ex1501)* 17/6/44 (63).
113 *(ex2148)* 12/10/46 (63A).
2467 *(ex9879)* 9/4/49 (63A).
24730 *(ex69853)* 23/4/52 (63B).
24689 *(ex69867)* 4/2/55 (63B).

SHEDS:
Heaton.
Scarborough 29/5/34.
Heaton 6/11/34.
Darlington 30/9/35.
Middlesbrough 20/3/39.
Blaydon 18/11/40.
West Hartlepool 27/12/41.
Middlesbrough 11/6/42.
Whitby 30/5/48.
Hull Botanic Gardens 25/9/55.

RENUMBERED:
9888 14/4/46.
69888 9/4/49.

CONDEMNED: 1/10/58.
Into Dar. for cut up 1/10/58.

1330

Darlington - Rebuilt
from Class H1.

To traffic 26/5/1934.

REPAIRS:
Dar. 30/10—27/12/35.**G.**
Dar. 19/12/38.*Weigh.*
Dar. 17/4—30/6/39.**G.**
Dar. 7—24/10/40.**N/C.**
Dar. 25/7—3/9/42.**G.**
Dar. 20/6—27/7/44.**G.**
Dar. 31/10/44.*Weigh.*
Dar. 9/3/45.*Weigh.*
Dar. 4/9/45.*Weigh.*
Dar. 11/1/46.*Weigh.*
Dar. 17/5/46.*Weigh.*
Dar. 14/6—4/10/46.**G.**
Dar. 18/11—24/12/48.**G.**
Dar. 6/11—9/12/50.**G.**

Positive lub. drive fitted.
Dar. 13/6—10/7/52.**G.**
Dar. 5/2/53.*Weigh.*
Dar. 27/5—26/6/54.**G.**
Dar. 18/4—18/5/57.**G.**
Dar. 20—21/5/57.**N/C.**
Dar. 3—6/6/57.**N/C.**

BOILERS:
2453 *(exH1 2149)* (63A).
D1310 *(ex1327)* 27/12/35 (63).
3040 *(new)* 30/6/39 (63B).
3059 *(ex2143)* 3/9/42 (63B).
3066 *(ex1519)* 27/7/44 (63B).
2822 *(ex9881)* 24/12/48 (63C).
24690 *(ex69892)* 9/12/50 (63A).
24736 *(exA7 69770)* 10/7/52
(63B).
24719 *(ex69886)* 26/6/54 (63B).
24757 *(exA7 69781)* 18/5/57
(63B).

SHEDS:
Middlesbrough 24/5/34.
Stockton 29/5/34.
Saltburn 11/9/42.
Middlesbrough 19/9/54.
Sunderland 15/9/57.

RENUMBERED:
9889 19/5/46.
69889 24/12/48.

CONDEMNED: 30/5/60.
Into Dar. for cut up 30/5/60.

1521

Darlington - Rebuilt
from Class H1.

To traffic 9/10/1935.

REPAIRS:
Dar. 11/10—27/11/37.**G.**
Dar. 30/10—29/11/39.**G.**
Dar. 2/8/40.*Weigh.*
Dar. 26/11—24/12/40.**L.**
Dar. 8/7—27/8/41.**L.**
Dar. 6/7—22/8/42.**G.**
Dar. 14/3—4/4/44.**L.**
Dar. 6/10—10/11/45.**G.**
Dar. 21/12/45—19/1/46.**L.**
After collision.
Ghd. 1—13/12/46.**L.**
Dar. 13/12/47—16/1/48.**G.**
Dar. 5/5—3/6/50.**G.**
Positive lub. drive fitted.
Dar. 5—7/6/50.**N/C.**
Dar. 26/2—1/4/53.**G.**
Dar. 13/3/56.*Weigh.*

WORKS CODES:- Cw - Cowlairs. Dar- Darlington. Don - Doncaster. Ghd - Gateshead. Gor - Gorton. Inv - Inverurie. Str - Stratford. Tux - Tuxford.
REPAIR CODES:- **C/H** - Casual Heavy. **C/L** - Casual Light. **G** - General. **H**- Heavy. **H/I** - Heavy Intermediate. **L** - Light. **L/I** - Light Intermediate. **N/C** - Non-Classified.

1521 cont./
Dar. 11/1/58. *Not repaired.*

BOILERS:
D1208 (63).
D1063 *(ex2143)* 27/11/37 (63).
D1208 *(ex2147)* 29/11/39 (63).
 2377 *(ex1522)* 22/8/42 (63).
 2456 *(ex2155)* 10/11/45 (63A)
 114 *(ex9874)* 16/1/48 (63A).
 3981 *(new)* 3/6/50 (63B).
 24684 *(ex69894)* 1/4/53 (63B).

SHEDS:
Gateshead 5/10/35.
Darlington 16/7/36.
Middlesbrough 20/3/39.
West Auckland 1/1/40.
Hull Botanic Gardens 4/1/41.
Whitby 15/8/48.
York 19/2/56.
Whitby 10/6/56.
Malton 30/6/57.

RENUMBERED:
 9890 12/10/46.
 69890 3/6/50.

CONDEMNED: 13/1/58.
Cut up at Darlington.

1328

Darlington - Rebuilt
from Class H1.

To traffic 14/5/1934.

REPAIRS:
Dar. 12/5—4/9/36.**G.**
Dar. 25/4/39.*Weigh.*
Dar. 4/12/39—16/1/40.**G.**
Dar. 10/12/40—9/1/41.**L.**
Dar. 15/4/42.*Weigh.*
Dar. 5/10—4/11/43.**G.**
Ghd. 30/11—20/12/44.**L.**
Dar. 26/3—17/4/45.**L.**
Dar. 21/6—20/7/46.**G.**
Dar. 2/7—6/9/47.**L.**
Dar. 29/9—22/10/48.**G.**
Dar. 27/6—5/8/50.**G.**
Positive lub. drive fitted.
Dar. 8—10/8/50.**N/C.**
Dar. 28/5—21/6/52.**G.**
Dar. 23—24/6/52.**N/C.**
Dar. 21/10—5/11/52.**C/L.**
After collision.
Dar. 8—15/7/53.**C/L.**
Dar. 18/9—30/10/53.**C/L.**
Dar. 28/6—24/7/54.**G.**
Dar. 24/6—8/7/57.**C/L.**
After collision.

BOILERS:
D1107 *(exH1 1500)* (63)

D1251 *(ex1529)* 4/9/36 (63).
 2455 *(ex2146)* 16/1/40 (63A).
 2463 *(ex1502)* 4/11/43 (63A).
 116 *(ex1502)* 20/7/46 (63A).
 2375 *(ex9885)* 22/10/48 (63).
 2455 *(ex69885)* 5/8/50 (63A).
 24733 *(ex69856)* 21/6/52 (63C)
 24769 *(new)* 24/7/54 (63B).

SHEDS:
Heaton.
Stockton 29/5/34.
West Hartlepool 25/8/42.
Saltburn 6/10/46.
Middlesbrough 19/9/54.
Thornaby 1/6/58.

RENUMBERED:
 9891 31/3/46.
 69891 22/10/48.

CONDEMNED: 16/9/58.
Into Dar. for cut up 16/9/58.

1326

Darlington - Rebuilt
from Class H1.

To traffic 4/3/1935.

REPAIRS:
Dar. 14/2—11/5/39.**G.**
Dar. 24/5—3/6/59.**N/C.**
Dar. 5—15/6/39.**N/C.**
Dar. 29/11/43—8/1/44.**G.**
Dar. 14/8/44.*Weigh.*
Dar. 15/10—16/11/46.**G.**
Ghd. 22/10—19/11/47.**L.**
Dar. 31/12/48—9/2/49.**G.**
Positive lub. drive fitted.
Dar. 11—16/3/49.**N/C.**
Dar. 30/11/49—5/1/50.**H.**
Dar. 6/3/50.*Weigh.*
Dar. 11/10—8/11/50.**G.**
Dar. 14—24/3/51.**C/L.**
After collision.
Dar. 24/3/52.*Weigh.*
Dar. 28/11/52—10/1/53.**G.**
Dar. 20/12/54—22/1/55.**G.**
Dar. 9—11/2/55.**N/C.**
Dar. 29/10—1/12/56.**H/I.**

BOILERS:
D1278 (63).
D1102 *(ex1530)* 11/5/39 (63).
D1282 *(ex2148)* 8/1/44 (63).
 2659 *(ex2159)* 16/11/46 (63A)
 2453 *(ex9862)* 9/2/49 (63A).
 24688 *(ex69855)* 8/11/50 (63A)
 24741 *(ex69874)* 10/1/53 (63C)
 24720 *(ex69865)* 22/1/55 (63B)

SHEDS:
Neville Hill.

Scarborough 12/3/35.
Starbeck 9/8/40.
West Hartlepool 28/6/43.
Saltburn 6/10/46.
West Hartlepool 10/11/57.

RENUMBERED:
 9892 1/9/46.
 69892 9/2/49.

CONDEMNED: 5/11/58.
Into Dar. for cut up 5/11/58.

1500

Darlington - Rebuilt
from Class H1.

To traffic 19/5/1934.

REPAIRS:
Dar. 16/3—22/5/36.**G.**
Dar. 26/5—6/6/36.**N/C.**
Dar. 18/6—9/7/36.**N/C.**
Dar. 19/1—24/3/39.**G.**
Dar. 20/8—8/10/41.**G.**
Dar. 28/1—4/2/42.**N/C.**
Dar. 10/7—17/8/42.**N/C.**
Dar. 1—29/3/44.**G.**
Dar. 6/2—16/3/46.**G.**
Dar. 10—30/1/48.**L.**
Dar. 27/10—26/11/48.**G.**
Dar. 22/10—17/11/51.**G.**
Positive lub. drive fitted.
Dar. 19—21/11/51.**N/C.**
Dar. 3/5—4/6/55.**G.**

BOILERS:
D1313 *(exH1 1328)* (63)
D1287 *(ex2155)* 24/3/39 (63).
 2373 *(ex2144)* 8/10/41 (63).
 2664 *(ex2162)* 29/3/44 (63A).
 2467 *(ex1522)* 16/3/46 (63A).
 2457 *(ex9855)* 26/11/48 (63A)
 24758 *(new)* 17/11/51 (63B).
 24715 *(exA7 69779)* 4/6/55
 (63B).

SHEDS:
Starbeck.
Darlington 29/5/34.
Middlesbrough 5/7/34.
West Auckland 1/1/40.
Hull Botanic Gardens 30/5/48.
Selby 17/7/49.
Scarborough 1/7/51.
Hull Botanic Gardens 25/9/55.

RENUMBERED:
 9879 16/3/46.
 E9879 30/1/48.
 69879 26/11/48.

CONDEMNED: 20/11/58.
Into Dar. for cut up 20/11/58.

1522

Darlington - Rebuilt
from Class H1.

To traffic 8/2/1934.

REPAIRS:
Dar. 26/11/35—22/1/36.**G.**
Dar. 30/5—22/7/38.**G.**
Dar. 25—29/7/38.**N/C.**
Dar. 1—8/8/38.**N/C.**
Dar. 9/7—21/8/40.**G.**
Dar. 14/9/40.*Weigh.*
Dar. 3/3—21/5/42.**G.**
Dar. 9/3—15/4/43.**H.**
After collision.
Dar. 16—21/4/43.**N/C.**
Dar. 27/9—28/10/43.**L.**
Dar. 17/10—16/11/44.**L.**
Dar. 14/12/45—26/1/46.**G.**
Dar. 19/2—1/3/46.**N/C.**
Dar. 9—19/3/46.**N/C.**
Dar. 26/6—24/9/48.**G.**
Dar. 12—15/10/48.**N/C.**
Dar. 22/1—17/2/51.**G.**
Positive lub. drive fitted.
Dar. 18/10—3/11/52.**C/H.**
Dar. 29/12/53—30/1/54.**G.**
Dar. 1—2/2/54.**N/C.**
Dar. 9/2—2/3/54.**N/C.**
Dar. 22/5—2/7/56.**G.**

BOILERS:
D1327 (63).
D1103 *(ex1531)* 22/1/36 (63).
 2466 *(ex2156)* 22/7/38 (63A).
 2377 *(ex2148)* 21/8/40 (63).
 2467 *(ex1499)* 21/5/42 (63A).
 3366 *(new)* 26/1/46 (63B).
 24695 *(ex69852)* 17/2/51 (63B)
 24708 *(ex69857)* 30/1/54 (63B)
 24743 *(ex69863)* 2/7/56 (63B).

SHEDS:
Blaydon.
Stockton 29/5/34.
Gateshead 27/6/35.
Darlington 31/12/36.
Saltburn 17/4/39.
West Hartlepool 28/2/42.
Durham 15/9/57.

RENUMBERED:
 9893 17/11/46.
 69893 24/9/48.

CONDEMNED: 19/11/58.
Into Dar. for cut up 19/11/58.

1530

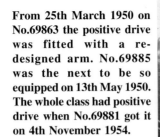

Darlington - Rebuilt
from Class H1.

To traffic 9/3/1935.

REPAIRS:
Dar. 15/2—5/4/37.**G**.
Dar. 27/2—8/6/39.**G**.
Dar. 24/12/41—31/1/42.**G**.
Dar. 17/11—16/12/44.**G**.
Dar. 18/5—15/6/46.**L**.
Dar. 12/9—17/10/47.**G**.
Ghd. 3—27/1/49.**L**.
Dar. 29/8—30/9/50.**G**.
Positive lubrication drive fitted.
Dar. 2—5/10/50.**N/C**.
Dar. 16—17/10/50.**N/C**.
Dar. 31/10—9/11/50.**N/C**.
Dar. 19/1—5/3/53.**G**.
Dar. 7/6—15/7/55.**G**.
Dar. 13/6—12/7/57.**G**.
Dar. 15—19/7/57.**N/C**.

BOILERS:
D1102 (63).
　3031 *(new)* 8/6/39 (63B).
　3069 *(new)* 31/1/42 (63B).
　3050 *(ex2158)* 16/12/44 (63B).
　3369 *(ex9861)* 17/10/47 (63B).
24684 *(ex69872)* 30/9/50 (63B).
24760 *(new)* 5/3/53 (63B).
24688 *(ex69869)* 15/7/55 (63A).
24719 *(ex69889)* 12/7/57 (63B).

SHEDS:
Starbeck.
Neville Hill 30/9/35.
Selby 19/10/42.
Scarborough 12/3/45.
Hull Botanic Gardens 4/6/50.
Saltburn 19/8/51.
West Hartlepool 10/11/57.

RENUMBERED:
　9894 20/10/46.
69894 27/1/49.

CONDEMNED: 23/6/60.
Into Dar. for cut up 23/6/60.

From 25th March 1950 on No.69863 the positive drive was fitted with a re-designed arm. No.69885 was the next to be so equipped on 13th May 1950. The whole class had positive drive when No.69881 got it on 4th November 1954.

When rebuilt to 4-6-2 type all the class had black paint with single red lining and with a lining panel on the front buffer beam on the first engine.

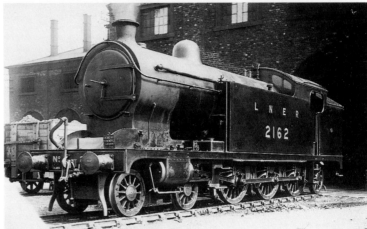

Single red lining continued to be used until the early days of the war, although with plain red front buffer beam.

From mid-1942 the 7½in. LNER was replaced by just NE but in 12in. transfers, and the black became increasingly roughly applied. Two had NE still when they were renumbered with Gill sans style unshaded figures. No.2145, ex works 8th December 1945 with NE was changed to 9852 on Sunday 20th October 1946 at Whitby shed whilst 2150, out on 11th August 1945, was made 9857 on Sunday 27th October at Blaydon shed. Another example was No.1499 which had NE when ex works 25th January 1945 and was renumbered 9878 on Sunday 14th July 1946 and continued as such until it next went for repair on 22nd August 1947.

From mid-January 1946 LNER in the smaller letters was restored and five engines got it in conjunction with their original numbers: 1522 ex works 26th January, reno.9893 17th November; 2162 ex works 2nd February, reno.9869 11th August; 1525 ex works 9th February, reno.9884 5th January 1947; 1528 ex works 23rd February, reno.9875 14th July; 1503 ex works 2nd March, reno.9882 15th September. Restoration of LNER was done at works and, apart from the above five, was combined with the 1946 number. No.9873 was ex works 6th April 1946.

Only nine months after its September 1947 general repair, No.9885 was in works again on 26th June 1948 for a change of boiler. When out 23rd August it had not been repainted but had got is BR number which was still on the tank, and had true Gill sans 6 and 9 which were also used on the front buffer beam as no smokebox plate was put on.

After the war, stocks of letter and figure transfers were not renewed to save the cost of them and by December 1946 Darlington had changed to yellow painted and unshaded Gill sans characters but with modified 6 and 9. One A8 got this style during 1946, nineteen in 1947 and one as late as January 1948: 9851 (7/11), 9853 (8/2), 9858 (26/4), 9859 (1/2), 9860 (11/1), 9861 (14/7), 9863 (7/11), 9864 (18/1), 9865 (15/2), 9870 (19/7), 9871 (7/12/46), 9874 (12/12), 9877 (14/6), 9878 (27/9), 9880 (10/10), 9883 and 9885 (both 12/9), 9886 (24/12), 9890 (16/1/48), 9891 (6/9), and 9894 (17/10).

Starting with No.69854, ex works 18th June 1948, a number plate was fitted on the smokebox door and the first five cast had modified 6 and 9 on them. On three, Nos.69854, 69857 (9th July) and 69884 (16th July), the figures on the bunker had been reduced to the same height as the letters on the tank. These figures also had the modified 6 and 9.

From mid January to mid March 1948, British Railways used a regional prefix letter E to the engine number. No.9879, last painted in March 1946 had a light repair 10th to 30th January 1948 when Darlington added the E. This was the only A8 so treated. Two others got the E prefix but combined with BRITISH RAILWAYS. They were: E9856 (28th March) and E9867 (20th February). Just one, 69875, had 12in. figures combined with 10in. BRITISH RAILWAYS (7th April).

Although the plates of 69873 (13th August) and 69852 (27th August) had modified 6 and 9, those on the bunker were true Gill sans, which was used thereafter.

From the end of August 1948 until November 1949 this was the standard painting - unlined black with 10in. high letters and figures in Gill sans and with a number plate on the smokebox door. No.69876 was ex works 3rd January 1949.

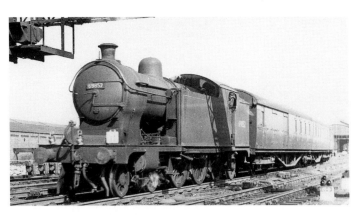

The five which had the modified 6 and 9 on the smokebox door plate continued to carry that style and were not corrected.

In July 1949 it was decided to discard the lettering to save the expense of applying it, and to use a transfer in its place showing the BR emblem. Supplies of the transfer were slow in reaching Darlington so some engines went back to traffic in unlined black and plain tank sides. Among them were three A8's Nos.69883 (27th August), 69853 (2nd September) and 69850 (17th September).

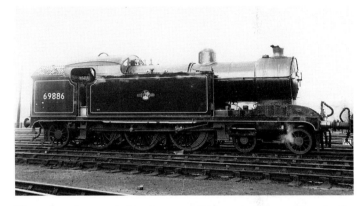

The only subsequent change was replacement of the emblem by the crest and only twelve were so done: 69850, 69861, 69869, 69870, 69874, 69878, 69880, 69883, 69885, 69886, 69889 and 69894. The first to get the crest was 69886, ex works 27th April 1957 and on the right hand side all had this wrong style with the lion facing forward to the right. None survived to have this heraldic gaffe corrected.

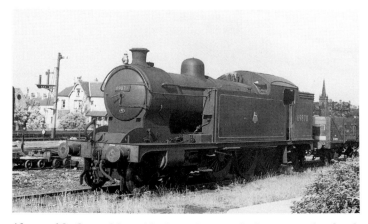

Along with the emblem A8 class also acquired two panels of red, cream and grey lining. No.69870, ex works 26th November 1949 being the first so treated. All then duly got the lining applied.

The class became extinct when Nos.69870 and 69878 were withdrawn 24th June 1960. Seen here at Darlington scrap yard, No.69860 had been withdrawn on 14th June 1960 and 69869 on the 13th June 1960.

(above) **During 1922 No.2143 was used for tests between Haxby and Strensall to see if bogie mounted pick-up shoes could successfully contact third-rail sections at 70 m.p.h.. The tests were in conjunction with the projected York to Newcastle electrification and to whether to use third rail in open country and overhead catenary at the bigger stations and junctions. The tests were completed and the trial equipment was removed from No.2143 during 1922, it having been decided to use overhead current collection only.**

(centre) **Until 1930 all forty-five had Schmidt superheater with a handwheel control valve mounted on the side of the smokebox to allow steam through the elements. These boilers were LNER Diagram 63.**

On replacement boilers built from July 1930 onwards, classified 63A, the Robinson superheater was used and a Gresley anti-vacuum valve provided protection from burning for the elements. No H1 chimney carried a capuchon.

CLASS H 1

2143

Darlington.

To traffic 10/1913.

REPAIRS:
Dar. ?/?—?/8/21.**G.**
Dar. 27/2—24/5/23.**G.**
Dar. 12/3—16/5/24.**L.**
Dar. 31/3—18/8/25.**G.**
Dar. 11/11/27—28/2/28.**G.**
Dar. 30/1—8/3/29.**L.**
Dar. 24/4—19/7/30.**G.**
Dar. 23/7—2/8/30.**N/C.**
Dar. 17/8—30/9/31.**H.**
Into Darlington 20/4/33
for rebuilding to Class A8.

BOILERS:
  D245.
D1107 *(new)* ?/8/21.
D1091 *(ex1528)* 30/9/31.

SHEDS:
Neville Hill.
Middlesbrough 12/6/33.

2144

Darlington.

To traffic 10/1913.

REPAIRS:
Dar. ?/?—?/5/22.**G.**
Dar. 11/1—26/3/24.**G.**
Dar. 26/1—18/6/26.**G.**
Dar. 14/10/27—23/1/28.**G.**
Ghd. 8/11/29—13/1/30.**G.**
Ghd. 22/3—29/4/32.**G.**
Into Darlington 16/1/35 for
rebuilding to Class A8.

BOILERS:
  D250.
  D245 *(ex2143)* ?/5/22.
D1282 *(ex1329)* 29/4/32.

SHEDS:
Saltburn.
Gateshead 28/5/28.

2145

Darlington.

To traffic 11/1913.

REPAIRS:
Dar. 6/12/22—24/2/23.**G.**
Dar. 24/1—28/3/24.**G.**
Dar. 23/11/25—27/4/26.**G.**
Dar. 20/9—30/12/27.**G.**
Dar. 25/3—7/6/29.**G.**
Dar. 20/6—31/7/30.**L.**
Dar. 5—18/8/30.**N/C.**
Ghd. 10/11—21/12/31.**G.**
Dar. 22/12/33—31/1/34.**G.**
Into Darlington 10/12/35 for
rebuilding to Class A8.

BOILERS:
  D252.
  D306 *(ex2162)* 7/6/29.
D1199 *(ex1499)* 31/1/34.

SHEDS:
Saltburn.
Middlesbrough 16/5/29.
Heaton 26/6/30.

2146

Darlington.

To traffic 11/1913.

REPAIRS:
Dar. 10/1—29/3/24.**G.**
Dar. 4/9—17/12/25.**G.**
Dar. 1/4—30/7/27.**G.**
Dar. 18/8—6/9/27.**L.**
Ghd. 20/6—21/8/29.**G.**
Ghd. 3/2—26/3/31.**G.**
Dar. 19/1—29/3/33.**G.**
Into Darlington 11/2/35 for
rebuilding to Class A8.

BOILERS:
D254.
D256 *(ex spare)* 30/7/27.
2455 *(new)* 29/3/33 *(63A).*

SHEDS:
Saltburn.
Gateshead 28/5/28.

2147

Darlington.

To traffic 12/1913.

REPAIRS:
Dar. 19/12/23—8/3/24.**G.**
Dar. 14—29/4/24.**L.**
Dar. 6/11/25—29/1/26.**G.**
Dar. 10/10/27—11/1/28.**G.**
Dar. 19/3—16/4/29.**N/C.**
Dar. 25/11/29—22/1/30.**G.**
Into Darlington 11/1/33 for
rebuilding to Class A8.

BOILERS:
  D256.
  D300 *(ex2161)* 19/1/26.
D1316 *(ex1326)* 22/1/30.

SHED:
Neville Hill.

2148

Darlington.

To traffic 12/1913.

REPAIRS:
Dar. 23/2—17/5/23.**G.**
Dar. 14—29/8/23.**L.**
Dar. 4/3—13/7/25.**G.**
Dar. 27—31/7/25.**N/C.**
Dar. 10—31/8/25.**L.**
Dar. 30/3—28/6/27.**G.**
Ghd. 19/2—16/4/29.**G.**
Ghd. 25/11/30—21/1/31.**G.**
Ghd. 29/1—17/2/31.**L.**
Ghd. 19/7—4/8/32.**L.**
Dar. 6/11—22/12/33.**G.**
Into Darlington 17/1/36 for
rebuilding to Class A8.

BOILERS:
  D261.
  2467 *(new)* 22/12/33 *(63A).*

SHEDS:
Saltburn.
Gateshead 28/5/28.
Heaton 19/6/34.
Neville Hill 28/6/34.

2149

Darlington.

To traffic 12/1913.

REPAIRS:
Dar. 27/9—13/11/23.**G.**
Dar. 17/6—29/9/25.**G.**
Dar. 29/10—9/11/25.**L.**
Dar. 7—16/7/26.**L.**
Dar. 12/4—17/8/27.**G.**
Ghd. 29/10—23/12/29.**G.**
Ghd. 7—15/1/30. *Paint.*
Ghd. 7/7—20/9/32.**G.**
Into Darlington 26/3/34 for
rebuilding to Class A8.

BOILERS:
D263.
  2453 *(new)* 20/9/32 *(63A).*

SHEDS:
Saltburn.
Blaydon 28/5/28.

2150

Darlington.

To traffic 1/1914.

REPAIRS:
Dar. 3/9—19/11/23.**G.**
Dar. 15/9—22/12/25.**G.**
Dar. 9/9—25/11/27.**G.**
Ghd. 23/9—12/11/29.**G.**
Ghd. 4/9—9/10/31.**G.**
Dar. 19/9—26/10/33.**G.**
Into Darlington 11/3/35 for
rebuilding to Class A8.

BOILERS:
D265.
  2373 *(new)* 9/10/31.

SHEDS:
Saltburn.
Blaydon 28/5/28.

WORKS CODES:- Cw - Cowlairs. Dar- Darlington. Don - Doncaster. Ghd - Gateshead. Gor - Gorton. Inv - Inverurie. Str - Stratford. Tux - Tuxford.
REPAIR CODES:- **C/H** - Casual Heavy. **C/L** - Casual Light. **G** - General. **H** - Heavy. **H/I** - Heavy Intermediate. **L** - Light. **L/I** - Light Intermediate. **N/C** - Non-Classified.

All twenty-eight built to June 1920 had three coal rails with plating on the inside of them, and nine of those, Nos.2153, 2154, 2157, 2159, 2160, 1517, 1519, 1523 and 1529 kept this arrangement.

The class was somewhat prone to rolling at speed and ex works 5th April 1929, No.1499 had been fitted with side bearings to its bogies. No others were so altered apart from No.2144, but their front bogies kept the side bearers to withdrawal.

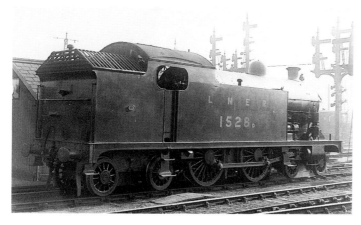

The other thirty-six had the rails replaced by a cage which had inward sloping sides but the three rails across the back were retained. The final seventeen - No.1499 built in June 1921 and those built later - had the cage from new.

From new Ross 'pop' safety valves were fitted and they had a circular casing around the base. All were fitted with Raven fog signalling apparatus, the striker being visible behind the trailing coupled wheels. Whilst they were still Class H1 it was removed from Nos.1503, 1517, 1526, 1527, 2145, 2148, 2151, 2152, 2156 and 2160.

In 1933 three, Nos.1530 (March) of Starbeck shed, 2161 (August) and 1520 (September), both of Neville Hill shed, had a hopper top added to aid coaling at the mechanical plant at the Leeds depot.

The 1930 built boilers were single plate and they did not have a casing at the base of the safety valves. Note the pipe from firebox to the cab.

CLASS H 1

2151

Darlington.

To traffic 12/1913.

REPAIRS:
Dar. 13/3—29/6/23.**G.**
Dar. 10/3—28/5/25.**G.**
Dar. 11/7—20/9/27.**G.**
Ghd. 9/7—5/9/29.**G.**
Ghd. 19—25/3/31.**L.**
Ghd. 9/10—13/11/31.**G.**
Dar. 3/10—17/11/33.**G.**
*Into Darlington 11/3/36 for
rebuilding to Class A8.*

BOILERS:
D269.
D254 *(ex2146)* 20/9/27.
2374 *(new)* 13/11/31.

SHEDS:
Saltburn.
Darlington 1-7/24.
Saltburn ?/2/25.
Blaydon 28/5/28.

2152

Darlington.

To traffic 12/1913.

REPAIRS:
Ghd. 22/9—3/12/23.**G.**
Dar. 3/6—25/9/25.**G.**
Dar. 30/9—9/10/25.**L.**
Dar. 12/7—7/10/27.**G.**
Dar. 19/10—3/11/27.**L.**
Ghd. 26/7—3/10/29.**G.**
Ghd. 10/11—8/12/30.**L.**
Ghd. 6/11—24/12/31.**G.**
Dar. 14/12/33—20/1/34.**G.**
*Into Darlington 7/1/36 for
rebuilding to Class A8.*

BOILERS:
D272.
2377 *(new)* 24/12/31.

SHEDS:
Saltburn.
Blaydon 28/5/28.

2153

Darlington.

To traffic 12/1913.

REPAIRS:
Ghd. 14/4—18/6/23.**G.**
Ghd. 25/6—18/7/23.**L.**
Ghd. 25/5—19/8/25.**G.**

Dar. 11/4—27/6/28.**G.**
Ghd. 8—21/8/29.**L.**
Ghd. 1/4—28/5/30.**G.**
Ghd. 11—22/7/30.**L.**
*Into Darlington 2/5/34 for
rebuilding to Class A8.*

BOILERS:
D276.
D1022 *(ex1520)* 27/6/28.

SHED:
Gateshead.

2154

Darlington.

To traffic 12/1913.

REPAIRS:
Ghd. 11/2—9/4/24.**G.**
Ghd. 6/2—25/4/28.**G.**
Ghd. 26/8—6/9/29.**L.**
Ghd. 2/6—25/7/30.**G.**
Dar. 27/4—30/5/33.**G.**
*Into Darlington 31/5/35 for
rebuilding to Class A8.*

BOILERS:
D280.
D294 *(ex2159)* 25/4/28.
1D/689 *(new exNBL)* 25/7/30
(63A).
D1106 *(ex2158)* 30/5/33.

SHED:
Gateshead.

2155

Darlington.

To traffic 2/1914.

REPAIRS:
Ghd. 23/1—12/4/23.**G.**
Ghd. 8/9/25—15/1/26.**G.**
Ghd. 12/9—18/10/27.**L.**
Dar. 5/3—25/5/28.**G.**
Dar. 16/9—4/10/29.**N/C.**
Dar. 27/6—12/9/30.**G.**
*Into Darlington 10/8/32 for
rebuilding to Class A8.*

BOILERS:
D283.
2D/689 *(new exNBL)* 12/9/30
(63A).

SHEDS:
Gateshead.
Middlesbrough 2/12/27.
Saltburn 16/5/29.
Heaton 26/6/30.

2156

Darlington.

To traffic 2/1914.

REPAIRS:
Ghd. 26/4—27/7/23.**G.**
Ghd. 25/2—16/6/27.**G.**
Ghd. 17/12/29—12/2/30.**G.**
Dar. 10/10—22/11/33.**G.**
*Into Darlington 11/6/35 for
rebuilding to Class A8.*

BOILERS:
D285.
D290 *(ex spare)* 16/6/27.
D280 *(ex spare)* 12/2/30.
2466 *(new)* 22/11/33 *(63A).*

SHEDS:
Gateshead.
Heaton 21/7/26.
Blaydon 27/6/28

2157

Darlington.

To traffic 2/1914.

REPAIRS:
Ghd. ?/?—29/12/22.**G.**
Ghd. 25/1/23—7/3/23.**L.**
Ghd. 28/4—17/8/25.**G.**
Ghd. 22/3—20/4/26.**L.**
Ghd. 12/12/27—7/3/28.**G.**
Ghd. 8—22/8/29.**L.**
Ghd. 22/7—17/9/30.**G.**
Ghd. 24/10—4/11/30.**L.**
Dar. 2/11/32—3/1/33.**G.**
*Into Darlington 12/3/35 for
rebuilding to Class A8.*

BOILERS:
D289.
D1102 *(ex 1529)* 17/9/30.
D1063 *(ex 1528)* 3/1/33.

SHEDS:
Heaton.
Gateshead 21/8/29.

2158

Darlington.

To traffic 3/1914.

REPAIRS:
Ghd. 14/6—9/9/24.**G.**
Ghd. 9/2—16/4/26.**G.**
Ghd. 22/12/27—8/3/28.**G.**
Ghd. 3—18/4/28.**L.**
Ghd. 25/9—11/10/29.**L.**

Ghd. 14/4—7/5/30.**G.**
Dar. 23/2—6/4/33.**G.**
*Into Darlington 18/3/35 for
rebuilding to Class A8.*

BOILERS:
D290.
D1106 *(new)* 9/9/24.
D1301 *(ex 1530)* 6/4/33.

SHEDS:
Heaton.
Gateshead 21/8/29.

2159

Darlington.

To traffic 3/1914.

REPAIRS:
Ghd. 20/3—28/5/24.**G.**
Ghd. 23/11/25—5/2/26.**G.**
Ghd. 6/10—15/12/27.**G.**
Ghd. 7/11—24/12/29.**G.**
Ghd. 11/5—4/7/32.**G.**
Dar. 16—22/6/33.**N/C.**
*Into Darlington 22/5/34 for
rebuilding to Class A8.*

BOILERS:
D294.
D1067 *(ex 1519)* 15/12/27.

SHED:
Heaton.

2160

Darlington.

To traffic 3/1914.

REPAIRS:
Ghd. 11/4—4/5/23.**L.**
Ghd. 6—19/9/24.**L.**
Ghd. 5/5—27/8/25.**G.**
Ghd. 14/2—8/3/27.**L.**
Ghd. 4/11/27—25/1/28.**G.**
Ghd. 10—25/4/29.**L.**
Ghd. 10/4—6/6/30.**G.**
Ghd. 26/11/31—8/1/32.**G.**
Dar. 5/10—4/11/33.**G.**
Dar. 12/9—9/11/34.**L.**
Dar. 6—14/12/34.**N/C.**
*Into Darlington 1/4/36 for
rebuilding to Class A8.*

BOILERS:
D298.
5D/689 *(new exNBL)* 6/6/30
(63A).
2465 *(new)* 4/11/33 *(63A).*

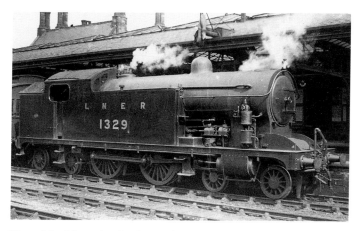

The original fastening for the smokebox door was by wheel and handle; a few kept this arrangement to rebuilding.

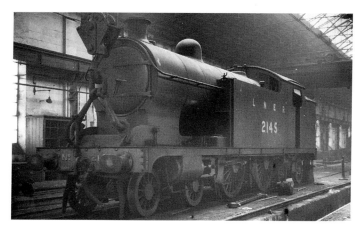

Until into the 1930's the front end of the frames did not have lifting holes in them. Apart from No.2162, the rest of the class were given lifting holes in the frames whilst they were still Class H1.

Even by 1923 the wheel on the smokebox door was being replaced by another handle and most were so altered.

At Grouping the whole class still had only Westinghouse brake on the engine and for train brakes. They had a short standpipe for connection.

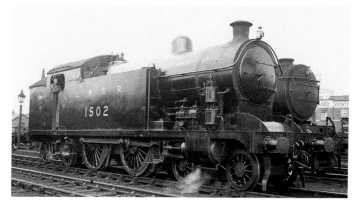

Steam reversing gear was standard on this class and was retained until rebuilding to Class A8.

In November 1923 No.1500, shedded at Starbeck, and in March 1924 No.1531, shedded at Neville Hill, had vacuum brakes added for train working. No standpipe was provided, the hose connection being from a union below the buffer beam. Note the number has been applied to the opposite side of the bufferbeam to what was customary. No.1500 stands alongside the south wall of Leeds (City) station awaiting a return working to Harrogate.

2160 cont./
SHEDS:
Heaton.
Gateshead 21/8/29.
Heaton 19/6/34.
Duns 12/7/34.

2161

Darlington.

To traffic 4/1914.

REPAIRS:
Dar. 7/5—31/7/24.**G.**
Dar. 7/7—7/9/25.**G.**
Dar. 21/10/27—28/1/28.**G.**
Dar. 5/7—16/8/28.**L.**
Dar. 22/11/28—4/1/29.**L.**
Dar. 17/6—19/7/29.**N/C.**
Dar. 5/5—15/8/30.**G.**
Dar. 8/5—27/8/33.**G.**
Into Darlington 4/11/35 for
rebuilding to Class A8.

BOILERS:
D300.
D250 *(ex2144)* 7/9/25.
2457 *(new)* 27/8/33 *(63A).*

SHED:
Starbeck.

2162

Darlington.

To traffic 4/1914.

REPAIRS:
Dar. 23/2—11/5/23.**G.**
Dar. 12/11/24—27/2/25.**G.**
Dar. 17/11/26—30/3/27.**G.**
Dar. 28/6—10/8/28.**L.**
Dar. 12/3—10/5/29.**G.**
Into Darlington 6/3/31 for
rebuilding to Class A8.

BOILERS:
D306.
D276 *(ex2153)* 10/5/29.

SHEDS:
Saltburn.
Middlesbrough 16/5/29.
Heaton 26/6/30.

1517

Darlington.

To traffic 5/1920.

REPAIRS:
Ghd. 3/12/23—13/2/24.**G.**
Ghd. 6/8—27/10/25.**G.**
Ghd. 28/9/27—12/1/28.**G.**
Ghd. 5—22/11/29.**L.**
Ghd. 6/7—19/8/31.**G.**
Dar. 6/12/33—16/1/34.**G.**
Into Darlington 19/5/36 for
rebuilding to Class A8.

BOILERS:
D1064.
5D/689 *(ex2160)* 16/1/34 *(63A).*

SHEDS:
Gateshead.
Heaton 21/7/26.
Blaydon 27/6/28.
Heaton 12/7/34.

1518

Darlington.

To traffic 6/1920.

REPAIRS:
Dar. 8/12/23—15/3/24.**G.**
Dar. 8/9—7/10/24.**L.**
Dar. 29/9/25—7/1/26.**G.**
Dar. 28/5—30/8/27.**G.**
Dar. 25/4—25/6/29.**G.**
Dar. 10—11/7/29.**N/C.**
Dar. 28/8—21/10/30.**G.**
Into Darlington 22/9/32 for
rebuilding to Class A8.

BOILERS:
D1063.
D1293 *(ex1327)* 21/10/30.

SHED:
Neville Hill.

1519

Darlington.

To traffic 6/1920.

REPAIRS:
Ghd. 26/9—28/11/23.**G.**
Ghd. 12/5—13/8/25.**G.**
Ghd. 4/7—3/10/27.**G.**
Ghd. 12/3—17/5/29.**G.**

Ghd. 3—18/6/29.**L.**
Ghd. 26/2—2/4/31.**G.**
Ghd. 16—23/4/31. *Returned to*
be painted.
Dar. 12/12/32—31/1/33.**G.**
Into Darlington 23/4/34 for
rebuilding to Class A8.

BOILERS:
D1067.
D285 *(ex2156)* 3/10/27.
3D/689 *(new exNBL)* 2/4/31
(63A).

SHED:
Heaton.

1520

Darlington.

To traffic 6/1920.

REPAIRS:
Dar. 20/10/23—12/1/24.**G.**
Dar. 12/6—7/7/24.**L.**
Dar. 16/4—17/7/25.**G.**
Dar. 21/8—18/9/25.**L.**
Dar. 24/11—30/12/25.**L.**
Dar. 16/7—29/10/27.**G.**
Dar. 29/4—3/7/29.**G.**
Dar. 8/9—30/10/31.**G.**
Dar. 17/8—21/9/33.**G.**
Into Darlington 17/1/35 for
rebuilding to Class A8.

BOILERS:
D1022.
D269 *(ex2151)* 29/10/27.
D252 *(ex2145)* 3/7/29.
2376 *(new)* 30/10/31.

SHEDS:
Starbeck.
Neville Hill 14/8/26.

1523

Darlington.

To traffic 6/1920.

REPAIRS:
Ghd. 15/11/23—1/2/24.**G.**
Ghd. 3/7—21/9/25.**G.**
Ghd. 21/10—3/11/25.**L.**
Ghd. 7/3—16/6/27.**G.**
Ghd. 13/1—28/3/29.**G.**
Ghd. 12/3/31—27/4/31.**G.**
Dar. 7/3—26/4/33.**G.**
Into Darlington 4/2/35 for

rebuilding to Class A8.

BOILERS:
D1019.
D289 *(ex2157)* 27/4/31.
2456 *(new)* 26/4/33 *(63A).*

SHEDS:
Heaton.
Blaydon 27/6/28.
Heaton 12/7/34.

1528

Darlington.

To traffic 6/1920.

REPAIRS:
Dar. 5/11/23—7/2/24.**G.**
Dar. 21/5—11/9/25.**G.**
Dar. 16/6—9/9/27.**G.**
Dar. 14/3—24/5/29.**G.**
Dar. 20/10—8/12/30.**G.**
Dar. 22—31/12/30.**N/C.**
Into Darlington 7/6/32 for
rebuilding to Class A8.

BOILERS:
D1091.
D1063 *(ex1518)* 8/12/30.

SHED:
Starbeck.

1529

Darlington.

To traffic 6/1920.

REPAIRS:
Ghd. 30/7—28/9/23.**G.**
Ghd. 18/2—9/4/25.**G.**
Ghd. 17/11/26—7/3/27.**G.**
Ghd. 24/8—1/11/28.**G.**
Ghd. 14—27/3/29.**L.**
Ghd. 8—17/4/29.**L.**
Ghd. 18/7—4/9/30.**G.**
Ghd. 14/3—21/4/32.**G.**
Into Darlington 31/1/34 for
rebuilding to Class A8.

BOILERS:
D1102.
D1251 *(ex1328)* 4/9/30.

SHED:
Heaton.

WORKS CODES:- Cw - Cowlairs. Dar- Darlington. Don - Doncaster. Ghd - Gateshead. Gor - Gorton. Inv - Inverurie. Str - Stratford. Tux - Tuxford.
REPAIR CODES:- **C/H** - Casual Heavy. **C/L** - Casual Light. **G** - General. **H**- Heavy. **H/I** - Heavy Intermediate. **L** - Light. **L/I** - Light Intermediate. **N/C** - Non-Classified.

89

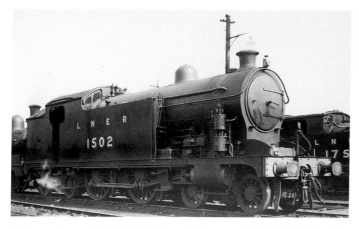

Between August 1928 (No.1527) and February 1930 (No.2156) all the others had vacuum brake equipment added, and these had a standpipe fitted at the front end.

The front windows of the cab were shaped to suit the firebox profile and roof curves. They were split and hinged vertically so that the outer section could be opened (*see* page 84, centre).

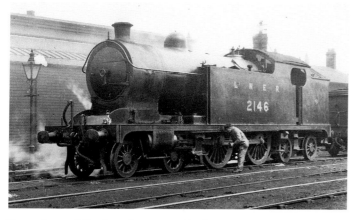

For a short while after the vacuum brake was put on, Westinghouse was retained with two standpipes, also carriage heating connection, fitted at the front end.

There were two whistles; an organ pipe on the driver's side and a small bell-shape on the fireman's side. No changes took place on either the original Diagram 63 boiler or on the Diagram 63A boilers introduced in 1930.

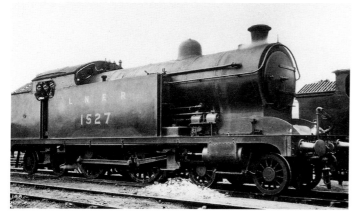

On rebuilding to A8 the Westinghouse equipment was removed and this applied in twenty cases. Between July 1932 (No.2159) and March 1934 (No.1526) the other twenty-five lost the Westinghouse gear prior to rebuilding; the engine then relied on steam brakes.

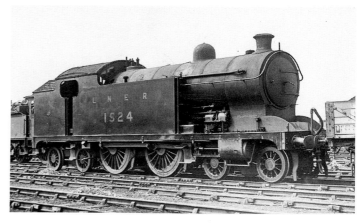

Whilst H1 class, all had the same type of buffers, circular flange, taper shank, and large oval head.

1531

Darlington.

To traffic 6/1920.

REPAIRS:
Dar. 2/11/23—17/3/24.**G.**
Dar. 31/7—20/10/25.**L.**
Dar. 25/3—11/8/26.**G.**
Dar. 24/8—17/9/26.**L.**
Dar. 27/5—17/6/27.**L.**
Dar. 17/9—15/11/28.**G.**
Into Darlington 23/10/33 for rebuilding to Class A8.

BOILER:
D1103.

SHEDS:
Neville Hill.
Starbeck 14/8/26.

1499

Darlington.

To traffic 6/1921.

REPAIRS:
Ghd. 9/11/22—16/1/23.**G.**
Ghd. 26/4—23/6/24.**G.**
Ghd. 29/9—4/12/25.**G.**
Ghd. 18—20/8/26.**L.**
Ghd. 24/8—10/11/27.**G.**
Dar. 29/1—5/4/29.**G.**
Special bogie fitted.
Ghd. 24—28/7/30.**L.**
Ghd. 1/12/30—23/1/31.**G.**
Dar . 15/5—23/6/33.**G.**
Into Darlington 23/3/36 for rebuilding to Class A8.

BOILERS:
D1199.
1D/689 *(ex2154)* 23/6/33 *(63A).*

SHED:
Heaton.

1501

Darlington.

To traffic 6/1921.

REPAIRS:
Ghd. 19/1—9/4/23.**G.**
Ghd. 28/7—2/10/24.**G.**
Ghd. 17/2—15/6/26.**G.**
Ghd. 24/3—24/5/28.**G.**

Ghd. 25/9—17/10/28.**L.**
After derailment.
Ghd. 16/11—12/12/28.**L.**
Ghd. 11—22/7/29.**N/C.**
Ghd. 20/5—10/7/30.**G.**
Into Darlington 11/10/33 for rebuilding to Class A8.

BOILERS:
D1202.
   D290 *(ex2156)* 10/7/30.

SHED:
Heaton.

1502

Darlington.

To traffic 7/1921.

REPAIRS:
Dar. 23/2—15/5/23.**G.**
Dar. 30/11—5/12/23.**L.**
Dar. 27/2—29/5/25.**G.**
Dar. 10—15/6/25.**L.**
Dar. 30/4—10/8/27.**G.**
Dar. 12/4—25/6/29.**G.**
Dar. 23/9—8/10/30.**N/C.**
Dar. 6—19/5/31.**N/C.**
Dar. 7/11—30/12/31.**G.**
Dar. 21/6—11/8/33.**G.**
Into Darlington 29/1/36 for rebuilding to Class A8.

BOILERS:
D1208.
   2463 *(new)* 11/8/33 *(63A).*

SHEDS:
Darlington.
Heaton 19/6/34.

1503

Darlington.

To traffic 7/1921.

REPAIRS:
Dar. 31/10/23—21/1/24.**G.**
Dar. 19/11/25—8/3/26.**G.**
Dar. 24/8—24/11/27.**G.**
Dar. 26/11—28/12/28.**L.**
Dar. 20/8—10/9/29.**N/C.**
Dar. 31/10—24/12/29.**G.**
Dar. 30/11/31—26/1/32.**G.**
Dar. 16/1—19/2/34.**G.**
Into Darlington 25/11/35 for rebuilding to Class A8.

BOILERS:
D1254.
D1064 *(ex1517)* 19/2/34.

SHEDS:
Darlington.
Blaydon 9/10/34.

1524

Darlington.

To traffic 8/1921.

REPAIRS:
Dar. 10/12/23—22/2/24.**G.**
Dar. 5—21/3/24.**L.**
Dar. 13/1—19/2/25.**L.**
Dar. 12/10—31/12/25.**G.**
Dar. 3/4—14/6/28.**G.**
Dar. 24/9—25/10/28.**L.**
Dar. 9—18/7/29.**N/C.**
Dar. 27/12/29—17/2/30.**G.**
Dar. 29/1—20/2/31.**N/C.**
Dar. 11/4—18/8/32.**G.**
Dar. 29/9—19/10/32.**N/C.**
Into Darlington 22/3/34 for rebuilding to Class A8.

BOILER:
D1219.

SHED:
Darlington.

1525

Darlington.

To traffic 8/1921.

REPAIRS:
Dar. 9/8—27/10/23.**G.**
Dar. 25/3—20/8/25.**G.**
Dar. 15/12/27—25/2/28.**G.**
Dar. 24/9—26/10/28.**L.**
Dar. 2/1—25/2/29.**H.**
Dar. 17/9—31/10/29.**H.**
Dar. 8/8—15/10/30.**G.**
Dar. 28/10—10/11/30.**N/C.**
Dar. 6/5—1/6/31.**N/C.**
Into Darlington 9/12/32 for rebuilding to Class A8.

BOILER:
D1267.

SHED:
Darlington.

1526

Darlington.

To traffic 9/1921.

REPAIRS:
Dar. 10/8—25/10/23.**G.**
Dar. 3—8/9/24.**L.**
Dar. 13/1—8/4/26.**G.**
Dar. 6/2—12/5/28.**G.**
Dar. 4—19/7/29.**N/C.**
Dar. 15/3—23/5/30.**G.**
Dar. 7/3—21/4/32.**G.**
Dar. 21—25/8/33.**N/C.**
Dar. 26/1—2/3/34.**G.**
Into Darlington 27/2/36 for rebuilding to Class A8.

BOILERS:
D1274.
D1254 *(ex1503)* 2/3/34.

SHEDS:
Darlington.
Blaydon 24/5/34.

1527

Darlington.

To traffic 9/1921.

REPAIRS:
Dar. 28/5—30/7/23.**G.**
Dar. 21/2—18/5/25.**G.**
Dar. 29/3—17/6/27.**G.**
Dar. 21/6—9/8/28.**G.**
Dar. 16/7—30/9/29.**G.**
Dar. 11/8—24/9/31.**G.**
Dar. 21—25/8/33.**N/C.**
Dar. 2/1—13/2/34.**G.**
Into Darlington 2/3/36 for rebuilding to Class A8.

BOILERS:
D1278.
   D269 *(ex1520)* 30/9/29.
4D/689 *(new exNBL)* 24/9/31 *(63A).*

SHEDS:
Darlington.
Heaton 12/7/34.

WORKS CODES:- Cw - Cowlairs. Dar- Darlington. Don - Doncaster. Ghd - Gateshead. Gor - Gorton. Inv - Inverurie. Str - Stratford. Tux - Tuxford.
REPAIR CODES:- **C/H** - Casual Heavy. **C/L** - Casual Light. **G** - General. **H** - Heavy. **H/I** - Heavy Intermediate. **L** - Light. **L/I** - Light Intermediate. **N/C** - Non-Classified.

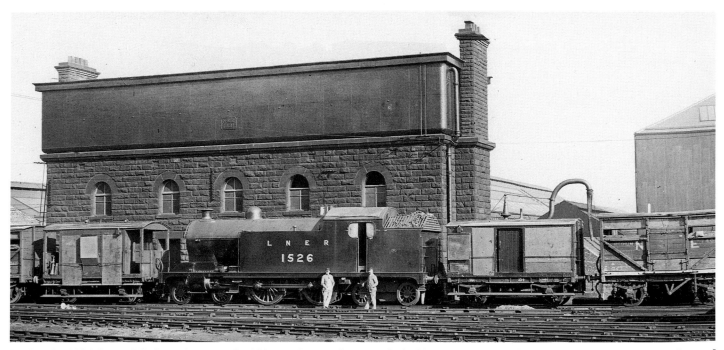

During the 1926 General Strike, miners north of Newcastle caused some ugly incidents and so No.1526 had extra protection in the shape of steel plates put in the cab opening and around the safety valves so that it could run with two similarly re-inforced brake vans and two cattle wagons which had been equipped to carry troops. Fortunately this proved un-necessary and was soon removed.

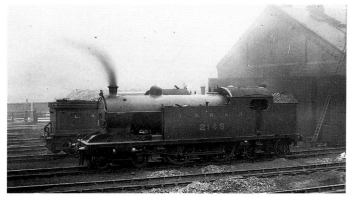

Hitherto in fully lined North Eastern green, the LNER changed them to black, beginning in April 1923. By the end of June, nine had gone to black with L.& N.E.R.. These were: 1501 (9th April), 2155 (12th April), 1330 (3rd May), 2162 (11th May), 1502 (15th May), 2148 (17th May), 2143 (24th May), 1329 (31st May) and 2153 (18th June).

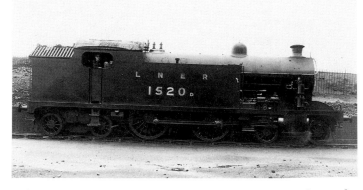

Before the Area suffix D was introduced, the ampersand was also dropped and two just got LNER and number, although it was another six months before that style became the all-line standard. These two were: 1527 (30th July) and 1328 (3rd August). In the six months that the Area suffix D was applied, sixteen were repainted and had it added to the number. They were: September - 1522 (24th), 1529 (28th), October - 1526 (25th), 1525 (27th), November - 2149 (13th), 2150 (19th), 1519 (28th), 1327 (29th), 1500 (30th), 2152 (3rd December), all 1923, and in 1924: January - 1520 (12th), 1503 (21st), February - 1523 (1st), 1528 (7th), 1326 (11th) and 1517 (13th).

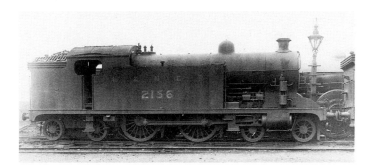

The next two still had the ampersand but the full points had been discarded. They were: 2151 (29th June) and 2156 (27th July).

(right) From mid-February 1924 standard painting to rebuilding was black with single red lining. The last two in green were Nos.2157 and 2160 which went to works 28th April 1925 and 5th May 1925 respectively.

1327

Darlington.

To traffic 10/1921.

REPAIRS:
Dar. 21/9—29/11/23.**G.**
Dar. 13/7—14/10/25.**G.**
Dar. 25/8—17/11/27.**G.**
Dar. 12—30/8/29.**N/C.**
Dar. 7/7—30/9/30.**G.**
Into Darlington 13/9/33 for
rebuilding to Class A8.

BOILERS:
D1293.
D1310 *(ex1500)* 30/9/30.

SHEDS:
Darlington.
Middlesbrough 19/7/28.
Saltburn 16/5/29.
Heaton 26/6/30.

1329

Darlington.

To traffic 11/1921.

REPAIRS:
Ghd. 5/4—31/5/23.**G.**
Ghd. 5/9—19/11/24.**G.**
Ghd. 2/9—2/12/26.**G.**
Ghd. 22/6—11/9/28.**G.**
Ghd. 20/5—7/7/30.**G.**
Ghd. 23/2—24/3/32.**G.**
Into Darlington 19/1/34 for
rebuilding to Class A8.

BOILERS:
D1282.
D1202 *(ex1328)* 24/3/32.

SHEDS:
Blaydon.
Heaton 21/7/26.

1330

Darlington.

To traffic 12/1921.

REPAIRS:
Ghd. 23/2—3/5/23.**G.**
Ghd. 3/3—28/4/24.**G.**
Ghd. 25/11/25—2/3/26.**G.**
Ghd. 18—28/3/27.**L.**
Ghd. 4/1—21/3/28.**G.**

Ghd. 7—21/10/29.**N/C.**
Ghd. 26/2—14/4/30.**G.**
Ghd. 22/2—1/4/32.**G.**
Into Darlington 12/3/34 for
rebuilding to Class A8.

BOILER:
D1287.

SHED:
Blaydon.

1521

Darlington.

To traffic 12/1921.

REPAIRS:
Ghd. 6/2—3/4/25.**G.**
Ghd. 20/5—2/8/27.**G.**
Ghd. 17/5—26/7/29.**G.**
Ghd. 29/6—11/8/31.**G.**
Ghd. 19/9—27/10/33.**G.**
Into Darlington 8/7/35 for
rebuilding to Class A8.

BOILERS:
D1313.
D1019 *(ex1523)* 11/8/31.
D1208 *(ex1502)* 27/10/33.

SHEDS:
Blaydon.
Gateshead *at 1/1/35.*

1328

Darlington.

To traffic 2/1922.

REPAIRS:
Ghd. 1/6—3/8/23.**G.**
Ghd. 11—21/9/23.**L.**
Ghd. 5/1—4/3/25.**G.**
Ghd. 30/12/26—22/4/27.**G.**
Ghd. 5/5—11/6/27.**L.**
Ghd. 30/10—21/12/28.**G.**
Ghd. 15—19/11/29.**N/C.**
Ghd. 2/7—20/8/30.**G.**
Ghd. 22/1—26/2/32.**G.**
Into Darlington 16/2/34 for
rebuilding to Class A8.

BOILERS:
D1251.
D1202 *(ex1501)* 20/8/30.
D1313 *(ex1521)* 26/2/32.

SHEDS:
Blaydon.
Heaton 21/7/26.

1326

Darlington.

To traffic 2/1922.

REPAIRS:
Dar. 3/11/23—11/2/24.**G.**
Dar. 15/12/24—10/2/25.**G.**
Dar. 28/10—5/11/25.**L.**
Dar. 1/3—30/6/26.**G.**
Dar. 5/11/26—22/2/27.**L.**
Dar. 6—15/9/27.**L.**
Dar. 17/2—25/4/28.**G.**
Dar. 9/4—10/5/29.**N/C.**
Dar. 8/11/29—3/1/30.**G.**
Dar. 3/11—18/12/31.**G.**
Into Darlington 6/12/34 for
rebuilding to Class A8.

BOILERS:
D1316.
D1278 *(ex1527)* 3/1/30.

SHED:
Neville Hill.

1500

Darlington.

To traffic 3/1922.

REPAIRS:
Dar. 10/8—30/11/23.**G.**
Dar. 7/2—19/3/24.**L.**
Dar. 13/6—14/7/24.**L.**
Dar. 23/10—5/2/26.**G.**
Dar. 31/5—10/8/28.**G.**
Dar. 25/4—14/7/30.**G.**
Dar. 16/11/31—18/1/32.**G.**
Into Darlington 6/3/34 for
rebuilding to Class A8.

BOILERS:
D1310.
D300 *(ex2147)* 14/7/30.
D1107 *(ex2143)* 18/1/32.

SHED:
Starbeck.

1522

Darlington.

To traffic 5/1922.

REPAIRS:
Ghd. 20/7—24/9/23.**G.**
Ghd. 19/6—2/7/24.**L.**
Ghd. 27/3—11/6/25.**G.**
Ghd. 1/12/27—7/2/28.**G.**
Ghd. 9—18/4/29.**N/C.**
Ghd. 28/5—16/7/30.**G.**
Ghd. 15—18/6/31.**L.**
Ghd. 22/9—29/10/31.**L.**
Into Darlington 20/10/33 for
rebuilding to Class A8.

BOILER:
D1327.

SHED:
Blaydon.

1530

Darlington.

To traffic 5/1922.

REPAIRS:
Dar. 16/1—31/3/24.**G.**
Dar. 21/9—9/12/25.**G.**
Dar. 16/8—14/11/27.**G.**
Dar. 1—8/12/27.**L.**
Dar. 29/4—5/7/29.**G.**
Dar. 2—16/10/29.**N/C.**
Dar. 5/1—17/2/31.**G.**
Dar. 17—31/3/31.**N/C.**
Dar. 20/1—2/3/33.**G.**
Dar. 2—10/8/34.**N/C.**
Into Darlington 12/12/34 for
rebuilding to Class A8.

BOILERS:
D1301.
D1102 *(ex2157)* 2/3/33.

SHED:
Starbeck.

WORKS CODES:- Cw - Cowlairs. Dar- Darlington. Don - Doncaster. Ghd - Gateshead. Gor - Gorton. Inv - Inverurie. Str - Stratford. Tux - Tuxford.
REPAIR CODES:- **C/H** - Casual Heavy. **C/L** - Casual Light. **G** - General. **H-** Heavy. **H/I** - Heavy Intermediate. **L** - Light. **L/I** - Light Intermediate. **N/C** - Non-Classified.

Before becoming LNER they had three other designations on their tanks. The first change, probably from their first shopping, retained only Metropolitan and in a straight line. The maker's plate was also replaced by a smaller one.

In April 1934 No.105 suffered further abbreviation to MET. but (fortunately) was the only one of the eight so maltreated. It also lost the maker's plate.

Several of the original details had been changed before LNER take-over, although odd items remained as detailed later. Note they first had Robinson superheater header discharge valve but all had been altered to a pair of Maunsell anti-vacuum valves by 1937. The original safety valves were Ramsbottom type which only three still had with LNER painting. All but one had different fastening for the smokebox door.

CLASS H 2

103/6415

Kerr Stuart 4088.

To traffic 10/1920.

REPAIRS:
Nea. ?/?—?/12/34.**G.**
Str. ?/?—4/3/38.**G.**
Str. ?/?—?/9/43.**G.**

BOILERS:
 LT4.
 LT4 reno.1421 4/3/38.
1426 *(ex6420)* ?/9/43.

SHEDS:
Neasden.
Colwick 6/12/41.

RENUMBERED:
6415 4/3/38.
7510 allocated.

CONDEMNED: 4/3/46.
Cut up at Stratford.

104/6416

Kerr Stuart 4089.

To traffic 10/1920.

REPAIRS:
Nea. ?/?—6/37.**G.**
Str. ?/?—22/9/38.**G.**
Str. ?/?—?/7/42.**G.**
Str. ?/?—?/3/45.**G.**

BOILERS:
LT16.
LT16 reno.1422 22/9/38.
1427 *(ex6421)* ?/7/42.
1424 *(ex6418)* ?/3/45.

SHEDS:
Neasden.
Colwick 5/12/41.

RENUMBERED:
6416 22/9/38.
7511 8/12/46.

CONDEMNED: 20/11/47.
Cut up at Darlington.

105/6417

Kerr Stuart 4090.

To traffic 11/1920.

REPAIRS:
Nea. ?/?—?/4/34.**G.**
Str. 25/6/37—3/3/38.**G.**
Str. 12/2—14/4/45.**G.**
Str. 11—25/5/46.**L.**

BOILERS:
LT15.
LT15 reno.1423 3/3/38.
1427 *(ex6416)* 14/4/45.

SHEDS:
Neasden.
Colwick 7/12/41.

RENUMBERED:
6417 3/3/38.
7512 29/9/46.

CONDEMNED: 17/10/47.
Cut up at Darlington.

106/6418

Kerr Stuart 4091.

To traffic 11/1920.

REPAIRS:
Nea. ?/?—?/6/35.**G.**
Str. ?/6/37—11/3/38.**G.**
Str. ?/?—?/3/44.**G.**

BOILERS:
LT28.
LT28 reno.1424 11/3/38.
1418 *(ex M2 6157)* ?/3/44.

SHEDS:
Neasden.
Colwick 4/12/41.

RENUMBERED:
6418 11/3/38.
7513 allocated.

CONDEMNED: 21/5/46.
Cut up at Stratford.

107/6419

Kerr Stuart 4092.

To traffic 3/1921.

REPAIRS:
Nea. ?/?—?/1/37.**G.**
Str. ?/?—17/6/38.**G.**

BOILERS:
LT7.
LT7 reno.1425 17/6/38.

SHEDS:
Neasden.
Colwick 5/12/41.
RENUMBERED:
6419 17/6/38.
7514 allocated.

CONDEMNED: 23/9/43.
Cut up at Stratford.

108/6420

Kerr Stuart 4093.

To traffic 4/1921.

REPAIRS:
Nea. ?/?—?/9/35.**G.**
Str. ?/?—25/3/38.**G.**
Str. ?/?—?/7/43.**G.**

BOILERS:
LT31.
LT31 reno.1426 25/3/38.
1422 *(ex6416)* ?/7/43.

SHEDS:
Neasden.
Langwith Jct. 12/12/41.
Colwick 14/8/42.

RENUMBERED:
6420 25/3/38.
7515 allocated.

CONDEMNED: 3/1/46.
Cut up at Stratford.

109/6421

Kerr Stuart 4094.

To traffic 6/1921.

REPAIRS:
Nea. ?/?—?/1/36.**G.**
Str. ?/?—24/3/38.**G.**

BOILERS:
LT35.
LT35 reno.1427 24/3/38.

SHEDS:
Neasden.
Colwick 6/12/41.
Langwith Jct. 12/12/41.

RENUMBERED:
6421 24/3/38.

CONDEMNED: 15/4/42.
Cut up at Stratford.

110/6422

Kerr Stuart 4095.

To traffic 6/1921.

REPAIRS:
Nea. ?/?—?/5/36.**G.**
Str. ?/?—8/4/38.**G.**

BOILERS:
LT10.
LT10 reno.1428 8/4/38.

SHEDS:
Neasden.
Colwick 4/12/41.
Langwith Jct. 12/12/41.
Colwick 18/7/42.

RENUMBERED:
6422 8/4/38.
7516 allocated.

CONDEMNED: 4/5/46.
Cut up at Stratford.

WORKS CODES:- Cw - Cowlairs. Dar- Darlington. Don - Doncaster. Ghd - Gateshead. Gor - Gorton. Inv - Inverurie. Nea - Neasden LPTB. Str - Stratford. Tux - Tuxford.
REPAIR CODES:- **C/H** - Casual Heavy. **C/L** - Casual Light. **G** - General. **H**- Heavy. **H/I** - Heavy Intermediate. **L** - Light. **L/I** - Light Intermediate. **N/C** - Non-Classified.

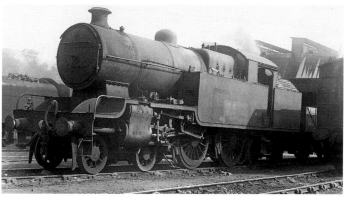

(above) From December 1934 on No.103, the tank lettering became London Transport and apart from MET. on No.105, the other seven had that wording at take-over. Note the smokebox door changed to fastening around the rim by six dog clips and that a handgrip was added at the left hand side.

Only No.105 (which became LNER 6417, and 7512 later) kept the original pattern of door with central fastening and during the war its wheel was replaced by a second handle. This door was kept to withdrawal on 17th October 1947.

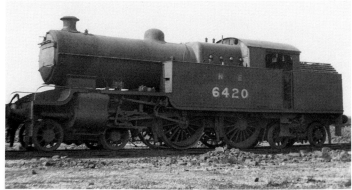

(above) Although never required to work where height would have been restrictive, in 1941, a shorter chimney was fitted, dome and cab heights were also reduced. Change of safety valves to 'pops' on Nos.6415, 6417 and 6420 also cut their height.

(left) The class had a maximum height from rail of 13ft 3in. but on the GC Section this did not cause any problem. Note Ramsbottom safety valves retained, also on Nos.6415 and 6417.

This class had 'trip cock' gear fitted on the right hand side of the front bogie and on the left hand side of the rear bogie.

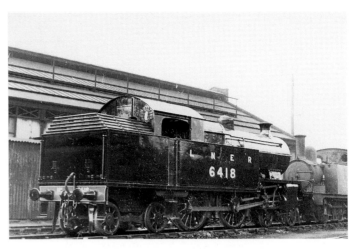

At its 11th March 1938 repair at Stratford, No.6418 also retained the destination board holders on the back of the bunker.

When all eight were sent in December 1941 to work in the Nottingham area, the trip cock gear was superfluous and so was removed.

During the war all went into unlined black except Nos.6421 and 6419 which were withdrawn on 15th April 1942 and 23rd September 1943 respectively. The other six had a 1943-5 repair at which LNER was reduced to only NE. At least Nos.6416, 6417, 6418, 6420 and 6422 changed to Group Standard buffers and No.6415 could have done at a 1943 general repair.

Between 3rd March (No.6417) and 22nd September 1938 (No.6416), all received LNER numbers, and black paint with single red lining. Only Nos.6415 and 6418 kept the Metropolitan type of destination board holders carried at the front end of the frames, and these were also taken off later. At take-over they were still fitted with safety chains on the buffer beam. Although retained at first, the LNER gradually took these off during the war.

Only two received 1946 numbers and neither had LNER restored. On Sunday 29th September 1946 Colwick shed changed 6417 to 7512, and on Sunday 8th December 1946 they changed 6416 to 7511 using painted figures without shading for both. Withdrawal of No.7511 on 20th November 1947 made Class H2 extinct and 7511, along with 7512, was cut up at Darlington in May 1948.

The LNER soon removed the superheater steam circulating valve from the L1's and replaced it with the Gresley anti-vacuum valve on the end of the header.

There was a Gresley anti-vacuum valve at both ends of the header.

By the 1930's there was a further change to a single Gresley valve in the usual central position behind the chimney.

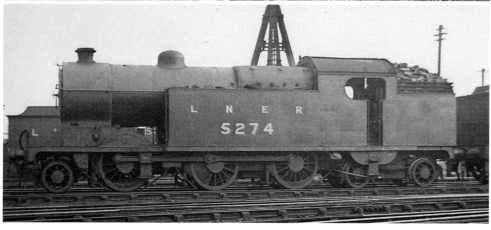

As late as 1938 four, Nos.5272, 5274, 5339 and 5344, did not have anti-vacuum valve on the header, relying on the cylinder mounted valves for protection.

CLASS L 1 (L 3 from May 1945)

5272

Gorton.

To traffic 12/1914.

REPAIRS:
Gor. 27/1—10/3/17.**G.**
Gor. 7/8—30/10/20.**G.**
Gor. 17/3—30/6/23.**G.**
Gor. 22/11/24—17/1/25.**G.**
Gor. 30/4—30/6/27.**G.**
Gor. 27/7—31/8/29.**G.**
Gor. 16/1—6/2/32.**G.**
Gor. 7/10—4/11/33.**G.**
Gor. 9/1—6/2/37.**G.**
Gor. 29/6—27/7/40.**G.**
Gor. 1/7—21/8/43.**G.**
Gor. 8/3—26/4/47.**G.**
New cylinders.
Gor. 11/3—1/4/50.**G.**
Heating apparatus removed.
Gor. 22/11—20/12/52.**G.**
After collision.

BOILERS:
668.
683 17/1/25.
682 6/2/32.
645 4/11/33.
3103 6/2/37.
60 27/7/40.
759 21/8/43.
3128 26/4/47.
649 1/4/50.
22025 20/12/52.

SHEDS:
Immingham.
Sheffield 2/10/29.
Retford 6/10/29.
Mexborough 9/3/33.
Sheffield 21/11/42.
Mexborough 20/2/44.
Neasden 21/7/46.
Mexborough 30/4/47.
Woodford 17/8/47.

RENUMBERED:
5272 17/1/25.
9050 18/8/46.
69050 1/4/50.

CONDEMNED: 12/3/55.
Into Gor. for cut up 12/3/55.

5273

Gorton.

To traffic 12/1914.

REPAIRS:
Gor. 2/12/16—17/2/17.**G.**
Gor. 2/4—7/5/21.**G.**
Gor. 24/11/23—16/2/24.**G.**
Gor. 26/12/25—20/2/26.**G.**
Gor. 11/2—14/4/28.**G.**
Gor. 19/10—23/11/29.**G.**
Gor. 2/4—7/5/32.**G.**
Gor. 11/4—9/5/36.**G.**
Heating apparatus removed.
Gor. 6/5—24/6/39.**G.**
Gor. 18/5—13/6/42.**G.**
Gor. 10/2—17/3/45.**G.**
New cylinders.
Gor. 6/7—24/8/46.**L.**
Gor. 18/10—1/11/47.**H.**
Secondhand cyls. exB8 1356.
Gor. 2/10—6/11/48.**G.**

BOILERS:
670.
1890 16/2/24.
340 23/11/29.
3101 9/5/36.
724 13/6/42.
645 17/3/45.
3123 6/11/48.

SHEDS:
Gorton.
Annesley 8/11/19.
Immingham 10/3/23.
Keadby 24/6/29.
Immingham 30/11/29.
Frodingham 15/9/32.
Mexborough 16/11/44.
Darnall 8/9/46.
Northwich 16/2/47.
Darnall 2/4/47.
Mexborough 7/5/47.
Frodingham 22/2/48.

RENUMBERED:
5273 16/2/24.
9051 1/12/46.
69051 6/11/48.

CONDEMNED: 14/5/51.
Into Gor. for cut up 26/5/51.

5274

Gorton.

To traffic 2/1915.

REPAIRS:
Gor. 28/4—16/6/17.**G.**
Gor. 12/3—16/4/21.**G.**
Gor. 25/8—10/11/23.**G.**
Gor. 6/12/24—17/1/25.**G.**
Gor. 5/5—23/6/28.**G.**
Gor. 2/5—6/6/31.**G.**
Gor. 18/5—8/6/35.**G.**
Gor. 30/7—3/9/38.**G.**
Gor. 2/12/41—10/1/42.**G.**
Gor. 13/3—22/4/44.**G.**
Heating apparatus removed.
Gor. 9/3—20/4/46.**G.**
Gor. 9—23/8/47.**H.**
Gor. 5—26/6/48.**G.**
Gor. 22—30/7/49.**C/H.**
Gor. 5—26/8/50.**G.**
Gor. 12/1—9/2/52.**G.**
Gor. 8/8—5/9/53.**C/L.**

BOILERS:
673.
492 10/11/23.
334 6/6/31.
988 8/6/35.
590 3/9/38.
687 10/1/42.
649 22/4/44.
683 20/4/46.
3105 26/6/48.
3134 26/8/50.
22016 9/2/52.

SHEDS:
Gorton.
Annesley 8/11/19.
Immingham 10/3/23.
Neasden 31/1/25.
Woodford 28/3/29.
Mexborough 29/6/29.
Woodford 6/8/42.
Northwich 19/1/43.
Gorton 9/12/45.
Northwich 12/5/46.

RENUMBERED:
5274 17/1/25.
9052 20/10/46.
69052 26/6/48.

CONDEMNED: 9/8/54.
Into Gor. for cut up 14/8/54.

5275

Gorton.

To traffic 3/1915.

REPAIRS:
Gor. 13/1—17/2/17.**G.**
Gor. 24/4—3/7/20.**G.**
Gor. 16/12/22—27/1/23.**G.**
Gor. 17/1—7/3/25.**G.**
Gor. 5/11/27—7/1/28.**G.**
Gor. 2/11—7/12/29.**G.**
Gor. 26/12/31—23/1/32.**G.**
Gor. 24/3—28/4/34.**G.**
Heating apparatus removed.
Gor. 13/2—13/3/37.**G.**
Gor. 23/3—27/4/40.**G.**
Gor. 5/4—3/5/41.**L.**
Gor. 7/1—12/2/44.**G.**
Gor. 6/12/47—17/1/48.**G.**

BOILERS:
682.
163 23/1/32.
977 28/4/34.
1675 13/3/37.
3107 27/4/40.
707 12/2/44.
3104 17/1/48.

SHEDS:
Gorton.
Mexborough 27/4/40.
Woodford 5/8/42.
Neasden 31/1/43.

RENUMBERED:
5275 7/3/25.
9053 18/8/46.
ᴇ**9053** 17/1/48.

CONDEMNED: 17/7/50.
Into Gor. for cut up 22/7/50.

5276

Gorton.

To traffic 4/1915.

REPAIRS:
Gor. 21/10—18/11/16.**L.**
Gor. 22/12/17—23/2/18.**G.**
Gor. 7/5—2/7/21.**G.**
Gor. 15/9—17/11/23.**G.**
Gor. 21/8—30/10/26.**G.**
Gor. 20/10—1/12/28.**G.**
Gor. 2/5—6/6/31.**G.**
Gor. 31/3—28/4/34.**G.**
Gor. 13/2—6/3/37.**G.**

Gor. 16/12/39—27/1/40.**G.**
Heating apparatus removed.
Gor. 15/6—20/7/40.**L.**
After collision.
Gor. 15/12/43—22/1/44.**G.**
Gor. 10—17/2/45.**L.**
Gor. 6/3—10/4/48.**G.**

BOILERS:
  683.
    60 17/11/23.
1671 6/6/31.
  163 28/4/34.
  645 6/3/37.
1672 27/1/40.
  657 22/1/44.
3119 10/4/48.

SHEDS:
Gorton.
Neasden 20/10/22.
Immingham 10/3/23.
March 17/8/29.
Immingham 16/3/31.
Neasden 18/1/41.
Woodford 2/2/41.
Neasden 27/9/41.

RENUMBERED:
5276 30/10/26.
9054 25/8/46.
69054 10/4/48.

CONDEMNED: 29/8/49.
Cut up at Gorton.

5336

Gorton.

To traffic 4/1915.

REPAIRS:
Gor. 6/10—17/11/17.**G.**
Gor. 25/5—17/8/18.**G.**
After collision.
Gor. 4/6—23/7/21.**G.**
Gor. 5/7—23/8/24.**G.**
Gor. 14/8—23/10/26.**G.**
Gor. 28/2—28/3/31.**G.**
Gor. 2/12/33—13/1/34.**G.**
Gor. 11/4—16/5/36.**G.**
Heating apparatus removed.
Gor. 6—27/2/37.**L.**
Gor. 16/9—7/10/39.**G.**
Gor. 12/3—17/4/43.**G.**
Gor. 11/8—22/9/45.**G.**
Gor. 21/8—25/9/48.**G.**

BOILERS:
  953.
  977 23/8/24.

1673 28/3/31.
3113 7/10/39.
3112 17/4/43.
3123 22/9/45.
  657 25/9/48.

SHEDS:
Gorton.
Neasden 14/10/21.
Immingham 24/6/31.
Neasden 26/10/39.
Woodford 2/2/41.
Neasden 27/9/41.

RENUMBERED:
5336 23/8/24.
9055 3/2/46.
69055 25/9/48.

CONDEMNED: 23/7/51.
Cut up at Gorton.

5337

Gorton.

To traffic 5/1915.

REPAIRS:
Gor. 2/12/16—6/1/17.**L.**
Gor. 4—25/8/17.**G.**
Gor. 5/2—9/4/21.**G.**
Gor. 13/10—8/12/23.**G.**
Gor. 1/5—3/7/26.**G.**
Gor. 25/8—13/10/28.**G.**
Gor. 2/8—20/9/30.**G.**
Gor. 14/1—18/2/33.**G.**
Gor. 11/4—9/5/36.**G.**
Gor. 4—25/3/39.**G.**
Gor. 17/5—28/6/41.**G.**
Gor. 1—25/12/43.**G.**
Gor. 31/12/47—7/2/48.**G.**
Gor. 23/12/50. *Not repaired.*

BOILERS:
  977.
  987 8/12/23.
  339 18/2/33.
  687 9/5/36.
  163 25/3/39.
  648 28/6/41.
3119 25/12/43.
  614 7/2/48.

SHEDS:
Gorton.
Annesley 8/11/19.
Immingham 10/3/23.
Woodford 18/2/43.
Mexborough 21/6/43.
Neasden 25/8/46.

RENUMBERED:
5337 3/7/26.
9056 24/3/46.
E9056 7/2/48.

CONDEMNED: 22/1/51.
Cut up at Gorton.

5338

Gorton.

To traffic 6/1915.

REPAIRS:
Gor. 23/6—28/7/17.**G.**
Gor. 10/1—6/2/20.**G.**
Gor. 11/11—30/12/22.**G.**
Gor. 3/1—28/2/25.**G.**
Gor. 3/3—5/5/28.**G.**
Gor. 10/1—7/2/31.**G.**
Gor. 10/2—31/3/34.**G.**
Gor. 13/6—4/7/36.**G.**
Gor. 9/12/39—13/1/40.**G.**
Gor. 9/9—23/10/43.**G.**
New cylinders.
Gor. 18/1—1/3/47.**G.**

BOILERS:
  987.
1577 30/12/22.
1556 28/2/25.
  334 5/5/28.
  997 7/2/31.
  745 31/3/34.
  342 4/7/36.
1673 13/1/40.
    60 23/10/43.
3126 1/3/47.

SHEDS:
Woodford.
Neasden *by* 9/8/25.
Mexborough 1/7/29.
Sheffield 21/11/42.
Mexborough 20/2/44.
Darnall 28/8/46.
Frodingham 9/3/47.

RENUMBERED:
5338 28/2/25.
9057 24/3/46.

CONDEMNED: 10/10/49.
Cut up at Gorton.

5339

Gorton.

To traffic 11/1915.

REPAIRS:
Gor. 13/7—9/11/18.**G.**
Gor. 4/6—27/8/21.**G.**
Gor. 26/7—27/9/24.**G.**
Gor. 21/9—2/11/29.**G.**
Gor. 30/12/33—27/1/34.**G.**
Gor. 27/11—25/12/37.**G.**
Gor. 12—19/2/38.**L.**
Trip cock gear fitted.
Gor. 31/5—28/6/41.**G.**
Gor. 29/4—10/6/44.**G.**
Gor. 26/10—23/11/46.**G.**
Heating apparatus removed.

BOILERS:
  988.
  163 27/8/21.
  953 27/9/24.
  260 27/1/34.
1909 25/12/37.
3111 28/6/41.
  687 10/6/44.
  670 23/11/46.

SHEDS:
Neasden.
Darnall 20/10/46.
Frodingham 16/2/47.

RENUMBERED:
5339 27/9/24.
9058 5/5/46.

CONDEMNED: 29/8/49.
Cut up at Gorton.

5340

Gorton.

To traffic 12/1915.

REPAIRS:
Gor. 7/7—11/8/17.**G.**
Gor. 17/7—28/8/20.**G.**
Gor. 30/12/22—24/2/23.**G.**
Gor. 25/4—27/6/25.**G.**
Gor. 30/6—11/8/28.**G.**
Gor. 11/1—15/2/30.**G.**
Gor. 20/8—24/9/32.**G.**
Gor. 29/10—3/12/32.**L.**
Gor. 13/2—13/3/37.**G.**
Gor. 16—23/3/40.**L.**
Gor. 5/10—2/11/40.**G.**
Gor. 4/9—16/10/43.**G.**
Gor. 18/5—29/6/46.**G.**

WORKS CODES:- Cw - Cowlairs. Dar- Darlington. Don - Doncaster. Ghd - Gateshead. Gor - Gorton. Inv - Inverurie. Str - Stratford. Tux - Tuxford.
REPAIR CODES:- **C/H** - Casual Heavy. **C/L** - Casual Light. **G** - General. **H**- Heavy. **H/I** - Heavy Intermediate. **L** - Light. **L/I** - Light Intermediate. **N/C** - Non-Classified.

100

Beginning in February 1924 with No.5273 (*see* page 108), the top feed was taken off, and all the class duly lost them.

From June 1939 (No.5273) to December 1944 (No.5341) all had the Intensifore removed and replaced by a Wakefield mechanical lubricator which was fitted with an anti-carboniser.

Seven of the twenty had lost the top feed by 1926 but No.5370 still had it until it went to works on 31st March 1934. This was the boiler originally fitted to No.367 in March 1917.

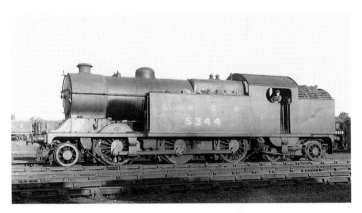

Originally all had a high curved back plate to the bunker and there were six coal rails on each side.

When taken over by the LNER, all twenty L1's had Robinson's 'Intensifore' sight feed lubrication for cylinders and valves.

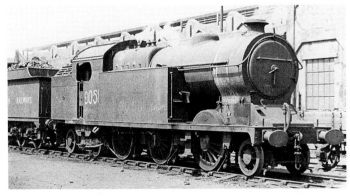

The six rails restricted the bunker opening and were a handicap to those using mechanical coaling plants at Neasden and Immingham. Three, Nos.5276, 5336 and 5339 (9054, 9055, 9058) were altered to three rails, with a substantial angle iron above them and No.5369 (9068) also got this type, which these four then retained.

By 1933 it had been found that the three rails and angle iron still did not give enough access and at least twelve, Nos.5272, 5274, 5337, 5338, 5340, 5341, 5343, 5344, 5345, 5366, 5367 and 5370, were altered to three rails set vertically at each side of the bunker.

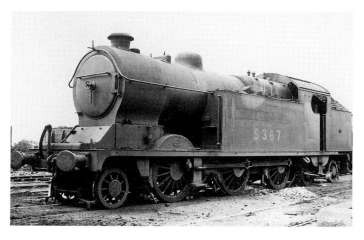

From about 1925 all twenty had chimney changed to the built-up 'plantpot' type but still 1ft 3in. high.

Three, Nos.5275, 5342 and 5368 (9053, 9061, 9067) retained the original arrangement through to withdrawal, even though No.5342 spent most of its life working from Neasden shed.

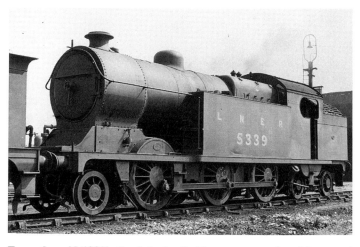

From the mid-1930's the 'plantpot' chimney was replaced by a cast type of very similar shape to the original and also of 1ft 3in. height.

Only one, No.5340 (9059) is known to have had the coal rails plated to prevent spillage of small coal.

The Diagram 14 boiler was also used by Classes D10 and D11 on which a low dome was needed and interchanging brought that type on to Class L1.

5340 cont./
Gor. 18—25/10/47.**L**.

BOILERS:
997.
1674 27/6/25.
 339 11/8/28.
1574 24/9/32.
 649 13/3/37.
3103 2/11/40.
 649 29/6/46.

SHEDS:
Langwith Jct..
Annesley 10/3/23.
Mexborough 18/2/29.
Neasden 15/8/33.
Sheffield 16/12/37.
Neasden 15/1/38.
Woodford 2/2/41.
Neasden 27/9/41.
Mexborough 28/10/47.
Neasden 11/4/48.

RENUMBERED:
5340 27/6/25.
9059 29/6/46.

CONDEMNED: 29/8/49.
Cut up at Gorton.

5341

Gorton.

To traffic 6/1916.

REPAIRS:
Gor. 16/12/16—13/1/17.**L**.
After collision.
Gor. 14/12/18—22/2/19.**G**.
Gor. 30/7—1/10/21.**G**.
Gor. 22/12/23—1/3/24.**G**.
Gor. 27/2—17/4/26.**G**.
Gor. 28/9—9/11/29.**G**.
Gor. 16/9—21/10/33.**G**.
Gor. 29/5—19/6/37.**G**.
Gor. 5/8—2/9/39.**G**.
Gor. 3—29/8/42.**G**.
Gor. 4/11—9/12/44.**G**.
Heating apparatus removed.
Gor. 27/3—1/5/48.**G**.
Gor. 17/3—21/4/51.**G**.
New cylinders.
Gor. 12—26/12/53.**C/L**.
After collision.

BOILERS:
1574.
1813 1/3/24.
 614 17/4/26.
 605 21/10/33.
1672 19/6/37.
3112 2/9/39.

3101 29/8/42.
 590 9/12/44.
3122 1/5/48.
22007 21/4/51.

SHEDS:
Neasden.
Woodford 28/3/29.
Neasden 19/2/31.
Mexborough 7/9/33.
Neasden 18/11/39.
Woodford 2/2/41.
Neasden 27/9/41.
King's Cross 31/5/53.
Frodingham 21/6/53.

RENUMBERED:
5341 1/3/24.
9060 31/3/46.
69060 1/5/48.

WITHDRAWN: 7/6/54.
*Used as stationary boiler at
Stratford works until condemned
in August 1957.*
Cut up at Stratford.

5342

Gorton.

To traffic 6/1916.

REPAIRS:
Gor. 14/6—16/8/19.**G**.
Gor. 2/7—24/9/21.**G**.
Gor. 15/4—3/6/22.**G**.
Gor. 24/1—28/3/25.**G**.
Gor. 26/1—9/3/29.**G**.
Gor. 10/1—14/2/31.**G**.
Gor. 30/12/33—20/1/34.**G**.
Gor. 9/4—14/5/38.**G**.
Gor. 16/2—21/3/42.**G**.
Gor. 22/8—23/9/44.**G**.
Gor. 25/10—6/12/47.**G**.
Gor. 6/11/48.**L**.
Firebox fracture.
Gor. 11/3—15/4/50.**G**.
Heating apparatus removed.

BOILERS:
1575.
1673 28/3/25.
1812 14/2/31.
 331 20/1/34.
 724 14/5/38.
 590 21/3/42.
 163 23/9/44.
 648 6/12/47.
3115 15/4/50.

SHEDS:
Neasden.
Woodford *after* 9/8/25.

March 11/5/29.
Woodford 8/3/31.
Neasden 17/3/31.
Woodford 2/2/41.
Neasden 27/9/41.

RENUMBERED:
5342 28/3/25.
9061 9/11/46.
69061 6/11/48.

CONDEMNED: 9/2/53.
Into Gor. for cut up 14/2/53.

5343

Gorton.

To traffic 6/1916.

REPAIRS:
Gor. 17/3—21/4/17.**G**.
Gor. 1/11/19—17/1/20.**G**.
Gor. 15/7—26/8/22.**G**.
Gor. 20/12/24—7/2/25.**G**.
Gor. 24/10—28/11/25.**H**.
Gor. 20/3—12/6/26.**G**.
Gor. 24/11/28—19/1/29.**G**.
Gor. 20/6—18/7/31.**G**.
Gor. 23/12/33—10/2/34.**H**.
Re-tubing.
Gor. 12/3—9/4/38.**G**.
Gor. 8/7—16/8/41.**G**.
Gor. 3/12/43—8/1/44.**G**.
Gor. 4/8—8/9/45.**G**.
Heating apparatus removed.
Gor. 1—29/3/47.**G**.
Gor. 5—19/6/48.**L**.
Gor. 17/9—15/10/49.**G**.

BOILERS:
1576.
 339 7/2/25.
1675 12/6/26.
 492 18/7/31.
 340 9/4/38.
 707 16/8/41.
 614 8/1/44.
3101 8/9/45.
3127 29/3/47.
3124 15/10/49.

SHEDS:
Gorton.
Annesley 12/3/20.
Mexborough 9/2/29.
Woodford 4/8/42.
Northwich 22/1/43.
Gorton 2/2/47.
Northwich 2/4/47.

RENUMBERED:
5343 7/2/25.
9062 13/10/46.

Woodford 15/2/43.
Mexborough 21/6/43.
Darnall 10/9/46.

RENUMBERED:
5344 11/7/25.
9063 11/8/46.

CONDEMNED: 25/7/47.
Cut up at Gorton.
69062 19/6/48.

CONDEMNED: 14/5/51.
Into Gor. for cut up 26/5/51.

5344

Gorton.

To traffic 8/1916.

REPAIRS:
Gor. 8/3—7/6/19.**G**.
Gor. 28/1—22/4/22.**G**.
Gor. 2/5—11/7/25.**G**.
Gor. 29/12/28—16/2/29.**G**.
Gor. 30/5—4/7/31.**G**.
Gor. 22/8—3/10/36.**G**.
Gor. 3/9—25/10/41.**G**.
Gor. 14/4—20/5/44.**G**.
Gor. 18/1—9/2/46.**L**.
After collision.

BOILERS:
1577.
1559 22/4/22.
1674 16/2/29.
 60 4/7/31.
 657 3/10/36.
3105 25/10/41.
 611 20/5/44.

SHEDS:
Gorton.
Woodford 8/11/19.
March 11/5/29.
Gorton 1/8/31.
Trafford Park 18/10/32.
Mexborough 27/12/33.
Doncaster 10/2/34.
Neasden 29/12/35.
Woodford 2/2/41.
Neasden 27/9/41.
Woodford 4/8/42.
Neasden 31/1/43.
Woodford 15/2/43.
Mexborough 21/6/43.
Darnall 10/9/46.

RENUMBERED:
5344 11/7/25.
9063 11/8/46.

CONDEMNED: 25/7/47.
Cut up at Gorton.

5345

Gorton.

To traffic 1/1917.

REPAIRS:
Gor. 6/9—22/11/19.**G.**
Gor. 18/2—15/4/22.**G.**
Gor. 26/9—28/11/25.**G.**
Gor. 2/2—9/3/29.**G.**
Gor. 22/8—3/10/31.**G.**
Gor. 11/8—15/9/34.**G.**
Heating apparatus removed.
Gor. 26/6—31/7/37.**G.**
Gor. 2—30/11/40.**G.**
Gor. 14/1—19/2/44.**G.**
Gor. 10/10—4/11/44.**L.**
New cylinders.
Gor. 31/8—12/10/46.**G.**
Gor. 24/6—12/8/50.**G.**
Gor. 21/10/50.**C/L.**

BOILERS:
1578.
1814 28/11/25.
1578 9/3/29.
1674 3/10/31.
 648 15/9/34.
 605 31/7/37.
 649 30/11/40.
 670 19/2/44.
3103 12/10/46.
 659 12/8/50.

SHEDS:
Gorton.
Annesley 7/1/20.
Mexborough 12/3/29.
Sheffield 21/11/42.
Mexborough 20/2/44.
Darnall 12/10/46.
Neasden 20/10/46.
New England 9/3/47.
Neasden 10/12/50.
King's Cross 31/5/53.
Frodingham 21/6/53.

RENUMBERED:
5345 28/11/25.
9064 12/10/46.
69064 12/8/50.

CONDEMNED: 24/1/55.
Into Gor. for cut up 29/1/55.

5366

Gorton.

To traffic 2/1917.

REPAIRS:
Gor. 20/3—14/8/20.**G.**
Gor. 28/10—16/12/22.**G.**

Gor. 30/1—3/4/26.**G.**
Gor. 27/10—8/12/28.**G.**
Gor. 14/3—9/5/31.**G.**
Gor. 24/3—28/4/34.**G.**
Gor. 20/3—17/4/37.**G.**
Gor. 20/11—11/12/37.**L.**
Gor. 17/8—21/9/40.**G.**
Gor. 23/12/41—21/2/42.**L.**
R.H. frame patched.
Gor. 17/12/43—29/1/44.**G.**
Gor. 21/7—4/8/45.**L.**
R.H. cylinder welded.
Gor. 17/11—1/12/45.**L.**
New cylinders.
Gor. 7/12/46—4/1/47.**G.**
Gor. 17—31/1/48.**L.**
After collision.
Gor. 1/7—12/8/50.**G.**

BOILERS:
1671.
1909 14/8/20.
1556 8/12/28.
1672 28/4/34.
 977 17/4/37.
 611 21/9/40.
 648 29/1/44.
 687 4/1/47.
 683 12/8/50.

SHEDS:
Langwith Jct..
Annesley 2/2/23.
Mexborough 23/2/29.
Neasden 25/8/46.
Mexborough 22/4/47.
Neasden 11/4/48.
King's Cross 31/5/53.
Frodingham 21/6/53.

RENUMBERED:
5366 3/4/26.
9065 11/8/46.
E9065 31/1/48.
69065 12/8/50.

CONDEMNED: 10/5/54.
Into Gor. for cut up 15/5/54.

5367

Gorton.

To traffic 3/1917.

REPAIRS:
Gor. 18/10—20/12/19.**G.**
Gor. 3/3—12/5/23.**G.**
Gor. 3/7—9/10/26.**G.**
Gor. 4/2—31/3/28.**G.**
Gor. 19/10—23/11/29.**G.**
Gor. 2/5—13/6/31.**G.**
Gor. 3/3—7/4/34.**G.**
Gor. 2—30/10/37.**G.**
Gor. 12/4—24/5/41.**G.**

Gor. 24/12/43—5/2/44.**G.**
Gor. 14/6—9/8/47.**G.**

BOILERS:
1672.
1909 23/11/29.
 648 30/10/37.
 670 24/5/41.
3120 5/2/44.
 605 9/8/47.

SHEDS:
Gorton.
Neasden 20/10/22.
Immingham 10/3/23.
Keadby 24/6/29.
Immingham 21/11/29.
Mexborough 29/10/37.
Woodford 7/8/42.
Mexborough 21/6/43.
Neasden 25/8/46.
Mexborough 11/8/47.
Frodingham 22/2/48.

RENUMBERED:
5367 9/10/26.
9066 11/8/46.

CONDEMNED: 17/4/50.
Into Gor. for cut up 22/4/50.

5368

Gorton.

To traffic 3/1917.

REPAIRS:
Gor. 5/4—21/6/19.**G.**
Gor. 3/12/21—8/4/22.**G.**
Gor. 2/8—27/9/24.**G.**
Gor. 3/8—21/9/29.**G.**
Gor. 29/8—10/10/31.**G.**
Gor. 31/12/36—6/2/37.**G.**
Gor. 27/11—31/12/37.**L.**
After collision.
Gor. 23/3—27/4/40.**G.**
Gor. 4—18/1/41.**L.**
After collision.
Gor. 5/2—13/3/43.**G.**
Gor. 10/2—3/3/45.**L.**
Main frame damaged.
Gor. 29/11/47—10/1/48.**G.**

BOILERS:
1673.
 163 27/9/24.
1675 10/10/31.
 678 6/2/37.
 342 27/4/40.
3120 10/1/48.

SHEDS:
Gorton.
Woodford 8/11/19.

Neasden *by* 1/8/26.
Woodford 25/3/29.
Neasden 29/6/29.
March 24/9/29.
Gorton 3/10/31.
Trafford Park 18/10/32.
Mexborough 27/12/33.
Doncaster 27/1/34.
Mexborough 30/5/34.
Immingham 24/1/36.
Gorton 13/3/43.
Mexborough 11/4/44.
Neasden 21/7/46.

RENUMBERED:
5368 27/9/24.
9067 21/7/46.

CONDEMNED: 19/2/51.
Into Gor. for cut up 24/2/51.

5369

Gorton.

To traffic 4/1917.

REPAIRS:
Gor. 31/1—13/3/20.**G.**
Gor. 10/12/21—8/4/22.**G.**
Gor. 8/11/24—3/1/25.**G.**
Gor. 24/8—5/10/29.**G.**
Gor. 31/12/31—30/1/32.**G.**
Gor. 9/3—6/4/35.**G.**
Gor. 27/8—8/10/38.**G.**
Gor. 24/5—28/6/41.**G.**
Gor. 20/5—1/7/44.**G.**
Gor. 5—23/9/44.**L.**
After collision.
Gor. 17/1—14/2/48.**G.**

BOILERS:
1674.
1574 3/1/25.
 988 30/1/32.
 707 6/4/35.
 163 28/6/41.
3105 1/7/44.
 342 14/2/48.

SHEDS:
Gorton.
Woodford 16/5/20.
Neasden *by* 30/1/25.
Woodford 25/3/29.
Neasden 29/6/29.
Immingham 5/11/29.
Frodingham 20/9/32.
Neasden 4/10/41.

RENUMBERED:
5369 3/1/25.
9068 25/8/46.
E9068 14/2/48.

No attempt was ever made to bring this class within the 13ft 0in. Composite Load Gauge, and on some the height to dome remained at 13ft 3⅜in. to withdrawal.

This boiler built in October 1919 served two D11 and two D10 engines before being put on No.5342 in February 1931. By then, Ross 'pops' had been put on the original Ramsbottom base.

The 'plantpot' chimney survived longer on this class than on most of the others which were so fitted. No.9057 still had one when it went to works 18th January 1947 for its final repair.

Two types of Ross 'pops' were used, No.5370 has the taller, thinner type mounted directly on to the firebox. Here at sometime prior to November 1937, No.5370 which was working from Mexborough shed, has banked a westbound goods train up to the east end of Woodhead tunnel at Dunford Bridge.

The 4-column Ramsbottom safety valves fitted when new had all been replaced by about 1935, two Ross 'pops' taking their place, and all replacement boilers had Ross type. This boiler built in February 1933 started work in November 1933 on No.5272 seen here in February 1936.

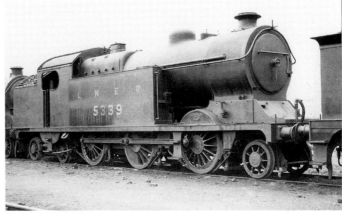

Gravity sanding was fitted to all coupled wheels and there were two feeds for both directions of running.

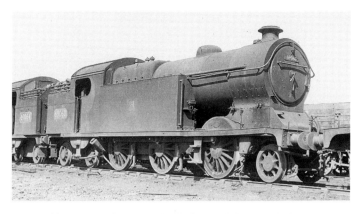

From 1945 at least four, Nos.9052, 9060, 9061 and 9064 changed to steam applied sanding but only from the leading sandbox. Note LNER load class 6 was still being shown on the vacuum standpipe in this May 1953 photograph.

The carriage heating was rarely used and from 1935 was gradually taken off those that had been so fitted, although they retained screw coupling.

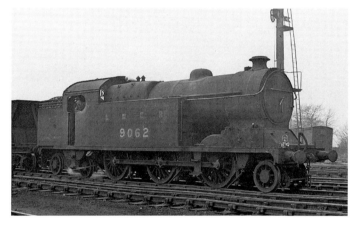

All except No.9062 are believed to have kept GC type buffers, only this one getting Group Standard type and then with oval heads.

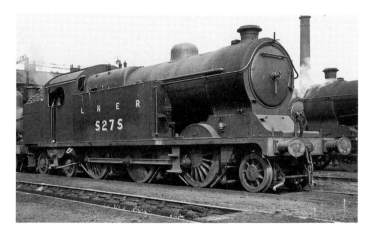

In 1935 No.5275 was an oddity in having a short handrail across the top of its smokebox door. No other was so fitted.

Built for heavy mineral train haulage, they proved deficient in brake power and so many were fitted with screw couplings and carriage heating apparatus (for which they had hose connections at both ends) so they could perform passenger duties.

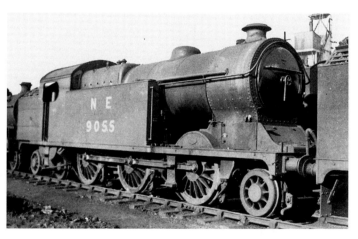

Until 1945, smokebox door fastening was by wheel and handle and the top lamp iron was fixed on the handrail above the door.

5369 cont./
CONDEMNED: 5/6/50.
Into Gor. for cut up 10/6/50.

5370

Gorton.

To traffic 5/1917.

REPAIRS:
Gor. 17/1—21/2/20.**G.**
Gor. 6/5—1/7/22.**G.**
Gor. 31/1—21/3/25.**G.**
Gor. 14/1—17/3/28.**G.**
Gor. 14/6—12/7/30.**G.**
Gor. 31/3—12/5/34.**G.**
Gor. 17/4—29/5/37.**G.**
Gor. 27/1—24/2/40.**G.**
Heating apparatus removed.
Gor. 13/11—18/12/43.**G.**
Gor. 24/11/45—5/1/46.**G.**
Gor. 14/6—5/7/47.**G.**
Gor. 20/8—17/9/49.**G.**
Gor. 9/8—6/9/52.**G.**

BOILERS:
 1675.
  338 21/3/25.
 1672 12/7/30.
 1556 12/5/34.
  645 24/2/40.
 1909 18/12/43.
 3114 5/1/46.
  745 17/9/49.
22021 6/9/52.

SHEDS:
Gorton.
Annesley 9/4/20.
Gorton 2/11/27.
Annesley 14/4/28.
Mexborough 23/2/29.
Immingham 11/11/37.
Neasden 20/1/41.
Woodford 14/8/47.

RENUMBERED:
 5370 21/3/25.
 9069 25/8/46.
69069 17/9/49.

CONDEMNED: 7/7/55.
Into Gor. for cut up 9/7/55.

(right) **The bogie brakes were seldom used after the class ceased hauling heavy mineral trains but they were only taken off during the 1939-45 war period.**

After the war the wheel was replaced by another handle, but the lamp iron remained on the handrail for a while longer.

The opposite order of change also occurred, No.5368 (9067) having its lamp iron moved on to the smokebox door, whilst retaining wheel and handle for fastening.

All had steam brake on the engine and vacuum ejector for train brakes. In addition, they had steam operated brakes to all four wheels of the bogie.

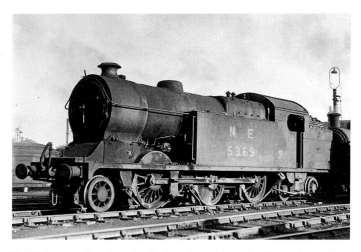

No.5369 was a Neasden shedded engine with coal rails cut from six to four during the 1939-45 war. Note cylinder snifting valves were also taken off.

No.276, here at Immingham in 1923, had the suffix applied and became 276c on the 17th November 1923.

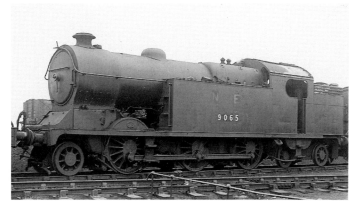

No.9065 did not have smokebox door changes until it went to works on 7th December 1946.

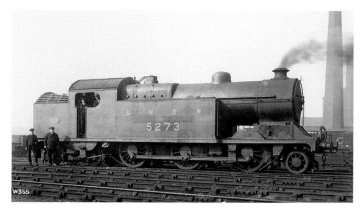

The first to get LNER numbers 5273, (16th February 1924) and 5341 (1st March 1924), kept their GC oval brass numberplate on the bunker. The paint appears to have been touched up enough to hide Great Central and the coat-of-arms.

As Great Central engines they were in lined green passenger livery with that company's coat-of-arms on the cab side. Note that by 1st July 1922 No.339 was already fitted for passenger train working, having a screw coupling and carriage heater connection at the front end.

Although scheduled for black with red lining, Gorton applied GCR goods and mixed traffic lining to No.5274, ex works 17th January 1925.

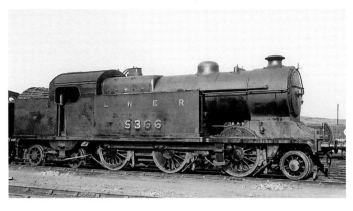

No.5366, ex works 3rd April 1926 was another to be simply touched up to hide the previous ownership as the original lining can still be discerned.

Before LNER was restored many were renumbered. No.5276 became 9054 on Sunday 25th August 1946 at Neasden shed and although shaded transfers were used they were only 9in. high.

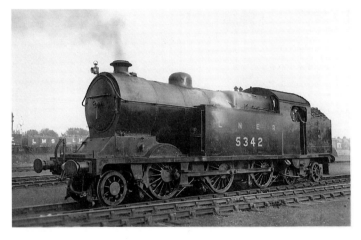

By the 1930's all had duly acquired black with single red lining. From November 1941 lining ceased to be applied and all then remained plain black to withdrawal.

No.5337 was changed to 9056 by Mexborough shed on Sunday 24th March 1946 using stencilled figures only 6in. high. That shed also used the same treatment for Nos.9067 (21st July 1946) and 9065 (11th August 1946). *See* pages 107 and 108.

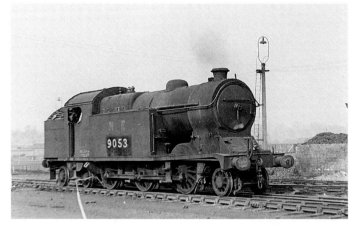

From July 1942 to early January 1946 only NE was used, No.5275 getting it ex works 12th February 1944. The number was changed to 9053 by Neasden shed on Thursday 18th April 1946 and shaded 12in. transfers were provided.

No.5340 was renumbered 9059 ex works 29th June 1946 from a general repair and LNER was put on in 12in. figures, probably due to retaining existing NE. Note that it had no change to the lamp iron and smokebox door fastening.

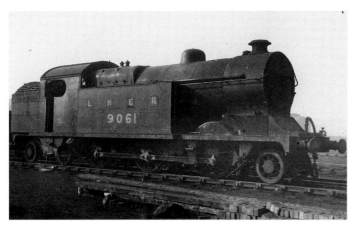

Ex works 6th December 1947, No.9061 got standard treatment. The 12in. NE, put on 23rd September 1944, was replaced by 7½in. LNER and that and the 12in.figures were all applied by shaded transfers. The lamp iron was moved from handrail to the door and a second handle replaced the wheel.

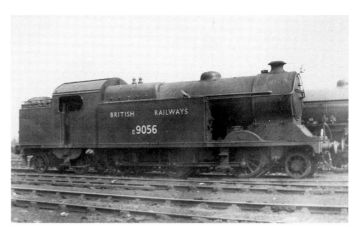

Ex works 7th February 1948 No.E9056, and 14th February 1948 No.E9068 were the earliest to show change of owners and the demise of LNER shaded transfers. The position and size was unaltered but in yellow painted and unshaded Gill sans, with modified 6 and 9.

From stencilled figures No.9065 went to 12in. LNER and number when ex works from a general repair on 4th January 1947. After a collision it had a light repair and when ex works on 31st January 1948, the regional prefix E had been added.

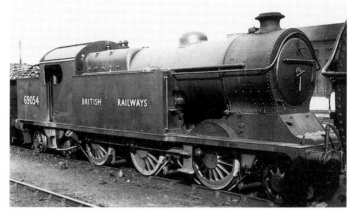

With the change from E to 6 as the number prefix, came the move of the number from the tank to bunker but 7½in. letters and 12in. figures were still used. Three got this style at general repairs in 1948: 69054 (10th April), 69060 (1st May) and 69052 (26th June), whilst 69062 got it when out from a light repair on 19th June.

No.9053 was another hybrid being in works at Nationalisation. It went in on 6th December 1947 with 12in. NE, put on in February 1944. It came out on 17th January 1948 with standard 7½in. LNER and 12in. figures, all in shaded transfers but prefix E had been added. Note the lamp iron was still on the rail. E9053 is seen at Gorton works in July 1950 awaiting scrapping, the collision damage suffered at the front end no doubt hastening its demise.

The next change was to 12in. letters and 10in. figures, including correct Gill sans 6 and 9. Four got this style: 69055 (25th September 1948), 69051 (6th November 1948) and 69069 (17th September 1949). Cast smokebox number plate was also fitted. No.69061 emerged from a light repair on 6th November 1948 but without smokebox number plate, instead the front bufferbeam number was retained.

The final change was effective from October 1949, the 15½in. emblem taking the place of the lettering. Eight achieved this guise: 69062 (15th October 1949), 69061 (15th April 1950), 69064 and 69065 (12th August 1950), 69052 (26th August 1950), 69060 (21st April 1951), 69069 (6th September 1952) and 69050 (20th December 1952).

Northwich allocated 9062 on a train of ICI lime stone hoppers on 7th March 1948.

(below) 69061 working over the single line loop to Wembley stadium in 1949, ferrying football fans from Marylebone station.

No.69069 of Woodford shed was the last of the class in traffic and its withdrawal on 7th July 1955 effectively made Class L3 extinct. Although not withdrawn until 7th June 1954, No.69060 was put to work in February 1954 as stationary boiler No.3293 at Stratford works where it served until condemned in August 1957. After ceasing work as stationary boiler, 69060 was disconnected and then remained at Stratford for cutting up.

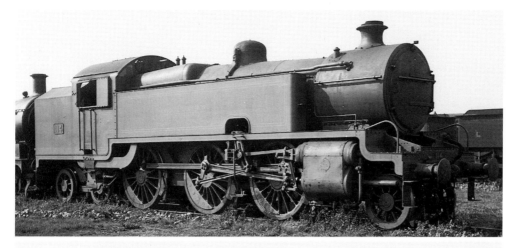

On 1st November 1937 these six were sold to the LNER who sent them to Stratford works to be renumbered and repainted, and to have the box-type lamp brackets replaced by LNER pattern.

They were given Nos.6158 to 6163 which they acquired from 26th July 1938 to 6th May 1939. All were painted unlined black. Their previous lining was so good that it could still be discerned through the black. Note the very wide spacing of LNER.

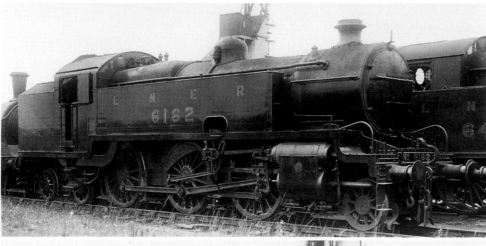

When taken into LNER stock, the smokebox door was Maunsell type with six dog clips around the rim for fastening. The top lamp bracket was fixed above the door.

Ex works 1st September 1945, No.6160 (9071 from 5th January 1947) had been fitted with an LNER type door having dart and crossbar fastening by two handles. It was the only one so altered.

CLASS L2

111/6158

Armstrong Whitworth 702.

To traffic 21/3/1925.

REPAIRS:
Nea. ?/?—?/8/36.**G.**
Str. ?/?—6/5/39.**G.**
Str. ?/?—?/7/41.**G.**
Str. ?/?—?/1/43.**G.**
Str. 2/12/44—24/2/45.**L.**
Str. 31/3—14/4/45.**L.**
Str. 24/8—19/10/46.**G.**
Str. 29/8/48. *Not repaired.*

BOILERS:
LT33.
LT33 reno.1429 6/5/39.
1430 *(ex6159)* ?/7/41.
1434 *(ex6163)* ?/1/43.
1435 *(ex6160)* 19/10/46.

SHED:
Neasden.

RENUMBERED:
6158 6/5/39.
9070 5/1/47.

CONDEMNED: 22/10/48.
Cut up at Stratford.

112/6159

Armstrong Whitworth 703.

To traffic 21/3/1925.

REPAIRS:
Nea. ?/?—?/4/35.**G.**
Str. ?/?—4/10/38.**G.**
Str. ?/?—?/5/41.**G.**

BOILERS:
LT2.
LT2 reno.1430 4/10/38.
1435 *(ex spare)* ?/5/41.

SHED:
Neasden.

RENUMBERED:
6159 4/10/38.

CONDEMNED: 2/1/43.
Cut up at Stratford.

For working on electrified routes, trip cock gear was provided. This was fitted on the left side frame of the bogie, and under the cylinder on the right hand side. Note the destination board brackets still on the rear of the bunker although, from 1925, the use of these 2-6-4T's on passenger trains was limited almost entirely to emergencies.

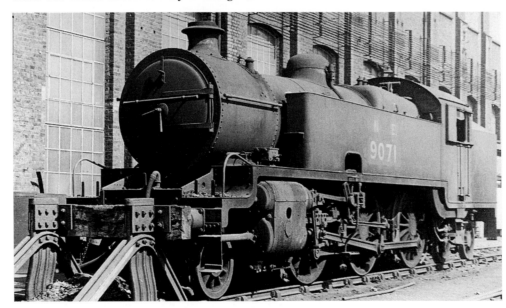

Sometime in 1947 No.9071 had the trip cock gear removed. It was still in place after No.6160 was changed to 9071 on 5th January 1947 but not whilst the engine stood at Stratford on 4th May 1947 as seen here. It went for light repair 15th March and was not ex works until 16th August, 1947.

Normal warning was by deep tone Caledonian Railway style hooter mounted horizontally, but No.6163 was changed to a vertical bell-shape whistle. It was also one of the L2's changed to Group Standard buffers.

Nos.6159 and 6161, withdrawn in January and March 1943, still had LNER, but from January 1943 the other four were reduced to just NE and on much closer spacing. This took place January (6158), April (6160), August (6162) and October (6163).

Only one, No.6158, had LNER restored when ex works after a general repair 19th October 1946. It was also renumbered 9070 but only on the tanks and No.6158 still existed on the rear bufferbeam. Note that the destination board brackets were retained, as were the original style buffers although changed to Group Standard at the front.

LNER smokebox door and Group Standard buffers.

113/6160

Armstrong Whitworth 704.

To traffic 23/3/1925.

REPAIRS:
Nea. ?/?—?/2/37.**G.**
Str. ?/?—6/4/39.**G.**
Str. ?/?—?/1/42.**G.**
Str. ?/?—?/4/43.**G.**
Str. 14/7—1/9/45.**G.**
Str. 15/3—16/8/47.**L.**
Str. 29/8/48. *Not repaired.*

BOILERS:
LT30.
LT30 reno.1431 6/4/39.
1433 *(ex6162)* ?/1/42.
1435 *(ex6159)* ?/4/43.
1430 *(ex spare)* 1/9/45.

SHED:
Neasden.

RENUMBERED:
6160 6/4/39.
9071 5/1/47.

CONDEMNED: 6/10/48.
Cut up at Stratford.

114/6161

Armstrong Whitworth 705.

To traffic 23/3/1925.

REPAIRS:
Nea. ?/?—?/4/36.**G.**
Str. ?/?—22/11/38.**G.**
Str. ?/?—?/2/42.**G.**

BOILERS:
LT5.
LT5 reno.1432 22/11/38.
1431 *(ex6160)* ?/2/42.

SHED:
Neasden.

RENUMBERED:
6161 22/11/38.

CONDEMNED: 26/5/43.
Cut up at Stratford.

115/6162

Armstrong Whitworth 706.

To traffic 28/3/1925.

REPAIRS:
Nea. ?/?—?/10/36.**G.**
Str. ?/?—26/7/38.**G.**
Str. ?/?—?/9/41.**G.**
Str. ?/?—?/8/43.**G.**

BOILERS:
LT11.
LT11 reno.1433 26/7/38.
1429 *(ex6158)* ?/9/41.
1433 *(ex6160)* ?/8/43.

SHED:
Neasden.

RENUMBERED:
6162 26/7/38.
9072 allocated.

CONDEMNED: 26/1/46.
Cut up at Stratford.

116/6163

Armstrong Whitworth 707.

To traffic 28/3/1925.

REPAIRS:
Nea. ?/?—?/10/35.**G.**
Str. ?/?—4/11/38.**G.**
Str. ?/?—?/3/42.**G.**
Str. ?/?—?/10/43.**G.**

BOILERS:
LT37.
LT37 reno.1434 4/11/38.
1432 *(ex6161)* ?/3/42.
1429 *(ex6162)* ?/10/43.

SHED:
Neasden.

RENUMBERED:
6163 4/11/38.
9073 allocated.

CONDEMNED: 12/5/45.
Cut up at Stratford.

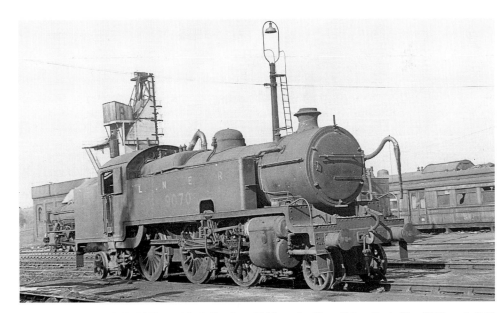

6162 with original smokebox door and buffers which it kept to withdrawal in January 1946.

The withdrawal of No.9070 on 22nd October 1948 made Class L2 extinct. Nos.6162 and 6163 had been allocated Nos.9072 and 9073 but never carried them as they were withdrawn on 26th January 1946 and 12th May 1945 respectively.

No.116 at Chorley Wood on 5th June 1938 unusually in charge of a passenger train.

6148

Kitson & Co. 4246.

To traffic 5/1904.

REPAIRS:
Tux. 30/3—2/9/09.**G.**
Tux. 3—31/3/11.**G.**
Tux. 23/12/12—1/3/13.**G.**
Tux. 3/9—23/10/14.**G.**
Tux. 29/7—29/9/16.**G.**
Tux. 3/8—21/11/18.**G.**
Tux. 10/5—8/7/20.**G.**
Tux. 24/10—31/12/21.**G.**
Tux. 25/4—13/7/23.**G.**
Tux. ?/?—26/7/24.**L.**
Tux. 19/12/24—26/2/25.**G.**
Don. 14/10—17/12/27.**G.**
Don. 3—28/12/29.**G.**
Gor. 9/7—13/8/32.**G.**
Gor. 22/9—20/10/34.**G.**
Gor. 30/7—20/8/38.**G.**
Gor. 26/4—7/6/41.**G.**
Gor. 1—26/9/42.**L.**
Main frame fractured.
Gor. 20/1—4/3/44.**G.**
Gor. 2/3/46. *Not repaired.*

BOILERS:
1354 *(ex??)* 31/3/11.
1338 *(ex1149)* 1/3/13.
 903 *(ex1146)* 23/10/14.
 254 *(ex1153)* 29/9/16.
 903 *(ex1151)* 21/11/18.
1729 *(ex1146)* 8/7/20.
 501 *(ex1150)* 31/12/21.
 433 *(new)* 13/7/23.
1733 *(ex1150)* 26/2/25.
 238 *(ex6153)* 17/12/27.
 268 *(ex6149)* 28/12/29.
 484 *(ex6147)* 13/8/32.
4132 *(new)* 20/8/38.
8220 *(ex6151)* 4/3/44.

SHED:
Tuxford.

RENUMBERED:
6148 26/2/25.
9080 allocated.

CONDEMNED: 4/3/46.
Cut up at Gorton.

6149

Kitson & Co. 4247.

To traffic 6/1904.

REPAIRS:
Tux. 16/10—11/11/08.**G.**
Tux. 6/9—11/10/10.**G.**
Tux. 17/8—30/9/12.**G.**
Tux. 20/8—23/9/14.**G.**
Tux. 4—31/3/16.**G.**
Tux. 3/10—21/12/17.**G.**
Tux. 23/1—26/4/19.**G.**
Tux. 4/3—28/4/21.**G.**
Tux. 28/7—9/10/22.**G.**
Tux. 6/11—21/12/23.**G.**
Tux. 14/5—3/7/25.**G.**
Tux. 9/12/26—29/1/27.**G.**
Don. 23/10—13/11/28.**G.**
Don. 3—29/11/30.**G.**
Gor. 22/4—6/5/33.**G.**
Gor. 9/2—9/3/35.**G.**
Gor. 31/7—21/8/37.**G.**

BOILERS:
1338 *(ex1153)* 11/10/10.
 254 *(new)* 30/9/12.
 592 *(ex1153)* 23/9/14.
1354 *(ex1151)* 31/3/16.
1338 *(ex1150)* 21/12/17.
 903 *(ex1148)* 28/4/21.
 445 *(ex1146)* 9/10/22.
 268 *(ex1153)* 21/12/23.
1354 *(ex1153)* 3/7/25.
 268 *(ex spare)* 29/1/27.
 570 *(ex6151)* 13/11/28.
 268 *(ex6148)* 6/5/33.
8222 *(ex6146)* 9/3/35.
 232 *(ex6145)* 21/8/37.

SHEDS:
Tuxford.
Ardsley 20/8/27.
Langwith Jct. 24/9/27.
Tuxford 1/1/28.
Lincoln 27/10/34.
Tuxford 10/11/34.

RENUMBERED:
6149 3/7/25.

CONDEMNED: 9/12/39.
Into Gor. for cut up 16/12/39.

6150

Kitson & Co. 4248.

To traffic 6/1904.

REPAIRS:
Tux. 25/5—18/7/08.**G.**
Tux. 8/11/09—6/5/10.**G.**
Tux. 25/10—7/12/11.**G.**
Tux. 1/8—16/9/13.**G.**
Tux. 29/10—16/12/14.**G.**
Tux. 1/7—28/8/16.**G.**

Tux. 28/3—23/5/17.**G.**
Tux. 11/12/17—12/4/18.**G.**
Tux. 8/9—24/10/19.**G.**
Tux. 6/9—12/10/20.**G.**
Tux. 20/8—28/9/21.**G.**
Tux. 19/3—18/5/23.**G.**
Tux. 2/7—26/8/24.**G.**
Tux. 23/3—5/5/26.**G.**
Don. 3—26/1/29.**G.**
Don. 3—22/11/30.**G.**
Gor. 11/6—2/7/32.**G.**
New cylinders.
Gor. 1/9—6/10/34.**G.**
Gor. 18/12/37—8/1/38.**G.**
Gor. 15/2—8/3/41.**G.**
Gor. 12/11—4/12/43.**G.**
Gor. 10/8/46. *Not repaired.*

BOILERS:
 570 *(ex??)* 6/5/10.
 268 *(new)* 16/9/13.
1338 *(ex1148)* 16/12/14.
 592 *(ex1149)* 28/8/16.
1379 *(ex1152)* 23/5/17.
 445 *(ex1145)* 12/4/18.
 501 *(ex1146)* 24/10/19.
 254 *(ex1145)* 28/9/21.
1733 *(ex1152)* 18/5/23.
 236 *(ex1151)* 26/8/24.
 484 *(ex6152)* 5/5/26.
 445 *(ex6147)* 26/1/29.
 433 *(ex6151)* 22/11/30.
1729 *(ex6145)* 6/10/34.
8222 *(ex6149)* 8/1/38.
1729 *(ex6146)* 8/3/41.
 484 *(ex6147)* 4/12/43.

SHED:
Tuxford.

RENUMBERED:
6150 26/8/24.
9081 allocated.

CONDEMNED: 10/8/46.
Cut up at Gorton.

6151

Kitson & Co. 4249.

To traffic 6/1904.

REPAIRS:
Tux. 30/1—14/4/08.**G.**
Tux. 26/7/09—4/1/10.**G.**
Tux. 20/7—19/9/11.**G.**
Tux. 19/6—20/8/13.**G.**
Tux. 25/1—3/5/15.**G.**
Tux. 24/4—9/5/17.**G.**
Tux. 30/8—13/2/19.**G.**
Tux. 13/11—15/12/20.**G.**

Tux. 6/10—20/12/22.**G.**
Tux. 5/1—25/2/24.**G.**
Tux. 24/6—9/9/25.**G.**
Don. 3/1—10/3/28.**G.**
Don. 27/2—22/3/30.**G.**
Gor. 17/12/32—21/1/33.**G.**
Gor. 17—24/6/33.**L.**
Gor. 16/11—14/12/35.**G.**
Gor. 15/10—12/11/38.**G.**
Gor. 27/12/41—31/1/42.**G.**
Gor. 18—28/11/42.**L.**
Frame fractures.
Gor. 14/1—19/2/44.**G.**
Gor. 13/4—4/5/46.**G.**
Gor. 4/7/47. *Not repaired.*

BOILERS:
 592 *(ex??)* 4/1/10.
1354 *(ex1148)* 20/8/13.
 153 *(ex1152)* 3/5/15.
 903 *(ex1148)* 9/5/17.
 268 *(ex1153)* 13/2/19.
1354 *(ex1147)* 15/12/20.
 236 *(new)* 20/12/22.
 570 *(ex1145)* 25/2/24.
 433 *(ex1148)* 9/9/25.
 232 *(ex6147)* 22/3/30.
8221 *(ex6146)* 21/1/33.
8220 *(new)* 14/12/35.
4132 *(ex6148)* 19/2/44.
 430 *(ex6153)* 4/5/46.

SHED:
Tuxford.

RENUMBERED:
6151 25/2/24.
9082 4/5/46.

CONDEMNED: 4/7/47.
Cut up at Gorton.

6152

Kitson & Co. 4250.

To traffic 6/1904.

REPAIRS:
Tux. 13/11/08—8/1/09.**G.**
Tux. 16/12/09—10/6/10.**G.**
Tux. 16/1—20/3/12.**G.**
Tux. 14/4—28/5/13.**G.**
Tux. 28/10—26/11/14.**G.**
Tux. 5/6—5/7/16.**G.**
Tux. 7/6—12/8/18.**G.**
Tux. 13/12/19—10/3/20.**G.**
Tux. 16/3—22/8/22.**G.**
Tux. 4/2—26/3/24.**G.**
Tux. 9/9—13/11/25.**G.**
Don. 3/1—3/3/28.**G.**
Don. 16/6—19/7/30.**G.**

In the months before they were absorbed, the L.D & E.C.R. had taken delivery of another three 0-6-4T from Kitson & Co., to which they gave Nos.A1 to A3. They had a longer smokebox with the frames built up to match. The GC numbered them 1145 to 1147. Note LNER load class 3 collar on the vacuum brake standpipe.

When new, the 1904 engines had Kitson design built-up chimney, but by Grouping all had changed to this Robinson pattern which the December 1906 engines had from new. Its height from rail was 13ft 1⁵⁄₁₆in.

From the late 1920's, all had the chimney changed to 'plantpot' type, which they then kept to withdrawal. This reduced the height to 12ft 11¼in., but did not bring them into Composite Load Gauge because the height over dome stud was 13ft 0⁵⁄₁₆in.. This was no handicap as they were never shedded where height was limited.

The original boilers had two-column Ramsbottom safety valves, but on the three 1906 boilers these had been changed to four-column and only one of the 1904 boilers was still in service (*see* below). The GC-built replacement boilers had four-column Ramsbottom safety valves.

After Grouping, Ross 'pop' valves became standard and by 1936 all nine were so fitted.

(left) From 3rd July 1925 to 9th December 1926 No.6149 had the single 1904 boiler which remained in service, and this had been built for two-column Ramsbottom valves. The branched mounting was retained and a Ross 'pop' was fitted on each outlet. This boiler came from No.1153 as shown in the Introduction.

(below) It was more usual to fit an adaptor when replacing Ramsbottom with Ross type and on these, the base of the Ross valve stood proud of the firebox casing.

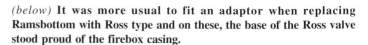

6152 cont./
Gor. 8/10—5/11/32.**G**.
Gor. 21/3—25/4/36.**G**.
Gor. 22/2/39. *Not repaired.*

BOILERS:
278 *(ex??)* 10/6/10.
153 *(ex??)* 28/5/13.
1379 *(ex1147)* 26/11/14.
278 *(ex1153)* 5/7/16.
1733 *(new)* 12/8/18.
232 *(new)* 22/8/22.
484 *(new)* 26/3/24.
430 *(new)* 13/11/25.
238 *(ex6148)* 19/7/30.
430 *(ex spare)* 5/11/32.
8221 *(ex6151)* 25/4/36.

SHED:
Tuxford.

RENUMBERED:
6152 26/3/24.

CONDEMNED: 22/2/39.
Cut up at Gorton.

6153

Kitson & Co. 4251.

To traffic 6/1904.

REPAIRS:
Tux. 6/9—15/10/08.**G**.
Tux. 1/6—25/7/10.**G**.
Tux. 17/4—28/6/12.**G**.
Tux. 20/10—13/11/13.**G**.
Tux. 2—24/2/15.**G**.
Tux. 5/7—11/8/16.**G**.
Tux. 1/2—7/3/18.**G**.
Tux. 1/5—20/6/19.**G**.
Tux. 21/2—23/3/21.**G**.
Tux. 22/1—23/3/23.**G**.
Tux. 9/10—19/11/24.**G**.
Tux. 26/8—4/11/26.**G**.
Don. 30/3—12/5/28.**G**.
Don. 16/4—2/5/30.**G**.
Gor. 10/12/32—21/1/33.**G**.
New cylinders.
Gor. 14/9—5/10/35.**G**.
Gor. 7—28/1/39.**G**.
Gor. 12/8—13/9/41.**G**.
Gor. 13—29/8/42.**L**.
Frame fractured.
Gor. 29/4—20/5/44.**G**.
Gor. 18/6/46. *Not repaired.*

BOILERS:
1338 *(ex??)* 15/10/08.
903 *(ex1146)* 25/7/10.
592 *(ex1151)* 28/6/12.
278 *(ex1152)* 13/11/13.
254 *(ex1149)* 24/2/15.
268 *(ex1145)* 11/8/16.

1379 *(ex1150)* 7/3/18.
570 *(ex1147)* 20/6/19.
268 *(ex1151)* 23/3/21.
1354 *(ex1151)* 23/3/23.
238 *(ex1146)* 19/11/24.
236 *(ex6150)* 4/11/26.
1354 *(ex6149)* 12/5/28.
236 *(ex spare)* 2/5/30.
238 *(ex6152)* 21/1/33.
430 *(ex6147)* 28/1/39.
4131 *(ex6147)* 20/5/44.

SHED:
Tuxford.

RENUMBERED:
6153 19/11/24.
9083 *allocated.*

CONDEMNED: 18/6/46.
Cut up at Gorton.

6145

Kitson & Co. 4435.

To traffic 12/1906.

REPAIRS:
Tux. 12—26/10/08.**L**.
Tux. 15/3—31/5/09.**G**.
Tux. 23/6—23/8/10.**G**.
After collision.
Tux. 11/11/11—25/1/12.**G**.
Tux. 16/5—9/7/13.**G**.
Tux. 28/11/14—26/1/15.**G**.
Tux. 11/2—8/3/16.**G**.
Tux. 15/6—2/11/17.**G**.
Tux. 12/7—26/8/19.**G**.
Tux. 24/5—9/7/21.**G**.
Tux. 13/7—12/9/23.**G**.
Tux. 3/9—10/10/24.**G**.
Tux. 26/5—21/7/26.**G**.
Don. 13/6—13/7/29.**G**.
Gor. 8/8—5/9/31.**G**.
Gor. 16/9—7/10/33.**G**.
New cylinders.
Gor. 15/8—5/9/36.**G**.
Gor. 2—23/4/38.**G**.
Gor. 16/12/39—6/1/40.**L**.
Wheels changed.
Gor. 10/9/41. *Not repaired.*

BOILERS:
445.
501 *(ex1147)* 9/7/13.
268 *(ex1150)* 26/1/15.
445 *(ex1147)* 8/3/16.
153 *(ex1151)* 2/11/17.
254 *(ex1148)* 26/8/19.
570 *(ex1153)* 9/7/21.
254 *(ex1150)* 12/9/23.
1729 *(ex1147)* 10/10/24.
254 *(ex spare)* 21/7/26.
1733 *(ex6148)* 13/7/29.

1729 *(ex6146)* 5/9/31.
232 *(ex6151)* 7/10/33.
236 *(ex6147)* 5/9/36.
4131 *(new)* 23/4/38.

SHED:
Tuxford.

RENUMBERED:
6145 10/10/24.

CONDEMNED: 16/9/41.
Cut up at Gorton.

6146

Kitson & Co. 4436.

To traffic 12/1906.

REPAIRS:
Tux. 1/1—8/2/09.**G**.
Tux. 25/7—4/11/10.**G**.
Tux. 10/10—13/12/12.**G**.
Tux. 21/2—22/4/14.**G**.
Tux. 23/10—19/11/15.**G**.
Tux. 10/4—25/6/18.**G**.
Tux. 10/11/19—5/2/20.**G**.
Tux. 20/4—23/6/22.**G**.
Tux. ?/?—28/9/23.**L**.
Tux. 6/3—3/6/24.**G**.
Tux. 3/2—19/3/26.**G**.
Don. 8/2—31/3/28.**G**.
Don. 2/7—2/8/30.**G**.
Gor. 8—29/10/32.**G**.
Gor. 22/12/34—26/1/35.**G**.
New cylinders.
Gor. 19/3—9/4/38.**G**.
Gor. 27/5—10/6/39.**L**.
Driving wheel spokes broken.
Gor. 18—25/5/40.Special **H**.
Gor. 21/7—16/8/41.**G**.

BOILERS:
903.
1379 *(ex1147)* 8/2/09.
903 *(ex1153)* 13/12/12.
570 *(ex1150)* 22/4/14.
501 *(ex1145)* 19/11/15.
1729 *(new)* 25/6/18.
445 *(ex1150)* 5/2/20.
238 *(new)* 23/6/22.
232 *(ex1152)* 3/6/24.
501 *(ex6147)* 19/3/26.
1729 *(ex6145)* 31/3/28.
8221 *(new)* 2/8/30.
8222 *(new)* 29/10/32.
1733 *(ex6147)* 26/1/35.
1729 *(ex6150)* 9/4/38.
8221 *(ex6152)* 25/5/40.

SHEDS:
Langwith Jct.
Tuxford 1/1/28.

RENUMBERED:
6146 3/6/24.

CONDEMNED: 12/7/43.
Into Gor. for cut up 24/7/43.

6147

Kitson & Co. 4437.

To traffic 12/1906.

REPAIRS:
Tux. 25/8—21/9/09.**G**.
Tux. 5/10—7/12/10.**G**.
Tux. 19/9/11—3/2/12.**G**.
Tux. 8/3—24/4/13.**G**.
Tux. 3—22/7/14.**G**.
Tux. 9/11/15—17/1/16.**G**.
Tux. 3/1—2/2/18.**G**.
Tux. 22/10—21/12/19.**G**.
Tux. 19/12/21—22/4/22.**G**.
Tux. 26/9—12/11/23.**G**.
Tux. ?/?—24/5/24.**L**.
Tux. 27/11—31/12/24.**G**.
Tux. 21/7—16/9/26.**G**.
Don. 17/5—22/6/29.**G**.
Gor. 24/10—19/12/31.**G**.
Gor. 1/9—6/10/34.**G**.
Gor. 8—29/8/36.**G**.
Gor. 26/11—24/12/38.**G**.
Gor. 4—22/11/41.**G**.
Gor. 25—28/8/43.**L**.
Frame fracture.
Gor. 12/2/44. *Not repaired.*

BOILERS:
1379.
501 *(ex??)* 21/9/09.
1379 *(ex1146)* 24/4/13.
445 *(ex1145)* 22/7/14.
570 *(ex1146)* 17/1/16.
1354 *(ex1149)* 2/2/18.
1379 *(ex1153)* 21/12/19.
1729 *(ex1148)* 22/4/22.
501 *(ex1148)* 12/11/23.
445 *(ex1149)* 31/12/24.
232 *(ex6146)* 16/9/26.
484 *(ex6150)* 22/6/29.
1733 *(ex6145)* 19/12/31.
236 *(ex6153)* 6/10/34.
430 *(ex6152)* 29/8/36.
484 *(ex6148)* 24/12/38.
4131 *(ex6145)* 22/11/41.

SHED:
Tuxford.
Langwith Jct. 28/2/30.
Tuxford 25/3/39.

RENUMBERED:
6147 31/12/24.
9084 *allocated.*

CONDEMNED: 16/2/44.
Cut up at Gorton.

Only five new boilers were built fitted with Ross 'pops', three in May/June 1929 and two in September/October 1937. On these the safety valves were mounted directly on to the firebox.

Nos.6145 and 6147 retained their longer smokebox until they went to works in August 1936. Both were then fitted with smokeboxes similar to Nos.6148 to 6153.

Both 6145 and 6147 then had a protruding portion of frame although not alike (*see* bottom photo, page 118) and their apron plates also differed.

No.6146 lost its longer smokebox when ex works 26th January 1935, the replacement being of intermediate length, but with an apron plate as on Nos.6148 to 6153.

Until February 1935, No.6149 had a short smokebox and GC built boiler which had two handholes for washout plugs on each side of the firebox.

Ex works 9th March 1935 No.6149 had been fitted with an intermediate length smokebox similar to that just fitted to No.6146 (*see* opposite, bottom). These two were the only ones noted so fitted, the boiler was one of the five built by the LNER and they had three handholes, with domed cover plates on the left hand side.

All the boilers for M1 class had only two washout plugs on the right hand side and only the five built in 1929 and 1937 had domed covers.

Until after Grouping the fastening of the smokebox door was by two handles.

(left) **From 1925 at least six, Nos.6145, 6148, 6149, 6150, 6151 and 6153, had the door fastening changed to a wheel and handle which was then retained, but No.6152 (*see* bottom photo page 117) still had two handles at its February 1939 withdrawal.**

(below) **Throughout, all had three coal rails round the top of the bunker, and these never had plating applied.**

(above) **Six of the class had a general repair at Tuxford works during 1923 but no evidence has been found that any got ampersand or suffix C. These were Nos.1153 (23rd March) which, as photograph in the Introduction shows, retained full GCR livery; 1150 (18th May); 1148 (13th July); 1145 (12th September); 1147 (12th November) and 1149 (21st December).**

(left) **Until 30th May 1927 maintenance was at Tuxford works and painting was black with single red lining. No.6149, photographed at Ardsley shed on 18th September 1927 was ex Tuxford 29th January 1927.**

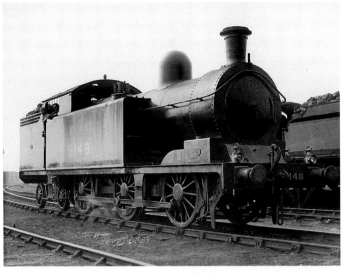

Doncaster then repaired M1 class and Nos.6146, 6148, 6151, 6152 and 6153, ex works from 17th December 1927 to 12th May 1928, still had red lining. No.6149 ex Doncaster 13th November 1928 was the first in plain black and when out again 29th November 1930 was the last repaired by Doncaster. Between those two dates all the others had a general repair at Doncaster and became unlined black. No.6148, shown here on 25th May 1931, was unlined when ex Doncaster 28th December 1929.

Practically all buffers remained GCR pattern and with circular head, but there were odd cases of oval head being fitted. The photograph left, middle, shows this type at the rear of No.6153 as does the photograph on the left, top showing them on the rear of No.6148.

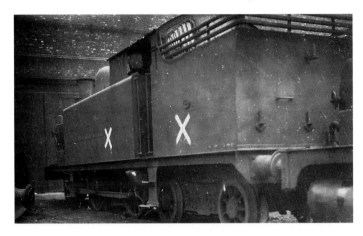

From July 1942 only NE was put on, but Gorton chose to use 12in. instead of 7½in. letters. Only four were so done: 6148 (4th March 1944), 6150 (4th December 1943), 6151 (19th February 1944) and 6153 (20th May 1944).

No.6148, shown standing outside Gorton works after its 4th March 1946 withdrawal, displays a Group Standard type buffer, the only example traced.

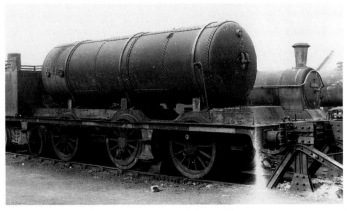

Only one survived to have LNER restored and that was in 12in. letters. No.6151 went into Gorton 13th April 1946 but came out on 4th May 1946 as LNER No.9082, in shaded transfers. Its withdrawal on 4th July 1947 made Class M1 extinct.

This air receiver at Gorton on 23rd September 1956, was carried on the remains of M1 No.6145, more than nine years after the class went out of traffic.

CLASS M 2

94/6154	95/6155	96/6156	97/6157
LORD ABERCONWAY.	*ROBERT H SELBIE.*	*CHARLES JONES.*	*BRILL*

94/6154

LORD ABERCONWAY.

Yorkshire Engine Co. 1283.

To traffic 12/1915.

REPAIRS:
Nea. ?/?—?7/33.**G.**
Str. ?/?—8/4/38.**G.**
Str. ?/?—?/9/42.**H.**
Str. ?/?—?/2/44.**G.**

BOILERS:
LT20.
LT20 reno.1417 8/4/38.
1419 (ex6156) ?/2/44.

SHED:
Neasden.

RENUMBERED:
6154 8/4/38.
9075 allocated.

CONDEMNED: 21/5/46.
Cut up at Stratford.

95/6155

ROBERT H SELBIE.

Yorkshire Engine Co. 1284.

To traffic 1/1916.

REPAIRS:
Nea. ?/?—?/11/36.**G.**
Str. ?/?—21/10/39.**G.**
Str. ?/?—?/1/42.**H.**
Str. ?/?—?/10/43.**G.**
Str. 12—26/1/46.**L.**
Str. 23/11/46—11/1/47.**G.**
Str. 8—14/3/47.**C/L.**
Str. 5/9/48. *Not repaired.*

BOILERS:
LT13.
LT13 reno.1418 21/10/39.
1420 (ex6157) ?/1/42.
1421 (exH2 6415) ?/10/43.
1423 (exH2 6417) 11/1/47.

SHED:
Neasden.

RENUMBERED:
6155 21/10/39.
9076 16/12/46.

CONDEMNED: 22/10/48.
Cut up at Stratford.

96/6156

CHARLES JONES.

Yorkshire Engine Co. 1301.

To traffic 2/1916.

REPAIRS:
Nea. ?/?—?/10/34.**G.**
Str. ?/?—1/4/38.**G.**
Str. ?/?—?/10/42.**H.**
Str. ?/?—?/1/44.**G.**
Str. 5—19/5/45.**L.**
Str. 26/4—10/10/47.**G.**
Str. 29/8/48. *Not repaired.*

BOILERS:
LT17.
LT17 reno.1419 1/4/38.
1420 (ex6157) ?/1/44.

SHED:
Neasden.

RENUMBERED:
6156 1/4/38.
9077 5/1/47.

CONDEMNED: 22/10/48.
Cut up at Stratford.

97/6157

BRILL

Yorkshire Engine Co. 1302.

To traffic 3/1916.

REPAIRS:
Nea. ?/?—?/11/34.**G.**
Str. ?/?—14/5/38.**G.**
Str. ?/?—?/3/42.**G.**

BOILERS:
LT3.
LT3 reno.1420 14/5/38.
1418 (ex6155) ?/3/42.

SHED:
Neasden.

RENUMBERED:
6157 14/5/38.

CONDEMNED: 2/1/43.
Cut up at Stratford.

In 1933 the Metropolitan Railway was merged into LPTB, and this is substantially the appearance when purchased by the LNER on 1st November 1937. The brackets for destination boards at the front had already been taken off but those on the bunker remained in place until withdrawal, though never used (*see* page 125). **At take-over, Nos.95, 96 and 97 had already been fitted with a Maunsell type snifting valve at both ends of the superheater header. These three also had wheel and handle for smokebox door fastening.**

The LNER renumbered the four engines 6154 to 6157 and ex Stratford 8th April 1938 No.6154 had still not been fitted with the Maunsell type snifters. In February 1944 it was fitted with a boiler from No.6156 so would then have got them.

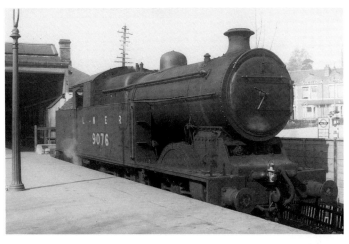

During the war, probably in October 1943, No.6155 was changed to Group Standard buffers. No.6154 and 6157 were taken out of stock 21st May 1946 and 2nd January 1943 and their buffer position is not known. No.6156 kept the original type buffers until withdrawn.

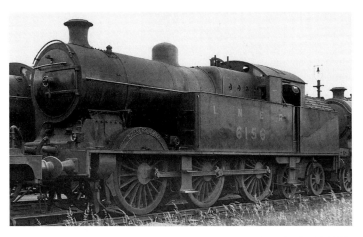

Nos.6156 (1st April), 6154 (8th April) and 6157 (14th May), all 1938, were soon into LNER black with single red lining. They also kept their original boiler mountings. Heights from rail were:- chimney 13ft 3in., dome 13ft 2⅛in., and cab ventilator 13ft 0½in.

For working on electrified lines, trip cock gear was fitted. On the right hand side it was mounted just ahead of the front footstep.

Having had a major repair and a boiler change in November 1936, No.95 did not go to Stratford until after the war had started. When ex works 21st October 1939 as No.6155 it had been brought within the Composite Load Gauge to give wider usage if needed. Heights from rail were now:- chimney and dome 12ft 11in., cab ventilator 12ft 10in. and, Ross 'pops' were put on in place of Ramsbottom safety valves. The others were altered similarly when they next went to Stratford during 1942.

On the left side the trip cock gear was fixed on the bogie frame between the wheels.

The original fastening for the smokebox door was by a wheel and handle. Note the studs where the draught retarder had been before snifting valves superseded it. The wheel and handle was retained on No.6156 to withdrawal as No.9077. It was the only one unaltered.

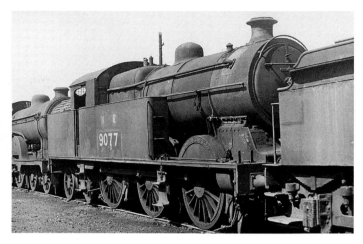

Although No.6157 kept LNER to its 2nd January 1943 withdrawal, the other three all had this cut to NE from October 1943 to February 1944 when they also lost the red lining. No.6154 had NE at its 21st May 1946 withdrawal. Note that in early 1947 trip cock gear was partially stripped from 9076 and 9077 but it was fully restored to both later.

No.6154 had, and retained, a Maunsell type door with six dog clips around the rim. The three repaired in April and May 1938 all kept box type lamp irons, although all were changed later to LNER type.

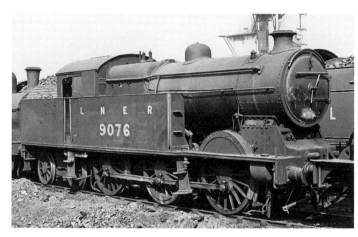

No.6155 was in Stratford for general repair from 23rd November 1946 to 11th January 1947, and on 16th December was renumbered 9076. When ex works it had LNER restored by 7½in. shaded transfers which were also used for the 12in. figures.

By October 1943, No.6155 (later 9076) had two handles for smokebox door fastening and it kept this type to withdrawal.

No.9077 went to Stratford on 26th April 1947 and, after a lengthy lay-by, was given a general repair. Ex works 10th October 1947 it too had LNER restored, but that and the figures were in yellow painted and unshaded Gill sans although with LNER modified 9. Both 9076 and 9077 were withdrawn on 22nd October 1948 making Class M2 extinct.